James E. Hill

Queen Charity

And other sermons

James E. Hill

Queen Charity
And other sermons

ISBN/EAN: 9783337086954

Printed in Europe, USA, Canada, Australia, Japan

Cover: Foto ©Lupo / pixelio.de

More available books at **www.hansebooks.com**

QUEEN CHARITY

AND

OTHER SERMONS.

BY

THE REV. J. EDGAR HILL, M.A., B.D. (Edin.),

Minister of St. Andrew's Church (Church of Scotland), Montreal.

MONTREAL:
W. DRYSDALE & CO.
C. ASHFORD.

Entered according to Act of the Parliament of Canada, in the year one thousand eight hundred and ninety, by Rev. J. Edgar Hill, at the Department of Agriculture.

MONTREAL:
PRINTED BY THE GAZETTE PRINTING COMPANY.
1890.

FOREWORDS.

These Sermons claim to be simple, practical, religious, and nothing more. John Wesley once said :—"I find more profit in sermons on either good tempers, or good works, than in what are commonly called Gospel Sermons. The term has now become a mere cant word. It has no determinate meaning." H. M. Stanley, a few weeks ago, in a speech at Edinburgh, bewailed the lack of helpful, practical preaching, in most of the pulpits of the great cities he had visited, both in Great Britain and America. The writer, after a seventeen years' ministry, has come to be much of the opinion of both Wesley nd Stanley. In the following discourses, he hopes the reader will find tangible token of this opinion.

ST. ANDREW'S DAY,
1890.

CONTENTS.

	PAGE.
PART I.—QUEEN CHARITY	1
1. The Greatest Grace.	7
2. The First Contrast	25
3. The Reason Why	43
4. Do.	61
5. Do.	68
6. The Second Contrast	101
7. The Third Contrast.	118
PART II.—JESUS, OUR LIGHT AND LIFE	137
1. The Compassionate Guest	139
2. The Mighty Worker	157
3. The Neighbourly Jesus	171
4. The Glad Master	189
5. In the Mount	209
6. The Agonised Messiah	224
7. The Rejected of Gadara	240
PART III.—WE SEE AS WE ARE	253
1. In Nature	260
2. In Man	274
3. In God	290
PART IV.—THE SEASONS	310
1. The Rossignol and the Anemone	314
2. The Oak and the Leaf	330
8. His Cold	346
PART V.—SPECIAL SERMONS	363
1. Thanksgiving Day	365
2. The Holy Sabbath	381
3. The Angelus	399

ERRATA.

Page 42, line 2.   For " their," *read* " there."
"   67, line 20.   For vi, *read* 6.
" 124, line 15.   For " Paronsia," *read* " Parousia."

PART I.
QUEEN CHARITY.

St. Paul has, by universal acclaim, been declared the poet, *par excellence*, of Christian love. Unapproached for depth of pathos, breadth of treatment, and fidelity of execution, this magnificent eulogy will ever stand without a rival, and without a peer, the wonder and the admiration of the world. Not a little enhanced, in the estimation of thoughtful Christians, is this glowing panegyric, that it is the product of a highly cultivated and well-balanced mind. St. Paul was no vapid sentimentalist nor one-ideaed, uncultured, religious enthusiast. Though he glorifies love as the Queen of the Holy Triad, he is not unfaithful to her noble sisters. They are all to him, "crowned virtues," and he lays at the feet of each, the homage which is hers, by right. More than once he uses Habakkuk's pithy maxim to sum up his high appreciation of Faith, "the just shall live by faith." He could hardly say more for Hope, than is conveyed in these words to the Roman Christians, "for we were saved by hope." Hope was the very wine of life in early Christian days—hope of the master's speedy return in glory and majesty. In Chapter XII, the Apostle extols many spiritual gifts

—the fruits of faith and the inspired of hope. In Chapter XIII, he magnifies love as the grand motive-principle of all religious activity, the inspiration of all Christian inspirations, But lest he should be misunderstood, lest it should be supposed, that in the glorification of love, he had forgotten the honour due to the sister graces, he returns in Chapter XIV, to magnify those spiritual gifts which, for the moment, he had seemed to forget. "Follow after love," he says, "but *desire earnestly* spiritual gifts." Thus he safeguards the rank of both Faith and Hope, and preserves his reputation as a broad, comprehensive exponent of Christian life and thought.

In this thirteenth chapter, he presents the supremacy of love among the graces:

1. By a comparison of certain great, and much prized religious gifts *without* love, and *with* love. Without love an individual may be eloquent, or scholarly, or charitable, or faithful, or heroic, and yet be nothing spiritually in the Christian sense. With love he will be something spiritually before God and man.

2. By an analysis of love into its principal component parts, if we may be allowed such an expression in treating of anything so spiritual as love, he shows how completely it covers the broad field of human thought and action, and how essential is the spirit of love to a worthy, helpful, and creditable life.

3. By urging the eternity of love alone among the graces. This thought is to be taken relatively only. Faith and Hope taken absolutely are as eternal as love. The apostle is writing with reference to the second advent. Faith and Hope, he asserts, will, in the Parousia, or second appearing of the Lord, be done away; but Love will abide.

These three chapters then, are to be studied as a complete practical instruction, concerning the comparative importance of the *gifts* of the Christian religion, and the *spirit* of the Christian religion. Spiritual gifts in the Corinthian church had been vastly overestimated, misunderstood, and therefore abused. The gifted ones claimed, that these gifts were the grand essentials of the Christian religion, and their devotees applauded the assumption to the echo. St. Paul says : " No ! the spirit is the grand essential, and that spirit is love. Gifted Christians, without the Christian spirit, are but as sounding brass, or a tinkling cymbal. On the other hand, loving Christians, without the gifts, are also lacking; not as individuals, but as helpers in the planting of the church." The gifted Christian and the loving Christian made up St. Paul's perfect man in Christ Jesus Our Lord. In thus exalting the *spirit* of Christianity, he would not disparage the *gifts* of Christianity. " Follow love," he says, " but covet earnestly the best gifts." While love is the elixir of the holy life, he knew very well that ungifted love would be less efficient, in those circumstances, than gifted love. He desired, for his Corinthian disciples, the highest rank in the Christian church. They were gifted above others, and so capable of being helpers-on of Christianity beyond any other church. But they did not love. Sectarian strife—that worst enemy of religion—had tarnished the Corinthian name, and the lustre of their gifts had been dimmed. Unloving, it had been better for themselves that they had been ungifted also; for their gifts were a snare, and their zeal a hindrance to the progress of the truth. The apostle realized most deeply, the highly critical condition of this famous church; for he tells them flatly, that while they were boasting of their spiritual gifts, their sectarianism showed that they were essentially carnal. In his intense anxiety, and yearning love for them, therefore, he breaks out into this splendid laudation of Queen Charity. It is a giant effort to arrest a giant evil; it is a special pleading to meet a special emergency. Nevertheless, it is so self-evidently true, so sublimely perfect, and so all-embracing, that there is no set of circumstances to which it cannot be applied with perfect propriety. More could not be said for any effort of inspired genius.

I.—THE GREATEST GRACE.

" The greatest of these is charity," 1 Cor., 13.13.

There was a dash of genius in the selection of the question which stands first in the General Assembly's, shorter catechism, " What is the chief end of man "? The reply, is a like splendid tribute to the wise appreciation our forefathers had, of the essential spirituality of our most holy religion, " Man's chief end is to glorify God and to enjoy him for ever." Nothing truer, simpler, fuller, within so limited a compass, has ever been written or spoken, as the statement of a manly Christian ambition. To make God glorious before men, to present in one's life and character the sublime spiritual characteristics of the supreme at their human best, to be so god-like in thought and act that the Divine Being shall be the companion, with whom we walk as Enoch of old walked with Him, and to find in that fittest companionship the earnest of the blessed fellowship which can know no ending—that surely must be the purest and noblest ambition of the human soul. It is, moreover, the highest dignity of man. Whatever can excite such a sublime ambition, and exalt to so high a dignity, must be what one has recently called it—the greatest thing in the world. That greatest thing is charity, the queen of the Christian graces. Charity or love is the greatest thing in the Holy Bible, it is the greatest thing in our Blessed Lord, it is the greatest thing in apostles and saints who have followed in the Lord's footsteps. Not only is it the greatest thing on earth, but it is the greatest thing in heaven—the very law and life of heaven—the very peace, and harmony, and fullness of energy, which make heaven the home of the saints' desire, the blessed everlasting rest, for which the tempest-tossed mariner on the ocean of life longs, like the sleepless sufferer for the first streaks of the golden dawn. Greater still than the greatest thing in earth or heaven, love is the greatest thing in the wide universe. For did not the apostle of love excel himself, when, with a pen plucked from an archangel's wing, and dipped in the hues of the rainbow, he touched the climax of all inspired thought and feeling, as he wrote these divine imperishable words, "God is love?" No higher could soul of genius soar. Here we are at the throne of the worlds, and its foundations are love.

Is it not passing strange, that this fundamental attribute of God and man, should not have been universally regarded throughout the Christian ages as the fundamental attribute of that religion in which God and man come into closest fellowship? Surely, if the great founder of Christianity had been made the living example of the Christian life, and his spirit the absorbing topic of Christian thought, there could never have been any rival to dispute with love the sovereignty of the soul's devotion. Surely, if apostolic words could illustrate and enforce the life, spirit, and teaching of the Master, the consensus of apostolic sentiment breathed in such phrases as this of St. Peter, "Above all things have fervent love among yourselves;" and this of St. John, "He that dwelleth in love dwelleth in God;" and these of St. Paul, "Walk in love," "Abound in love," "Knit together in love"—

surely if the precepts of the servants could commend the life, and the precepts, of the master, no better testimony to almighty love has ever been paid than by the apostolic writers. If everything else failed me, I should be content to rest my plea for Queen Charity on this thirteenth chapter of first Corinthians, and proclaim aloud to the four winds of heaven—Enough! this is enough! Love must be the greatest thing in the universe.

But the history of Christianity has no records to show, that the queen of the Christian graces has ever been reverenced with all true homage and fealty within the Christian church. It is a deplorably sad fact, but it is a fact, that the great names of history, which Christendom to-day delights to honour most, were not borne by men whose great inspiration in all their thought, and action was Queen Charity. Some names, indeed, are very highly honoured of men who were notoriously stout rebels against her supremacy. Some among them even died speaking with their latest breath the word, which caught up by zealous and indiscreet disciples, has gone across the world to be the tocsin of war and devastation in the Christian ranks wherever it has come. Christians have fought for theoretical faith like demi-gods. For the truth, as they believed it, they have been eager to face every foe, and bear every trial. And I am not here to speak lightly, for a moment, of faith. The faith, which has so often lit up with heavenly lustre the martyr's eye, and plucked up by the roots the sycamine tree of solid difficulty, and cleft its way through the stolid ranks of despotism, and battered to the dust the Babel-towers of horrid selfishness, can never be celebrated in too lofty strains. Our modern civilization owes too much to the pioneers who started out into the forest primeval of barbarism, and hewed down the monarchs of the wood, to make paths for the feet of men of leading and of light to walk in, that we should speak lightly of the triumphs of faith. Christian faith has lit up too many bonfires, on the hill-tops of these centuries, to be denied her rank among the sisters of the sacred three.

Neither would I speak lightly of the sparkling-eyed queen, who has gilded a thousand times, with her holy and blessed light, both the path of life, and the bed of death for the faithful and good. Rob human life of its hope, and the stainless banner, excelsior, will fall headlong from the firm grasp of youth, and the maiden's young love burn up her heart, as it burnt up the heart of the Lily Maid of Astolat; the mother's eye will droop in her watch by the couch where infant beauty sleeps, and the brand spring aimless from the lost patriot's hand. Blessed, beauteous hope! with thee to encourage us, farewell dread of coming ills, and welcome even the last enemy of man. The miserable have in thee their only solace, the afflicted their only medicine, the bereaved their only balm, the exile his only home.

While no one dare be-little the victories of faith, or bedim the sheen of the pleasures of hope, these two fair queens must both take their places at the feet of queen charity. For she is their life, and without her they are nothing. The faith, which goes forth uninspired by love, may strike many a deadly blow and take many a strong fortress; but she will be unable to hold what she has won. She may be like Elijah on Carmel or by the Kishon,

"Zealous even unto slaughter for the God of Israel,
'Gainst Ahab and the minions of the Tyrian Jezebel."

But though she has the glory of Carmel and the vengeance of Kishon behind her, she will as surely have the flight to Horeb, and the humiliation of the cleft in the rock, before her. Triumphant faith working without love has sooner or later to confess, like Elijah in the valley of repentance:

"I smote you there on Carmel as I thought by God's commands,
But I smote my own heart also when your blood was on my hands."

Hope without love has no pedestal for her feet. It is love that lends the brightness to the Christian mourner's eye; it is love that prompts the worn covenanter's cry to heaven at the grave of a martyred comrade, "O to be wi' Richie." Take the love out of hope, and faith, and you have nothing left with which to glorify God or bless mankind. As the heart and soul of faith and hope, love is pre-eminently the greatest of the three.

There is an agreeable disappointment about the uniform eulogy of love by the apostolic writers, inasmuch as it is precisely the Christian grace we should not have expected these old worthies to exalt. They had, one and all, been trained in a bad school. The religious atmosphere they breathed from infancy, and the religious life into which they grew up, were loveless. John, who sang like a seraph of love, reflected the religious sentiment of his education perfectly, when on a memorable occasion he said: "Master! wilt thou, that we command fire to come down from heaven and destroy them, as Elias did?" Peter was a foul traitor to love, when he swore his denial of the Master at a little serving-maid. And though Saul of Tarsus was the penman of the grandest eulogy of love, which genius has yet conceived, when we first meet with him, he is standing as the accepted champion of those, who were breathing out threatenings and slaughter against the disciples of the Lord. Depend upon it when John, and Peter, and Paul glorify love, they are not speaking out of the heart of early prepossession, or of maturer prejudice. I marvel at the fine development of the spirit of love, in the later years of men, who had so little of it to begin with. You may be sure, that nothing short of an overmastering conviction, ever brought Gamaliel's favourite pupil to proclaim as the very life of all human duty, "love is the fulfilling of the law." I cannot imagine a saying more likely to arouse and astound the Hebrew mind, steeped as it was in the narcotism of tradition and formula. Nevertheless it fell from the lips of one, who was educated in the straitest sect of Pharisaism, and who, before his conversion, had been regarded as the rising hope of his ancestral faith.

One can but ill conceive the shock which those devotees of an elaborate and conventional religious system received, when they were told that a new law, as brief as theirs was lengthy, simple as theirs was intricate, and easy as theirs was difficult, was destined to supersede the old, and eventually to command the homage, not only of one nationality, but of all the nations of the earth. These old loyal Judaists knew very well, how rocky was the road they had to travel to heaven. Still, with all its hardness, it was the path by which their fathers had ascended, and the glory of their national life haloed around the brows of the mighty dead. How should they abandon it for any untried path, and least of all for a path drenched with the blood of the crucified Nazarene? Moreover, was it not suspicious, that the substitute for their venerable and elaborate law should be presented, in the form of a single precept? To us, its simplicity is the charm, and the strength of the Christian law. But to them, the contrast was too striking, the change too risky, the good news too good to be true. It seemed, as if they were called to pass at a step, from climax to anti-climax—from a *law* which had authority to a *love* which had none. Indeed, the high spiritual teaching of Our Lord so transcended the current ideals of his countrymen, that they were actually unable to follow it; and in their incapacity to appreciate, they developed a remarkable capacity to depreciate. Those who stigmatised him, as a destroyer of the law and the prophets, were not the illiterate or the vicious, but educated, pious people, pure-motived and conscientious; very much indeed like those earnest evangelical Anglicans, who, in our own day, have believed that they could not honor God, and his Christ better, than by pointing the finger of scorn at such manly Christians as Charles Kingsley, and Frederick Denison Maurice, and Arthur Penrhyn Stanley. History is constantly repeating itself. The reign of law in the popular religion is far more popular to-day than the reign of love.

Saul of Tarsus was the very last man to surrender lightly his ancestral faith, and, by that act, brand his people as the betrayers and murderers of their noblest son and king. No one shall ever know what it cost that pharisee of the pharisees, to lay down the sword of the persecutor, and take up the cross of the persecuted. Only those know something of the ordeal through which he passed, who have had to fight, "foot to foot and hand to hand," spectre after spectre of the mind—those whose souls have been scarred and furrowed all over, in the struggle to reach the light and liberty of the spirit of the Christ. Only such as those know, that love and not law was their best ally in the battle, and, that it was only by her power they fought and endured hardness like good soldiers of Jesus Christ. Not every one is sufficient for this trial. But they, who can receive power from on high to fight that battle, need fear no other foe. St. Paul had that power in a remarkable degree; and he never gave better proof of it than when he put aside at one sweep the whole traditional code of his early training, and declared unhesitatingly that the simple law of love is " the law of laws, the rule for fulfilling all rules, the new commandment for keeping all the old commandments, the one secret of the holy, helpful life." It was the greatest triumph of Christianity, in the first age, this conversion of Saul, from the conventionalism of pharisaic law and tradition acquired by long and weary toil, to the simplicity of a single precept, self-evidently true, and so far-reaching, that it entirely superseded, not only the holy ten words, but all the wisdom of the Rabbis. Not only superseding them, but proving itself greater, just as simple nature is greater than elaborate art. It must have been a great shock to him to find, that without love not only does the life go out of the ten commandments, and all other commandments whatsoever, but that with love, whatever is good and true in all religious precept must be effective and immortal. And yet there is no evidence of the shock in the writings of St. Paul. Because the possession of this greatest gift grew into his consciousness, as the pale dawn grows into the midday glory. Could the history of those dark days of Damascus have been written, or of those two contemplative years in Arabia, one might have been able to trace his dolorous way, out of the darkness of the pharisee, into the light of the Christian apostle. As it is, we know that the knowledge of the heavenly love must have come to him as the most natural thing in the world. Marvellous though the change was, the method was most simple. He who had hounded his countrymen to death, because they dared to cling to the dear memory of the Crucified One—he who would sacrifice not a jot or a tittle of pharisaic tradition, to tolerate a brother who could not be recreant to the spirit of the Pure One—this man and persecutor, for the love of God, was destined to be willing to surrender his own hope of heaven, if thereby the veil might be lifted from the Hebrew mind, and Israel according to the flesh saved. What a magnificent victory was that for the spirit of love! It recalls the Master's words, "greater love hath no man than this that a man lay down his life for his friends." Nevertheless, the apostle was never so much himself, as when he was so possessed by the love of the Lord Jesus. Let no man dream—a woman cannot—that love is unnatural, and that when we celebrate the praises of this greatest power of the universe, we are speaking of that which is not humanity's very own. I protest that no one is ever so natural, as when he loves; nor so unnatural as when he hates. For proof of this assertion I ask: Is not the love of Jesus, the almighty and the most natural thing about his history, so far as we can apprehend it? His tenderness at Cana, his thoughtfulness at Bethsaida, his tears at Bethany, speak the most eloquent language that ever thrilled the human soul; because these episodes reach human nature deepest down. To him who can grasp it, the sublime love in those deeds awakens the echoes of his own affections and so possesses his whole being as to make him instinctively exclaim: "Surely, this son of man is the son of God." It is that true human naturalness, which makes this chief among the graces, the greatest thing in any man or woman to-day, as it was the greatest thing in the Apostle Paul. It is that same naturalness, which commends it to every one as a possible possession. It is that naturalness, which is love's true dignity in the soul of man or woman. Conversely, it is the absence of that grace, which makes man or woman the poorest, because the most unnatural, being in

God's creation. For the heartless villain, who casts from him the jewel of love, which his selfish nature cannot appreciate, and treads it beneath his feet, we do not pollute the sacred name of manhood by calling him a man. On the other hand, the mother who dashes forward to pluck her boy from the jaws of death, only to give up her own life in saving his, we canonise among the noblest of her sex. The soul of the world judges rightly in both cases, and, in its judgment, we recognise the innate testimony of the human bosom to the naturalness of love, and to the unnaturalness of anything else. A great modern poet has illustrated very strikingly this naturalness and unnaturalness: The scene is laid in a Russian village. A span of horses, with distended nostril and steaming flank, dash into the village, dragging a sleigh in which sits a lonely weeping mother, in widow's weeds. She draws up at the door of a former peasant-friend, and proceeds to unfold her sorrowful tale. The day before, she had left her distant home, rendered desolate by the death of her husband, to return with her three children to the scene of her childhood. On the way she had been overtaken by wolves, and despite the best efforts of herself and her team, one after another of her children fell a prey to the hungry pack. The peasant sat meanwhile nervously sharpening his pruning hook on his knee, while in broken accents the widow recited her mournful story. Springing to his feet, when she had ended, with a voice of thunder he shouted, "And are you there to tell the tale?" Then for an instant gleamed his sickle in the air, and that unloving, unnatural mother fell to the ground a headless corpse. So tragically natural was love's avenging.

This greatest thing of St. Paul may become the possession of every one who will be a true man or woman. It is the natural possession of every sharer of the divine image. "God is love," and God made us in the image of love. So true is this, that one must be deliberately unnatural not to love. Without love we are nothing, we have nothing, we can do nothing. With love we draw to ourselves all the gifts, treasures, powers, of life worth the having. The great man is not he who bears a great historic name, or fills a high place in the councils of his queen; but he is great with whose praises the world rings because of the greatness of his love. The rich man is not he whose coffers swell with yellow gold, or whose broad acres fill a country-side. Such an one may be the poorest of all who live on his bounty, or sweat in his fields. But that man is rich indeed, who has gathered to himself the rich endowments of love. He has a treasure which neither moth nor rust doth corrupt, and which thieves cannot break through to steal. He enjoys the warm glow of heavenly peace in his soul which no chills of adversity can quench, and no assaults of envious pride destroy. The strong man is not he, before whose feet thousands crouch, and at whose word the world trembles. Such an one may be the very weakest of mortals in the lonely silence of his own chamber. But he is strong who, in the love of God and man, goes forth to break the captives' chains, and to sanctify the sinner's soul, and to bid the demons depart who stalk through the earth working their wicked will. He is strong who can break the stubborn will of hardened vice, and lift to heaven the despairing eye, and send solace into the mourner's heart, and bring songs of joy into the widow's cheerless garret.

"Mightier far
Than strength of nerve or sinew, or the sway
Of magic potent over sun and star,
Is love, though oft to agony distrest,
And though its favourite seat be feeble woman's breast."

II.—THE FIRST CONTRAST.

"Though I speak with the tongue of men and of angels, and have not charity, I am become as sounding brass or a tinkling cymbal.

"And though I have the gift of prophecy, and understand all mysteries and all knowledge; and though I have all faith, so that I could remove mountains, and have not charity, I am nothing;

" And though I bestow all my goods to feed the poor, and though I give my body to be burned, and have not charity, it profiteth me nothing."—Verses 1-3.

This grand epic opens with a comparison. St. Paul takes certain great personal gifts, highly prized and honoured by society, and he declares, that the grand essential to the right use of these is love. A man eloquent or learned, or liberal, if he be withal a man of high Christian aims, will be a great boon to his age and people. Desiring the well-being of his fellow-men, he will employ his talent, for their good, and be himself richly blessed. If he be not a man of high character, that is to say, if he do not love, and exercise his gift at the bidding of love, then, however gifted he may be, he is nothing in any true, human, and Christian sense. Observe, St. Paul does not decry these great and estimable gifts. He does not say that these gifts are nothing; nor that even an unloving and selfish man may not do good to others by them. He says only, that the individual himself is nothing; because the possession of the gift has brought into his spiritual being no enrichment, however it may enrich others. This is an important distinction, which the author of the address I have already referred to has overlooked.

All good gifts have a twofold object. They are designed, on the one hand, to enrich those who possess them, by their lawful exercise; and, on the other hand, enrich all those who can be influenced and helped by them. Both objects must be gained, if any gift is to fulfil the full purpose of the Great Giver. Society is to be greatly blessed by the seven gifts which the apostle enumerates; but the gifted individuals are themselves also to be blessed in the blessing of society. Rightly prized and exercised, these gifts ought to be the sources of choice soul-enrichment to him who may be endowed with any or all of them. They should dignify him before his fellow-men, and elevate him before God. They ought to be great helps in the upbuilding of a noble character; and they are always a great stimulus in the enlightenment and progress of mankind. St. Paul does not deny that society will be a great gainer, even though the possessors of these seven renowned talents may lack love; he does deny, that the unloving possessors themselves can be any gainers whatever. The gifted may help to make something of their fellow-men even without love; they themselves without love must be nothing.

There are just these two alternative motives which primarily actuate men, self or sacrifice, Either men live, or think, or toil to promote what in common speech is called their own interests exclusively,—their pleasure, their fame, or their wealth; or they live, and think, and toil for the life, or well-being, or the prosperity of others. The former is the selfish policy; the latter is the policy of sacrifice, or love. Unfortunately, there is a widespread popular delusion, that one's own interests and the interests of others are mutually hostile. One who is wise for his own interests, it is alleged, must devote his energies exclusively to care for these; one who desires to promote the good of others is sure to neglect his own interests. Both assumptions I emphatically deny. On the contrary, I maintain, that he who starts out in life, determined to seek only his own interest, will never gain his object in any true sense; whereas, he who seeks the good of others is just the man, who really cares the most for his own good, and does the best for it, even while he is thinking the very least about it. For this good reason, that the one man girds himself for life's battle in the spirit of a slave; the other starts out a free man. Here is the dictum of the slave:—" This gift is mine, " and it is for me. It is to be strained to the " utmost to bring into my lap all the good " things it can. That will be my reward to be " enjoyed at my own pleasure. My own good " is the only good I know." Not the language that of a slave, you may say. But the speaker is a slave all the same; for while there can be no despotism so cruel and so wicked as a plutocracy, there is no slave like the plutocrat. And here is the dictum of the free man:—" I am a " steward. This gift is committed to me by the "good God, and I am to administer it, to the "best of my ability for his glory, which must "be also for my own good. My one talent shall "be made ten talents, if I can, that I may be "able to do ten-talent good in the world. I am "master of this thing by God's grace, and I "shall be master with his help."

There is a very simple and personal test which every one can apply to these alternative motives. It is the test by results—a test which a commercial people will readily appreciate. Have you ever got out of any object, on which you had set your heart selfishly, all that you expected? On the contrary, have you not oftentimes got some ill which you did not expect? Even at the very best, have you not felt that the good thing sought for itself, that is selfishly, always brought with it something which took the very heart out of the pleasure you had coveted? I put these questions straight to conscience, and I call upon conscience to stand up, and speak out like a man. Again, have you ever failed to get far more good than you ever imagined, out of something sought for what it could bring, in true blessing, to yourself and others? Even, when you did not win your object, was not the effort in seeking it so consecrated by the unselfish motive, that your regret was not that you had failed, but that you had been deprived of the delight of doing a good to others? No one shall ever sound the depths of unselfish tenderness implied in that poignant regret of the Master on the cross, "They know not what they do."

Everything in human life turns on the questions, Am I a free man? or a slave? Do I walk in the liberty of the spirit of God as I should? or am I controlled, ruled, commanded, by some selfish ambition? Do I rule my gifts or my possessions? or do they rule me? Do these things make my character what they please? or do I make them do just what I please? The right answer to these questions gives the key to the interpretation of this chapter. It will show very clearly in what direction one's real interests are to be sought. It will suggest, by contrast, the false and the true principles of living and working. It will illustrate most strikingly the pure and impure motives to duty.

1. What a splendid gift is eloquence! History presents no more striking examples of the

power of man over man, than in the charm of
eloquence, "potent to command a listening
senate," or, "to wield the wild democracy."
Warren Hastings said that he never thought he
was guilty, till he had heard Burke's magnificent impeachment. Nevertheless, there are few
great gifts which have been so fatally abused
in the lips of unprincipled and ambitious men.
Without love for the right, as the ruling passion
of the orator, the most eloquent speaker is
nothing better than sounding brass or a tinkling
cymbal. He is in society what the hypocrite is
in the church—a play-actor. And we know
what our Lord thought of that detestable type
of character. Eloquence inspired by love may
be one of the greatest blessings to an age and to
its possessor; eloquence uninspired by love may
be the greatest curse to both.

2. "Prophecy," is the interpretation and ex-
position of truth. The true prophet is a teacher
to the manner born, and the born teacher is the
hope of society. The future of both the church
and the state is in his hands.

> 'Tis education forms the common mind;
> Just as the twig is bent the tree's inclined.

The true prophet dignifies his office by his

high motive and his wise method. He educates, that is, leads out, by careful culture, the faculties of the young mind. His ambition is to develop a genuine love of learning, and a high standard of honour and righteousness. He never thinks for his pupils; but trains them to do their own thinking. He believes in God, and his great desire is that they should believe in, that is, as he explains, live-by, God. St. Paul could never say of such a prophet, "He is nothing." Pure love of human good inspires his every thought. Such an one is the greatest benefactor to his people; and as he blesses, his own nature is being more abundantly enriched. He is something to both God and man—a something increasing in value day by day.

But St. Paul thought of another prophet, of which class, unfortunately, Corinth had, at that time, too many specimens. He thought of the prophet whose motive is last of all the real good of his people. He is the creature of party, and system, and regulation. He crams his youthful charge with facts, and figures, and formulas, and thinks he has produced a perfect result, to do him credit as a teacher, when he has turned out a pupil, something on the principle of the manufacturer of glass jars stamped and warranted to contain just so much. Such a teacher is the greatest curse of society and religion. He is no true follower of the great prophet, whose standing order to the twelve was this, "Let *your* light shine." He himself has no light but that of his names and authorities, and too often these are in him but as darkness. Though the unthinking and unloving world of sect and party applaud such a prophet to the echo, he is nothing. Weighed in St. Paul's balances, he is light as thistle-down.

3. "Initiation into mysteries," and, "knowledge," may go together. Though, "initiation into mysteries," has no exact parallel in modern civilization, we may take it along with, "knowledge," as best represented by modern science. Who, in this nineteenth century, shall dare to speak lightly of the feats of literary and scientific genius? Speaking comparatively, all old things, in these last days, have passed away, and all things have become new. Nevertheless, while society must rejoice in the vast results of science, and honour the great toilers in her vineyard, it is quite possible to find the greatest scientific gifts allied to an ignoble character.

Who would exchange the lowliest lot for that of the great English Chancellor, whom Pope stigmatises truly?

> "If parts allure thee, think how Bacon shined,
> The wisest, brightest, meanest of mankind."

If science be sought for her own sake—if she be one's queen and not love—then

> "He may be wise, or rich or great,
> But never can be blest."

Though a man be as wise as Solomon, if he be as selfish, he will be only a good illustration of St. Paul's own words—"Knowledge puffeth up." But love buildeth up—buildeth up the world's good—buildeth up the builder's character.

4. Next comes, "the faith which can remove mountains." The faith here referred to is that intellectual gift called by theorists *faith*, and not that spiritual gift known in religion as *fidelity*. The loving man is greater than the man of intellectual faith—so much greater, indeed, that though a man may be distinguished for faith, if he lack fidelity, he is nothing. That is saying a great deal for love. Has not strong faith electrified the world a thousand

times by its indomitable heroism? Without faith no great thing has ever been achieved by man of woman born. Surely nothing can be greater than faith. But if we consider the end of our life, and of our religion, we shall discern that St. Paul is right. As I have already said, the end of our noblest ambition is Godlike, and God is not faith, but love. Faith is necessary to love, for, " He that cometh to God must believe that he is." But though the sunbeam is necessary to the peony, that gorgeous flower is greater than the light which plays upon its petals. Love is greater than faith in like manner; for it is the end to which faith is a means. Moreover, faith so-called may be where love is not, as in the case of St. James' devils, who "believe and tremble." Love cannot exist without faith. Faith has often tried to exist without love. Such faith not working by love is therefore, not entitled to be called *religious* faith. Though strong enough to perform wonderful works, yet its possessor is not entitled to be called a model Christian. Disciples of such like faith are evidently referred to by our Lord, in that passage, where, forecasting the day in which many will come to Him, protesting,

"Lord! have we not cast out devils in Thy name, and done many wonderful works,"? he will sadly but promptly answer, "I never knew you," to chill with horror every pleading lip.

> "In faith and hope the world will disagree,
> But all mankind's concern is charity."

5. One may be celebrated even for almsgiving, and yet not be charitable. "Though I give all my goods to feed the poor," I may be nothing. But is not alms-giving itself charity? one may ask. Yes, if the charitable hand is the messenger of the charitable spirit; but not otherwise. Alms bestowed, because one cannot deny a pitiful appeal, or because one does not like to risk refusing the poor, or because it is the easiest way to get rid of a disagreeable intruder, is not charity at all. A large proportion of the alms-giving of the world, for that reason, neither blesses him that gives nor him that takes. There is no love in it. It may temporarily help; it is sure to degrade permanently. It cannot make the giver anything. Judged by the Christian standard he is nothing.

6. We come now to the climax of the comparison. Martyrdom even may be no sure token

of a true Christian manhood or womanhood. It is possible to become a martyr by mistake. There could be no stronger form in which to express this antithesis. What will a man give in exchange for his life? What pledge like that of the genuineness of his devotion, and the thoroughness of his conscientious conviction? Can anything be more testing than the martyr's faith and courage? Has it not passed into a maxim?—" The blood of the martyrs is the seed of the church." Is it not an intolerable harshness for St. Paul to speak of giving one's body to the flames for nothing? The longer we reflect on the apostle's words, however, the more convinced are we that he is right. Take his word with you as a torch into the chambers of history, and you will be astonished at finding how much of Christian martyrology is a loveless story, and how much of it posterity has not been able to justify. After all, martyrdom only means the fruit of strong sincerity, which cannot bend; but strongly-sincere people, who were wrongly-sincere, have been as common as blueberries in all the ages. As a great English author very well says:—" 'Tis not the dying for a faith that's so hard—every man of every nation has done that—'tis the living up to it that is difficult." This climax of meritorious things, according to the popular acceptation, may be no true test, therefore, either of a lofty piety, or of an ardent loving-kindness. Many a man has mounted the stake, like a hero, to whom martyrdom profited nothing, dying for an opinion, and not for love. This greatest thing, as the world judges, is inferior to love.

What a splendid tribute this comparison furnishes to the peerless supremacy of queen charity! One after another Paul takes up the things most esteemed and honoured among men —things more or less worshipped by persons and classes as the chief good—and one after another he says to their possessors:—" You are " nothing, and you, and you. Ye are all noth- " ing without love's meritorious spell. Touched " by her magic wand, ye are all heroes and " great ones of the earth. Base metal, so to " speak, your gifts are made fine gold when " brought into touch with this divine philoso- " pher's stone. Pieces of dull, cold iron,—these " are instantly magnetised, making you magnets " also able to magnetize, when seized by love's " magnetic charm." The greatest force in the universe is charity. For it is the motive power, without which virtue cannot live, and selfishness must reign supreme, even in the most gifted of the sons and daughters of genius.

The high law of the Christian stewardship could not be more strikingly illustrated than in this grand panegyric. That law is really the secret of this eulogy of charity. He who is endowed with any of these great gifts, and realizes that his gift is his only in trust, is the only individual who ever knows how good and how great a thing he possesses. He will, moreover, be just the person likely to make the most of it, by doing the most good with it. Love is the soul of his stewardship, and you may as well bid the Evening Glory to shut its chaste petals against the soft twilight, as forbid the steward of love to share with the greatest number of his fellow-men, his good thing, whatever it be. Indeed, he never knows how good his gift is till he has seen how much good it can do. Is not this just the method of the divine love which bathes us round ?—distributing unstintedly, and being unstintedly enriched. How sublime then the dignity of the child of love! Eloquence, prophecy, faith, martyrdom

—how these have glorified men in the eyes of their fellows! Yet, all their dignity may be stained by self. Love's dignity is stainless and divine. How highly exalted the wise and good steward; how base and unworthy the lot of the faithless!

While all of these great and gifted ones, as men often judge greatness, may be, by St. Paul's test, nothing, many lowly ones, of whom the world never hears, and of whom she would, perhaps, think very little, even if she did hear of them, are, by the same test, declared to be something. Love is the sole ennobler. Without love no one is anything. This psalm of love is, therefore, a great leveller up as well as a great leveller down. It casts down the mighty from their seats, but exalts them of low degree. While it disqualifies the selfish and unbrotherly, however high his titles and proud his name, it qualifies the brotherly, and the loving, entirely unknown to fame though he be. Here, then, is a seat of honour for all who will fill it. Limited though our influence, scant though our gifts, poor though our graces; nevertheless, if whatever we have be inspired by a true and simple love, these insignificant things will bring to us the reward promised by our Lord, to all lowly good-doers, at the great day. They will be unable to recall, He tells us, when they did anything for their Master— so natural and so true was their good-doing. But the great judge cannot forget it. Modestly, they will blush to hear of a service they did not try to render, but rendered all the better on that account. And their embarrassment will pass into profound astonishment, when, for their poor service of love, the lips of the love divine will pronounce the invitation, " Come ye blessed of My Father." Among that shining band will be the widow with her rusty weeds and her two mites; and Mary, with flowing tresses and her box of spikenard; and the Good Samaritan, with his oil and wine; and they will take their places beside the apostle of love, and Peter, the Man of Rock, and Saul of Tarsus, and will not be ashamed. Cowper's Cottager will be there, and the sainted Queen Margaret; the hidden Village Preacher, and the martyred Williams; the silent Servitor, and the eloquent Chrysostom. All ranks and conditions of men will be there, levelled up by the love of God in Christ Jesus to be kings and priests in heaven.

The gifted loving, and the ungifted will be then—all filling the places they have made for themselves—no two alike in dignity, and none envious of another's place. Surely, she who can so dignify and crown is well-worthy the first place among the heavenly graces.

> Yes, love indeed is light from heaven;
> A spark of that immortal fire
> With angels shared, by Allah given,
> To lift from earth our low desire.

III.—THE REASON WHY.

> "Charity suffereth long,
> And is kind;
> Charity envieth not."
> —Verse 4.

While I have, in the two preceding discourses, been speaking of love as the essential element in all true human dignity and virtue, I have been, in reality, dealing with a principle or a spirit, rather than with an attribute, or a thing. For example, we do not accurately describe religion, when we speak of it, as a thing to be singled out from among many valuables, and exhibited, labelled in large letters, "Religion," in case society might not recognize it; or, as a thing to be put away for safe-keeping and preserved in our most secret repository, lest it should be stolen. On the contrary, enlightened Christians regard religion as the spirit of their life—the way the devout soul has of doing everything—the one divine method of fulfilling man's great destiny. In like manner, we say of love, that it is not a prize to be awarded for some meritorious act, but a principle to be lived-by in loyal devotion to the Christ. A religious man is not he who possesses a sacred treasure called religion ; a religious man is he who breathes the religious spirit. The way of his life is religious, the work of his life is religious, the worship of his life is religious. So, a loving man is a man of the loving spirit. His words of love, or his acts of love are the just expression of his loving character. The spirit of the man is, "love."

In these verses the writer is presenting certain great characteristics of the loving spirit. I do not suppose that he means to exhaust his great subject. That would be very hard to do. He takes certain outstanding features of this spirit, which are self-evident to all, as they appear in the man or woman of the loving spirit. His object is to supply Corinthian Christians with certain great test-marks, by which the loving man or woman, that is, the true Christian, can be easily known, and recognized in society and the church. I am quite sure the apostle is not theorizing in this analysis. I am sure he did not work out these features of the loving spirit, in his inner consciousness, by any powers of reasoning. Love won't stand to be manipulated in that fashion. I believe, that he simply took our Blessed Master, as the highest exemplar of all the virtues, and, with the eye of inspiration, perceiving in his divine subject those features of human character which were the grandest, strung them together with the hand of love, to be to mankind for ever, the finest tribute to the spirit of the Christian religion, which the human soul has ever conceived.

1. *Charity suffereth long.* She is patient. With this clause we will take verse 7, which is really only a restatement amplified of the, "long-suffering of love." Love, "beareth all things, hopeth all things, believeth all things, endureth all things."

No characteristic of any human faculty or emotion has so impressed the soul of the world as the hoping, the believing, the staying power of love. More than any other, if I may be allowed to discriminate where every grace is so divine, was this the, "feature most divine," of our Blessed Lord's character. More than any other, has it been the predominating feature, in the best loves of the best men and women. Well did the Hebrew singer carol:

> "Many waters cannot quench love;
> Neither can the floods drown it."

Could either result have been possible, the heartlessness of pride and selfishness should have often conquered love. These have succeeded occasionally; but their scant success has only thrown up into bolder relief the sublime long-suffering of love, in the finest examples of it. I have seen a poor wife, struggling like a heroine for years against both the wind and the tide of a weak husband's folly. Implored by relations to forsake him, and herself cast off because she would not cast him off; blamed by good friends because she would not, were it only for her children's sake, abandon to his sin and shame the wreck of humanity, who, in happier days, had wooed and won her maiden love. But nothing could turn her from what she believed to be her wifely trust. Clinging to him, like the affectionate hound which licks the hand stained with its life's-blood, doing her wisest, and hoping the best, her long-suffering devotion at last reaped its well-merited reward. In course of time the erring one was reclaimed—

rescued by the strong hand of her love, like a brand from the burning—and for the rest of his days the most devoted of husbands, never able to do enough for the love of the good woman who, at his very worst and wrongfullest, would not let him go.

I think, if I were asked to select, from the pages of history, episodes illustrative of man's native dignity, as an inheritor of the divine image; or if I were considering the best reply I could make, to the sternest censor of our peccant humanity, I should select the triumphs of long-suffering love and say:—"These present the godlike in humanity. These retrieve humanity's darkest disgrace. These are humanity's proudest victories." When every other power in man or woman has utterly failed—when the torch of hope in every other hand has burnt out, and faith even has gone down in the deep waters of sorrowing despair—love has kept alive her watch-fire, love has made her foot swift and steady, and her hand strong and sure, to seek out and to save the object of her undying solicitude. Take the triumphs of love from history, and the residuum is but a weary, wicked record of rapine, cruelty and blood.

The writer who should offer to the public a loveless tale would be pronounced, without a dissenting voice, a hopeless failure. The voice of humankind would proclaim: " It cannot be. Human story has no meaning without long-suffering love."

"They sin who tell us love can die."

Making our Blessed Master his great example, St. Paul, like a true disciple of love, followed bravely in his master's train. When he sang of long-suffering love, therefore, it was because his life was one long illustration of that whereof he sang. Master and disciple alike suffered wrongs the most terrible, were the objects of suspicions the most unjust, had accusations the most cruel hurled at them, and calumnies the most unworthy heaped upon them—all by those for whom they were living to do so much, and for whose good they were ready to die. Their best offices were scorned, their best gifts maligned, their best kindness flung back contemptuously in their face. Nevertheless, they held on heroically for the goal which love had planted for them. Neither shame, nor cruelty, nor death itself, was able to make them falter in the path which they had chosen to tread. Rather were their zeal rendered more ardent, and their labours more abundant, to rescue, if possible, from a fate they knew not, those who would not save themselves. Love long-suffering, and love triumphant were never so splendidly illustrated, as in the greatest gift of these greatest of the world's benefactors. On these resplendent orbs in the Christian firmament must the eye of toiling, tried, and weary mankind for ever rest, with consoling and inspiring interest. For do they not glitter only to reveal the glory of Him with whom we have all to do? Our Lord said : " He that hath seen Me, hath seen the Father," and all the lights of long-suffering love are but reflections, therefore, stronger or fainter, of the divine long-suffering love. What a gospel this is to erring mortals! Isaiah sang of it to sinful Judah, "If ye are willing and obedient, though your sins be as scarlet, they shall be white as snow." Hosea exemplified it, when he went out into the waste to rescue the unfaithful wife, who could be no longer wife to him, and, for the old affection, guard her fatherlike until the day she died. Our Lord fulfilled it to the height when He drew into the kingdom of God, because God loved them, and He loved them, harlots and thieves, publicans and sinners, leprous outcasts and souls tormented with devils—the very scum of humanity, at whom respectable society dare not look, and by whom she sweeps with lofty head and uplifted hands. And those who have come nearest to the stature of their Lord have ever been the most eager to gather in that moral, "flotsam and jetsam," of the sea of life, to gladden the great treasure-house above. What a gospel that is to raise and cleanse humankind, and save it for the royal love of our God and Father! Dearly beloved! I should not hold it worth my while to open my lips in this pulpit, could I not say to every son and daughter of Adam—the weakest, the waywardest, the wickedest—in spite of all the speculations of Christian theorists, " Brother! sister! " you shall not despair. The long-suffering love " of your Heavenly Father has been following " you, in tears, all through the days of your sin. " Look up to heaven's blue and say it if you " will—God loves me; Christ gave himself for " me; I have a place in that great, tender, " unquenchable love." What an encouraging, saving message is that, for every one of us, from

St. Paul's love "which beareth all things, hopeth all things, believeth all things, endureth all things," and yet will not be turned away by any sin of ours!

" Love is indestructible :
Its holy flame forever burneth ;
From Heaven it came ; to Heaven returneth."

2. *The kindness of love.* "Kind," comes from "kin," which means, of the same family. Kindness, is therefore a synonym for, brotherliness. The kind man is the brotherly, and the brotherly man makes his brother's case his own. He thinks, feels, acts, for and with another, as for himself. This is the second element in what may be called the *matter* of love.

Kindness is a great Christian virtue, much less appreciated than it deserves. More fully to express our author's meaning, I prefer the psalmist's word, loving-kindness. It is a virtue based on something broader than any religious system ; its foundation is humanity. For when we go back far enough we hear the whisper of primeval lips : " Be kind, not because thou art a Jew, nor because thou art a Christian ; but because thou art a man." Both Judaism and

Christianity have done much to celebrate kindness; although to be a good Jew, or a good Christian, has sometimes meant to be a most unkind man. Such unkindness, however, has always been in spite of, and not because of, the spirit of either religion : for the religion which has no loving-kindness in it, is no religion at all. Indeed, brotherliness or its lack must ever be the sure test of a rising or falling religion—of a religious or an irreligious man.

To coin a word, I might say that whole-kindness is what St Paul means here. I use whole-kindness, to distinguish the kindness of this passage, from much that passes muster in society for kindness; and by it I mean those kindnesses in word and manner, and work, all which are necessary, to adequately represent the kindness of St. Paul. Giving gifts, for example, is a popular and precious form of expressing good feeling. But if custom only, or fashion suggest such gifts, these may bear then very little of the virtue of kindness. Moreover, though with the hand we bestow many kind deeds, in all sincerity, if with the lips we needlessly inflict unkindness, our virtue, you can perceive, must be very much watered. Our author's is a whole-kindness, for it is the exponent of love, and love is careful in everything to do her very best. If one were asked to apply a single epithet to Our Lord, which should express the most characteristic feature of his ministry, perhaps the, " kind," would be the most appropriate. His sole effort and influence were calculated to make others happy. He had compassion, because he was kind ; and he constantly spoke and lived-out the kindness which reigned in his bosom. That is ever love's ambition. She rejoices with the joyful, to make their joy the purer ; she weeps with the sorrowful, to bring light and help into their sorrow ; she plays with the child, to intensify its playfulness ; she soothes tottering age, to crown with sweet Sabbath rest the close of an honourable life. Had she her will, love would sweep all pain, and sorrow, and misery from the face of this fair earth of ours. As she cannot have her will, she does the next best thing. She girds herself, with right good will, to breathe into all human relations as much light and pleasure as they can carry. She casts her purple robe around all who choose to wear it.

How much more all of us can do in loving-kindness, we know very well, to our deep regret. How little, comparatively speaking, most of us do in this regard, we also know to our shame, that we have tried to do it so little. How great a return is to be obtained, for a very little kindness bestowed in the spirit of love, those know well who rank these episodes among the choicest of all their experience—episodes they delight to refresh their spirit with, and which, most of all, they will desire to recall at the gates of eternity. The rose laid in the lonely sufferer's hand which lent a gleam to the glazing eye; the faithful, loving word to the erring one which made you his hope and his friend forever; the load lifted from the widow's heart, which took half the gloom out of her life, and gave back the spring to her footstep; the little attention that pleased, and the little comfort that cheered; the gracious look which charmed, and the pressure of the hand which thrilled—these all show how much the kind heart can do for others, and how much it can do also for itself.

God help us to apply duly this word of the Apostle. None of us, I hope, mean deliberately to be unkind: we know, however, that, without meaning it, we are all more or less guilty of unkindness, both by omission and by commission. Consider how it wrongs our nearest and dearest, how it wrongs far more ourselves through the wrong we do to them, how it mars our Christian influence by so misrepresenting the Christian character, how it taints the sweetest fountains of our peace by its unmanliness, and, worse still, by its unwomanliness. The love which has stood many a strain, oftentimes breaks down at the little unkindness, the trifling neglect, the hard look.

3. *Love envies not.* It is the severest test of many good people's virtue, to see something in another better than they have, or than they can ever hope to possess. How lamentably the companions of the Lord of love broke down at this point. When they saw an unknown philanthropist, achieving a success which they could not claim, they must arrest his good work if they can, and forbid the unauthorised worker, who had more of their Master's spirit than they had themselves. Probably, the finest lesson of the Baptist's life is his sublime generosity. When his friends announced, that the young

man whom he had baptized in Jordan, was now the centre of a vast popular enthusiasm, while his own power and influence were apparently on the wane, his quiet, shall we say pathetic, reply was only this : "He must increase, I must decrease." What a wealth of native generosity, in that unselfish remark of the once popular idol, concerning his more popular successor! What a height of spiritual grace one must have reached, to be able to utter such a divine sentiment! It is just the fulness of the divine Jesus, anticipated by his distinguished harbinger.

Ah! how hard it is for all of us, to follow in those footsteps! How easy for most of us, to imitate James and John! How ill the Christian churches have entered into the spirit of the Baptist! How quick sect is to underrate the good work of sect; and how slow to render fair and Christian justice. And yet the good of every church ought to be regarded, as it truly is, the good of all the churches. Whatever is good in the Catholic Church, is the common property of the Protestant Church, and *vice versa*. For every Christian talent is the property of Christianity, and every Christian heart should give thanks, that, in any way, and anywhere, Christianity at large is by so much the richer. If I were to quote Paul, to illustrate Paul, I would point to that strikingly generous word to the Phillipians, where he remarks sorrowfully that some preached Christ of envy and strife, in order to raise up affliction for him in his bonds. But that great heart, though sad, is not scornful. "What then?" he says. "Only that, in every way, whether in pretence or in truth, Christ is proclaimed; and therein I rejoice, and will rejoice." Noble, magnanimous words! Would to God, that we heard more of them in those days! It would be a triumph for the gospel of love, such as the world has never witnessed, to see Catholics blessing God for good done by Protestants, and Protestants thanking God for the good done by Catholics. The world would marvel at such a spectacle, and ask, What next? And why should the world marvel? Ought it not to marvel far more at another spirit prevailing? For are Catholic and Protestant not all one in Christ Jesus, whether they own the unity or no? Is not the weakness, the scandal, the superstition of any one branch of the Church, alike the weakness, the scandal, the superstition of

Christianity? Shall not likewise the good, the success, the prosperity of one, be the glory of all? Why in the name of all that is reasonable and sacred, have Christians dared ever to think anything else? Looking abroad across Christendom to-day, at the fierce sectarian rivalries and strifes which abound, there is no more glaring lack in Christian sentiment than the spirit of St. Paul's words, "love envieth not."

There is no order of plants which possesses more interest for botanists than the orchidaceæ. A bouquet of orchids is, to the skilled eye, one of the most magnificent, and marvellous of Nature's treasures. Every flower an exquisite in beauty, and design, and each markedly different from the rest, a lady may hold in her hand, a world's wonder of Heaven's elegance and loveliness. I call this grouping of love's excellencies by St. Paul a marvel of poetic genius, rich and rare, to be not inaptly compared with the orchid bouquet of Nature's divine handiwork. Both are supreme. One by one we take up these gems of floral excellence, and every one has a fresh fascination. One by one, we take up these flowers of spiritual beauty, and every turn reveals a new charm. Three of these flowers we have already attempted to examine and disclose its charms. We have looked at love in its passive aspect. We have seen it in suffering, revealing a power to endure, unparalleled for strength to stay, among the powers of humanity. The entire poetry and fiction of the world have been built up on long-suffering love ; and if, after we have exhausted the masterpieces of literary genius, we turn to some faithful son, bowed and broken for a father's sin and shame, taking his place in the dock beside his accused parent, and clinging to the last to the unworthy one, we shall say, poetry is grand, and fiction is strange, but common life is grander than poetry, and fact is stranger than fiction.

We have looked at love on its active side. We have seen it go out to work miracles of beneficence—subduing stubborn wills, inspiring callous natures, seizing the sinful with a grip of steel, and lifting the downcast from the abyss of despair to the heaven of hope. Time fails us to tell of the triumphs of divine loving-kindness. The psalmist could soar no higher when he touched the climax, "Thy loving-kindness is better than life." Shakspeare well described this virtue when he wrote—

"The milk of human kindness."

Yes, the milk—the very life-spring of the world.

We have considered love, looking not only on her own things, but also on the things of others. Our queen lives for others, is never so happy as when blessing others, and is not even satisfied when she is doing her very best. She would even do more for those she loves. Her joy is in the joy of others. Beholding others happy, she rejoices with them in their good. Envy does just the reverse of all that. Another's joys are envy's miseries, and his miseries, her joys. Whatever is taken from them seems to be so much personal gain to her. It is an abominable and inhuman spirit, though all the sects practice it. Love cannot share that detestable spirit. She cannot be jealous of another's good things or happiness. She is therefore her best friend, by being the best friend of others. Base envy feeds upon the heart that harbours it She kills the life that seeks its life in her.

What more shall I say? "If ye know these things, happy are ye if ye do them."

IV.—"THE REASON WHY."

"Charity vaunteth not itself,
Is not puffed up;
Doth not behave itself unseemly,
Seeketh not her own."
Verses 4-5.

That is a fine prophetic stratagem by which Nathan wins from the royal David his own conviction. Before the better nature of the unsuspecting monarch, the prophet sketches a picture of great simplicity and pathos. Cruel selfishness, in the person of a wealthy man, had worked its wicked will, in circumstances of extreme heartlessness. Promptly, the kingly conscience adjudges condign punishment for the ruthless reiver, who had not only broken his country's laws, but also foully defamed his manhood. Nathan then lifts the veil, and, to the royal consternation, reveals in the selfish rich man, who had so cruelly wronged the poor, a full-length portrait of himself; and the vision smote him to the heart.

The analysis of love is not to be understood, except in the concrete, nor its power felt, save like Nathan's parable. Loving-kindness has no meaning as an abstract term. No one ever failed to appreciate the philanthropy of the Good Samaritan. St. Paul is here simply depicting the Christ, and his own career as a Christian apostle, shows how truly the Christ character had been forming in his soul, making him, in fact, a Christly version of the love he eulogised. As he had seen he wrote, is true; it is truer, that as he felt and lived, he wrote. We also shall never know how great is the treasure which the human race possesses in his picture, till we have seen it in some measure realized in the life and character of some good man or woman, and especially, till we have educated ourselves up to living it.

4. *The fourth characteristic of the loving character is humility.* Love never vaunts of her works; love is never puffed up because of her gifts or graces. Like her Lord, she is among men as, "one that serveth." She is quite at home when she is ministering; she is positively uneasy when she is being ministered unto. This word, humility, is a contribution of Chris-

tianity, to the vocabulary of modern civilization. The old Roman was greatly insulted, if any one dared to hurl at him the epithet, "humilis." Every student knows that, "humilis" is the classical epithet for, "unmanly," "cowardly." The Roman piqued himself on being, "superbus," or proud, and his best friends could pay him no higher compliment. Christianity has changed all that. She has reversed the verdict of the ancient world. Her highest are her lowliest. Because her Lord could be the humblest, he is crowned, "Lord of All." Accordingly, just as His disciples can go down with Him, so shall they also rise with Him. Blessed truth that, for a society in which nobody serves from choice, but everybody pants to be served. Masterdom is the Paradise of modern society ; Jesus was ambitious to be a servant. Now, there is no reason in the world why any one should esteem it, the chief good of life, to rule. The highest success of life is to be a great ruler, by being the most helpful to one's fellow-men. To rule in the brighter, better lives of others is an immeasurably greater thing, than to rule over their bodies. Jesus, who lived the greatest, noblest, happiest life, and who was, moreover, the Master of Masters, was the Servant of Servants. That fact solves the problem of all modern ambitions. If the happiest life be your ambition, then let your life be the holiest, which is just the most helpful, and then the greatest master among you will be the greatest servant. This fourth flower of love is among the choicest in the garden of the soul.

> " Nothing so becomes a man
> As modest stillness and humility."

5. *The seemliness of love.* This is what may be called the first element of the *manner* of love. Seemliness has to do with the outward appearance, the grace of the loving one. It is not so easy to popularize this element of the manly character as some others. *Manner* is not of the essence of a thing, and it requires a certain degree of culture to give manner its just importance, either in religion or in common life. "The *matter* of duty and religion is the all-important thing," say many good people, "and it matters little how the duty or the religion may be performed, so long as the root of the matter is there. Give due heed to the thing itself; the way of doing it may be left to look after itself." And yet, it matters a good deal how a thing is

done. Every one recognizes the difference between a person with a good heart and an unfortunate manner; and a person with a good heart, and an attractive, graceful manner. The former may be capable of doing a great deal more real good than the latter, and yet how terribly will his manner detract from the quality of his service. The latter may do far less, and yet the charm of his manner may be so striking, that the lesser good will be enhanced a hundred-fold by his way of doing it. There are, for example, good people, to whom one goes in the interests of any charitable work only under pressure—so unfortunate is their way of bestowing gifts. Others, again, have such a natural grace of bestowing, that one goes away from their door feeling, that he has conferred a privilege rather than received a favour.

This is a failing for which many good people are to be blamed only with a qualification. An easy, natural grace of manner is greatly the product of early training and culture. Those who have this grace are to be congratulated on having had such good early advantages, that they have attained naturalness in a gift so important and so Christian. Those who lack it are to be greatly pitied, both for the pain they may give to others, and for the wrong they are certainly doing to themselves. The splendid Easter lily would be as truly a lily, though it did not fill the air with its rich and refreshing fragrance. But who will deny, that the fragrance is a vast additional charm to what is in itself so eminently charming? Likewise, the gruff, unseemly Christian may be as true a Christian as his most graceful, seemly neighbour Christian; and yet the soul of the world will draw to the one man rather than to the other. The one man's Christianity is very apt to be evil spoken of, because of his infirmity; the other man's has a fair field wherein to do its very best for God and for man.

Let no man, therefore, despise the *manner* of love. The Christian life is not the same without the Christian manner of it. These are significant words of St. Luke: " Jesus increased in wisdom and stature, and in favour with God and man." The holy child Jesus had the noble ambition " to behave Himself seemly," and He won a magnificent success. Shall we, who esteem it our highest honour to bear His name— shall we presume to esteem lightly a grace so precious in His eyes? Shall we not rather make it a great aim of our lives to cultivate this grace of a Christian manner? One's up-bringing has much to do, undoubtedly, with the grace of all his speech and action; but it is marvellous how much can be gained, even in this virtue, at a later age. Parents cannot overestimate the value of the grace of seemliness in the education of the young. Not that I would plead for the culture of a generation of mannerists. The dude is the last abomination of a superficial society. Above all things, let the young grow up simple and natural, true to their own character, and true to their neighbours. But simplicity and truth are nowise inconsistent with grace flowing from the lips, dropping from the hands, and incensing the life. No one should let his good be evil spoken of, and it will be often evil spoken of, if it be performed unseemly.

VI. *Love seeketh not her own.* On a Southern railroad a band of rough navvies were building a tunnel. In the progress of the undertaking an unforeseen accident occurred in the drift. The roof caved in; and several hapless victims were buried in the ruins. There was one hero, however, in that unfortunate band, rude navvy as he was, and his noble self-forgetfulness lit up with a heavenly light that terrible disaster. As the timbers were creaking and rending, he was seen to place his back to the wall and hold up both hands, as if to arrest, if he could, the falling mass, and heard to shout out in the darkness to a comrade whom he would save:

> Run for your life, Jake!
> Run for your wife's sake!
>   Don't wait for me.
> And that was all
> Heard in the din,
> Heard of Tom Flynn,—
>   Flynn of Virginia.

What a splendid touch of our better nature in what, the superficial student of human life would call, most unlikely circumstances! That rough navvy sought not his own.

It is ever a true feature of genuine affection and a test as well—self-forgetfulness. Love's own interests never come up in her devotion to the object on which she has set her heart. So true is this, that the greater the demands made upon love—the severer the strain put upon her strength—the more splendid becomes her self-forgetfulness. Who ever read, without deep emotion, Enoch Arden's prayer on the waste, beside the miller's home?

> Uphold me, Father, in my loneliness
> A little longer! Aid me, give me strength
> Not to tell her, never to let her know.
> Help me not to break in upon her peace.

I know no single feature of our social experience so helpful to faith in the power of the Christian religion, than the living examples of unselfish love which meet us among all ranks and conditions of men. When amid the frightful distortions of the Christian ideal, which appear in modern life, one is prompted, in a hesitating moment, to enquire, " Where are the signs of an enlightened, progressive Christianity? and, when so many perplexed minds are ready to answer, in anxiety or despair, where? the noble self-surrender of some good man or woman, on behalf of the waifs and strays of society, the beautiful devotion of daughter to aged parent, or of husband to stricken wife, or of friend to distressed friend, and their unselfish labours of a love that never can do enough, help more than anything else to encourage the desponding heart, and revive drooping faith in the divinity of the truth, and in the ultimate triumph of the gospel of love over all the delusions and falsehood of selfishness. For, wherever such a spectacle meets the eye, there is the Christ still walking the earth.

This spirit of self-forgetfulness runs right counter to the spirit of what is called, modern society. Society says: "Seek your own, and "only your own: gather into your bosom as "much as ever you can of life's good things— "religious things included Let others care for "themselves, and gather what they may. Make "you sure of all the pleasure possible in this "life, and, in case there should be a future life, "make its pleasures secure by all priestly "and other provision. Every one for himself, "in this rush and struggle of busy life. That "man will never come to anything who starts "out to 'seek not his own.' He will only find "sorrow and misery for his pains." This preaching is very plausible, but it is based on manifest error. It assumes that happiness is to be found without, rather than within, the circle of the spiritual life. It limits the rewards of Time to *getting* as much as one can: whereas, common sense and the Gospel teach that these consist in *being* as great as one can. Moreover, society has not yet produced a better way of becoming great, than by seeking not one's own. Put it to the test. I maintain, with the utmost confidence, that there is no record of any man or woman who ever became a living, helpful influence in the community on the principle of seeking only their own. I challenge the other side to produce a single individual whom the wise and the good have pronounced a blessing to their age—one whom posterity has cherished in its heart of hearts, and refused to let his name perish from among men —out of the ranks of those who sought only their own. Call for their noblest and their greatest, from the highest niche in the temple of fame to the lowest, and not one can be produced who will stand the test of contemporaneous history, far less the more trying test of the centuries. On the other hand, I offer the bright scroll of Christian apostles, prophets, saints and martyrs, and the unwritten story of those "hidden ones," the subtle power of whose thought and life has entered into what I may call the Christ-force in humanity—I offer these, and I declare fearlessly, that for all the power they

exerted in their day, and for all the greatness they have attained since, they were indebted to the ability to seek not their own. Whether it was as the intrepid missionary, whose only hire was the purer souls and the brighter lives of degraded men, or as the warrior, whose only thought was his country's honour and glory, or as the day-labourer every turn of whose spade, or every sweep of whose scythe reflected a service for wife, or parent, or child, in the highest degree religious and ennobling—in all, it is the same Christ-love inspiration which seeketh not its own.
. . Moreover, I challenge the other side to quote a single failure among the noble army of the self-forgetful through love, or a single success among the millions of the self-mindful against love. Love knows no failure. Though its object be unworthy, or though it receive not the blessing, through no fault of its own, there is no waste for love. How true are these words of the priest to Evangeline :—

Talk not of wasted affection, affection never was wasted;
If it enrich not the heart of another, its waters, returning
Back to their springs, like the rain, shall fill them full of
    refreshment;
That which the fountain sends forth returns again to the
    fountain.

Self-love is always love's labor lost. There is nothing to show for all its slavish struggling. Did I say, nothing? I retract the word. There is, alas, too much to show, in a degraded, polluted, inhuman character. Hear the sad, warning words of one, who had sounded all the depths and shoals of honour so-called, seeking only his own :—

> Love thyself last;
> Let all the ends thou aim'st at, be thy country's,
> Thy God's, and Truth's. Then, if thou fall'st,
> O Cromwell, thou fall'st a blessed martyr.

If anyone desire the best gift, the sure reward, the life that shall most certainly have success, let him make "seek not my own," and not "seek my own," the maxim of his daily life.

> Love took up the harp of Life, and smote on all the chords
>   with might;
> Smote the chord of Self, that, trembling, passed in music out
>   of sight.

There is a plant on this continent called the compass-plant, the leaves of which all point to the north, as truly as the magnetic needle. It is alleged, that oftentimes the weary and bewildered traveller has been directed on his journey, across the sea-like, pathless waste of the desert, by coming upon this delicate flower. In two respects, this panegyric of love is fitly emblematised by the compass-plant.

1. Every element, like a leaf of the compass-plant, points infallibly to the Christ—the pole-star of the Christian's devotion ; and we shall never know what these elements are, in any real sense, till we have not only perceived their loveliness, but felt their living power, in our Blessed Lord. Like the traveller, the Christian must study carefully the leaves of love's compass plant, and daily start out anew to seek the goal— the stature of the Lord. He must not halt at reverent study of the leaves, nor linger in doting admiration over the beauty of the flower, nor marvel in amaze at the wise design of the great Creator. Already the day is far spent. He is like a pilgrim on the march, who has to reach his journey's end before the shades of evening close over him. While it is day, therefore, and he is able to see clearly the leaves of this divine compass-plant, and trace accurately how they point, he must be active and energetic, watching and praying that he

may make straight and steady progress to the end of his journey. Specially trying for most of us may be the path, to which the three leaves, we have been studying this morning, point. Full of flints and thorns it may be, which wound the feet, and pierce to the very quick. Cutting off a right hand may be nothing to the agony of subduing the spirit of pride and vanity; or to the sacrifice of a cherished idol at the altar, over which is inscribed, "seeking not his own;" or to the casting of our behaviour in the mould of seemliness, that our character may be made over again, after a new image. But the path must be trodden, if we would be perfect, even though it be in tears of blood. The battle must be fought out, even though it be in the mist and hail of the valley of humiliation, with only God and his Christ to see. The one cry of the struggle must be, "Lord help me to be a man." His help and all help must be enlisted, in this hand to hand conflict with self. Friends must help by their sympathy, their moral support, and their wisdom. Circumstances must be utilized that they may also help; but, after all, the battle is really to be fought out, and victory gained, in the secret place of the soul, with all the good influences of the Gospel as allies.

2. Many a leal Christian heart, vexed and clouded by the faithlessness of Christian friend or the faultiness of Christian professor, has muttered in its perplexity, "When the Son of Man cometh, shall he find faith on the earth?" And many an honest and good heart, not claiming to be Christian, and ill at ease in unbelief, has been hindered from avowing Christianity, by some repelling presentation of the truth of the Gospel, delivered with all the terrors of apocalyptic thunderings. Such an one has many a time groaned forth, in heart-breaking misery, "O who will show us any good?" How often have both found a compass in these holy words, to point them to Him who is the way, the truth, and the life. When teachers have been but as false prophets, and churches but as miserable comforters, and theologies but as blind guides, the love of Christ which passeth knowledge, has upheld the fainting Christian, and directed the seeker after God.

"To Christ," then, be our watchword as we march toward the golden gates of the brighter morning. Old and young together, to Christ—

to his fullness of grace and truth, to his beauty and excellency of life, to his greatness, grandeur, goodness, of unselfishness and gentleness in the Great Salvation.

To proclaim one's self better is the sin of pride; to make herself of no reputation, and do her ministry in secrecy and silence is love's peculiar way. No trumpet heralds love's approach, nor banners gleaming in the orient light. Modest as the snowdrop bending her meek head to receive the blessing of the great Apollo, is love, who will not look into the eye of fame.

V.—THE REASON WHY.

> "Is not easily provoked,
> Thinketh no evil;
> Rejoiceth not in iniquity, but
> Rejoiceth in the truth."
>
> Verses, 5-6.

There remain but three characteristics of the "Loving One," to be considered; and these are among the choicest and the most suggestive of the series.

1. Calm, good temper.

> "Whose unclouded ray,
> Can make to-morrow cheerful as to-day.

2. Unsuspicion, that exquisite feature of the

> "Goodness which thinks no evil,
> Where no evil seems."

3. The grief at all iniquity, which so oppresses the good man,—a grief which is always allied in the same mind to rejoicing at the truth.

VII. *Seventh in order, among the graces of the spirit, comes good-temper.* Love's mission is to beautify and bless human life by her grace and sweetness; and to grow stronger in herself, as she fulfils her blessed functions. She knows very well that ill-temper means always weakness, and oftentimes defeat. So, to succeed in her beneficent work, and to make her success the very best, she will not be provoked. The New Version omits the adverb, "easily," and thereby intensifies the virtue of this grace. Divine Love will not only, "not be easily provoked;" she will not be provoked at all.

I do not know any feature of Queen Charity's character which has so pathetic and so searching a test for *most* of us—may I not say *all* of us? I speak feelingly on this topic; and you can all hear feelingly. For who amongst us can lay hand on heart and say, "I am guiltless?" Unfortunately, this infirmity is too often regarded as very venial. Indeed, so little is it thought of as an infirmity, that it is impossible to get many people to think of it as anything but an unamiable weakness, or as a fit topic for occasional ridicule and amusement. One has called ill-temper, "the vice of the virtuous."

Unprincipled people treat the victim of ill-temper like a troublesome child who has to be manœuvred. To gain their selfish ends, such persons always discredit themselves, and too often their unfortunate victim also—themselves by their contemptible trickery, and him by their gross insincerity. Wise men regard him with the deepest pity and regret. The Ancients used to say, "Anger is a brief madness;" and no one knows better than the unhappy victim who is easily provoked, how much truth there is in the aphorism.

What a strength resides in the mind calm, equable, self-possessed! How deep the faith such a mind generates in others! How vast the work such an one can accomplish, and how good the quality! By what means shall we promote the calm, strong, well-governed temper, so much needed, and so earnestly desired by the best men and women? Not I fear, by direct fighting with the foe. That method may bring a mechanical placidity, which in ordinary circumstances sometimes passes muster for natural self-possession; but in extraordinary circumstances, which are always the test of character, the old enemy will re-assert himself, and the fancied victory of half a life-time may vanish in a moment. A skilful physician will not attempt to cure nervous disease by prescribing to his patient, a hand to hand struggle with himself. Most probably such treatment would aggravate rather than alleviate the malady. Instead of advising his patient to think much about his troubles, he will do his utmost to divert his thoughts from himself and his ills. He will direct his skill to raise the tone of the sufferer's constitution generally, that constitutional strength may deliver him from the abnormal nervous state. So to subdue ill-temper, the true Christian method is to cultivate the spirit of Christ. The cure for avarice is to know the beauty of sacrifice; and the cure for ill-temper, is to acquire the character of Him who, though he was reviled, reviled not again, and in all his ministry lived up to the precepts, "Resist not evil," "If a man strike thee on the one cheek, turn to him the other also." Precepts these, to the slave of literalness, a snare, but to the Christian animated by the Spirit of Christ, a fountain of perennial health and refreshment. Do we not all need, to come to this physician of the Sermon on the Mount, for his healing balm? We can only counteract and cure this infirmity, which continually besets us, by the force of a good stronger than the evil. Love can, and will lay this intruder low, if we will yield our natures to her blessed charm. Then shall the one stain be taken from many a character capable of great nobility, the one hindrance lifted to a splendid spiritual progress, the one vitiating ingredient plucked from many an otherwise saintly life, the one false note struck from the discord of many a true soul, the one evil element eradicated which poisons so many good men's happiness and peace, and permeates the society they love with untold dispeace and misery.

VIII. *Unsuspicion.* Love's motives are pure, and she judges others by herself. She cannot suspect impurity of motive in others, her own thoughts being so pure. The best certificate of character, indeed, almost the only one Our Lord ever gave, was spoken of Nathanael. The guilelessness of the youth seems to have so struck Our Lord, that, for the moment, he departed from His usual custom, to pay it a compliment. Society never refuses her meed of praise for the simple, unsuspecting soul who sees the best in others because he cannot think evil. Nor is society ever so indignant, as when guilelessness is wronged and betrayed, by designing, wicked spirits. If the sharper is caught in his own trap, by one sharper than himself, society grins and chuckles, "The biter is bit," "Diamond has cut diamond," and then dismisses his case with scant sympathy. But when guileless youth is betrayed, or the helpless innocent wronged, the full, hearty indignation of a united people, rises up like a flood-tide, to avenge promptly and sternly the heartless offender. Such admiration for guilelessness, and indignation at her wrongs, are redeeming features of our much maligned, but still too selfish human-kind. That even the vicious will recognize the goodness in him who thinketh no evil, and be drawn instinctively to trust, and sometimes to shield him, is surely no slight testimony to the native dignity, and purity of our nature, as well as to the fidelity of the Christian's ambition, as illustrated by St. Paul's perfect man in love.

(a) Love thinketh no evil because love knoweth no evil. In some sense this is quite true ; although it is very difficult to be in the world and yet remain ignorant of its evil. I hold it true, as a general rule, that the less one knows of evil, the better for his purity of thought, and for his peace of mind. Only those, who have seen much of the shady side of human life, know how terribly depressing it is to contemplate the possibilities of degradation, to which men and women, made in the divine image, can descend. What I mean to say is, that unsuspecting love knows no evil, in the sense of the evil inclination. She knows not the influence of the evil desire, the strong pressure of the polluted imagination. She, like King Arthur, is

>Too wholly true, to dream untruth.

It is a sublime spectacle, to see friend believing in friend against the whole world, and standing up in his defence against all accusers. Sometimes love is blind, in her devotion to one notoriously unworthy of her confidence. The wish is father to the thought in such a case. Nevertheless, the sight is grand and impressive of friend confiding in friend so perfectly, that his mind is actually incapable of thinking evil in one, whom he has hitherto loved and trusted. It is a tribute, at least, to the sacredness of friendship, and the loyalty of soul to soul.

Although we may deeply regret it for the trusting one's own sake, still it is impossible not to admire the childlike simplicity of the faith that is so baseless, and the hope that will hold on against hope. How differently do many so-called lovers and friends behave. In the first mutterings of blame, they are found so lacking in faith, that by their sudden defection from their friend, credence is lent to suspicion, and public rumour is helped to become popular fact. Alas! for human nature, that so many are so much readier to take up an evil tale, than to circulate a good one.

(b) I would hardly venture to affirm that the converse of my last proposition must be equally true, viz:—That the mind which thinketh all evil must itself be evil. But I think I may say that the old English maxim, " Set a thief to catch a thief," and the old French motto emblazoned on the royal shield of Britain, " Evil be to him that evil thinks," and many such-like in every language, are not to be treated as the fruit of baseless and vain imaginings. One is very much tempted to believe, that the person who has always only one explanation for another's questionable conduct, and that a bad one, must himself have been there before his friend. His explanation may too often illustrate how he would behave in the same circumstances, or temptation. The ill-interpreter of motives cannot be a true friend. If he does not hate his neighbour, his behaviour bears a strong resemblance to the fruit of hatred. No one, judging of his sentiments by his speech, would ever construe his feelings into loving-kindness. Now, the very principle which leads us so properly to applaud the unsuspecting one, who thinks no evil, should bring us as properly to condemn the suspicious one, who thinks all evil. And it invariably does so. There are those of whom the community has nothing but good to speak. They are the simple, good hearts, who think and speak only the best of their fellow-men, and whom their fellow-men reward, by thinking and speaking only good of them. There are others, again, of whom the community at large, has hardly a good word to speak These are usually suspicious natures, who are always ready to think and speak the worst of their fellow-men, and whom their fellow-men repay, by thinking and speaking the worst of them.

Very seamy though the side of our nature be, which is turned to society, it must never be forgotten, that there is another side, which is turned from society, and which is apparent to the All-seeing Eye alone. If we could see both sides we should pronounce oftentimes a very different judgment on the conduct of our fellow-men. Our Lord never delivered a wiser practical precept than this—" Judge not that ye be not judged." It is an abominable maxim, and a stupidly absurd—" Take every man for a rogue and you will find the honest man ;" but it describes, alas! too truly, the policy of many men and women who do not yield their spirits to the spell of the charmer, " Love."

It is not a little interesting. to note the curious local, racial, and family traces of the suspicious spirit, to be met with up and down the world. The spirit of the savage is that of the Ishmaelite. He sees in every man a possible foe, and so he suspects. It is the same spirit which prevents races and families among civilised men, from being candid and open with one another, and with society. Do what.you will, you can rarely get from such people a downright "No," or a distinct " Yes," in reply to any question. They are constantly suspecting your motive, even when the slightest thought would suffice to show them that there can be nothing behind your question. There can be no character more opposed to the spirit of our holy religion than this. Where such a spirit rules, there can be no faith in God and his Christ. This is a terrible result of the spirit of suspicion. The man who has made suspicion an art for six days of the week, cannot, on the seventh, throw off the bias, and, with the congregation of the faithful, look up to heaven with the candour and simplicity of a little child. Do what he will, suspicion will conquer simplicity, and render his worship double. I think Our Lord must have had some some such thought in his mind, when he said to the twelve, " Except ye be converted and become as little children ye cannot enter the Kingdom of God." Converted to what? To simplicity of trust in God, and confidence in man. I never weary lingering over that type of heavenly citizenship. A guileless, innocent child, the spiritual type of highest manhood and womanhood! Childhood is open, candid, transparent as the day. True, and believing every one else true; loving, and desiring every one else to love it; pure, and taking every one else for pure. Oh, the Christ-likeness and the Christly blessedness, in such a character! Before the little child, the best of us can do little but stand self-condemned, and sigh to think how far short we come of the Christ ideal. No contrast could better convince us, that with all their learning, and all their ologies, nineteenth century Christians have yet to learn some of the simplest lessons of the Gospel of Christ.

Love unsuspecting does not mean love blind to evil, or love tolerant of evil. Love sees glaring wickedness, and as we shall immediately see, grieves over it as none other can ever grieve. What grief can there ever be like love's,— so pathetic and so powerful! No influence ever reaches the sinner so deep down, or brings into his soul such poignant repentance. Love is unsuspecting only so long as she can think no evil. The time may come, however, when she can be no longer unsuspecting, and then she can think all evil with an intensity of feeling, equalled only by the depth of her grief. The very depth of her sorrow at the sin then becomes the spring of her inspiration to save the sinner. Because none other sees so clearly as love the horrible degradation of sin, no other can put forth such efforts to wipe out the stain from God's universe, and bring back faith again to her own torn and bleeding bosom.

Many, as the temptations are to suspect and distrust one's fellow-men—Christian men, alas! as well as Non-Christian—I would plead for the sincere desire to retain, and where shaken, to regain, faith in human character. Not only is it a deplorably sad thing, that we should not be able to confide in others, but it is the very misery of miseries, for an honest and tender spirit to think all evil of those whom it once trusted, and whom it desires to trust still. I had rather be an optimist, believing in my fellow creatures and be deceived, than a pessimist doubting, and be miserable. Some years ago a friend said to me, in a time of great trial, brought on through the treachery of a partner in business :—"It is not the loss of the money, though I could ill spare it, which so troubles me, as the moral wrench which my nature has received by being compelled to distrust the man, in whom I had most implicit confidence." If you value your own peace of mind, try to find a foot-hold for faith in your fellow men, and try your best so to behave, that they may be attracted to believe in you. Try your best to think no evil, by thinking all the good you can. It is marvellous how much good we can find in our neighbours when we try to find it, and how little good we find when we don't. Do your best to be open, candid, transparent with others. It is the surest way to promote the same virtues in them. Abhor cunning, which is devilish in its origin, and devilish in all its ways. Promote among the young the Nathanael spirit. Encourage them to speak and act prudently, but, above everything, to be true to their inmost thoughts. There can be no fairer jewel on a young brow than guilelessness; there can be no rarer gem of righteousness than the fresh, firm eye of truth vieing with the gazelle's in its brilliance; there is no more eloquent appeal for honesty and honour than the simple, trustful countenance of a sweet, young, generous soul.

IX. "*Grieved with iniquity*," expresses better the meaning of the original, and besides, makes a better contrast with the, "rejoices with the truth," in the second clause. Grieving, and rejoicing, make the strong antithesis, which it was obviously the writer's intention to create. The sin of the world lies a heavy load on the soul of Love. She alone fully realizes what a loss iniquity is to the doer of it, to the society of which he forms a part, and to the God who made him for better things. She yearns over the sinner like Jeremiah over erring Judah, and, for every reason, she cannot but grieve, that he should choose to follow evil. Like her Lord, Love would follow the sinner in tears, sobbing, "Ye will not come unto me that ye might have life." Indeed, this may be another convenient test of the depth and intensity of one's love for his fellow man—the sense of his grief at the sin, in any relative, or friend, or Christian brother. If that sense be keen, then his love will be proportionally intense; if dull, then his love will be, in the same ratio, apathetic. Grief at sin is the true inspiration of all prophetic zeal, and evangelical enterprise. It will not be, primarily, because the other side is strong, or popular, or in error, that any really fine Christian spirit will assume the role of a reformer. He will not go in indignant wrath, or wild declamation, to champion the cause of truth or philanthrophy. He will be too grieved at the sad, dark plight of those for whose good he longs to labour. He will trust to his tears to melt, rather than to his lips to move, or his hands to crush. " Wise as a serpent, and harmless as a dove," was the standing command to the first missionaries, by the Master who grieved over iniquity, as none of women born ever grieved. Would to God that it were the " Vade Mecum," or, " Constant Companion," of every one who goes forth in the Master's name! Such an one will, like his Lord, bear on his sympathetic soul the sins and carry the sorrows of his people. Out of the depths of his sorrow he will plead with them, exhort, persuade, with all long-suffering and meekness. If man can do it, he will do it; and he will do it, by love. Not one word will fall from him which can rudely offend the objects of his interest. Love's ways, like wisdom's, will be ways of pleasantness, and all her paths will be peace. The reformer in love will not be content simply to legislate against iniquity, nor to pass strong resolutions against the workers of iniquity, nor to break the power of iniquity by main force. As he reads history, he perceives that these methods have never yet succeeded in creating any real and permanent great moral or religious reformation. He will go further back. He will strike at the root of the iniquity in the human soul, and he will woo the offender by the attractions of goodness, till ashamed of his sin he break with his enemy, for ever. "Reform yourself," is the true reformer's watchword, as he goes forth with the message of grieved love to the erring and the fallen. No other messenger, and no other message have ever yet succeeded, in uprooting iniquity. He, who would be free, himself must strike the blow; and it is the reformer's greatest grief, when the sinner will not, with God's help, strike off his fetters and be free. For he knows full well that no other hand can do it for him.

It is to be feared, that the grief at iniquity is not so lively with most Christians, even among those who talk the most bitterly about it, as it should be; and that, consequently, their love for their fellow-men must be judged to be all the less intense. This is Palm Sunday. Carry your thoughts backward to the triumphant episode, of which this is the commemoration. Watch those devoted disciples casting their garments before Jesus, and those enthusiastic multitudes waving their palm branches, and chanting their hosannas. It is a right royal welcome. And yet the central figure of that jubilant throng is riding with a grief-stricken heart that not all the rejoicings in His honour can soothe. There is a grief of griefs, and it stands out in bolder relief, because limned on the bright background of a people's joy. Our Lord realized the iniquity, which was to bring untold misery to the guilty Jerusalem; and His only comment on her past rejection of Him, and His near crucifixion, was this passionate outburst of a whole soul's anguish. What a wealth of meaning in those tears! Wrong, shame, cruelty, to be met only with tears of grief! Saw the earth ever such a sight as that? The world's best and bravest have died blaming and prophesying doom, or exhorting and praying for their persecutors and murderers; but only the Son of God ever died heart-broken for the wrong his foes were inflicting on themselves. Those salt tears of sorrow have done more for the human race than mind has ever conceived. They have inspired Christianity at her strongest and her best—in her pathos and her love. What a lesson here for every one of us—how to regard iniquity, and how to face, and conquer it! There is no other way, but by the grief of love inspiring both the head and the hands of love. Our Lord had no other, and he is a bold man who will suggest a more excellent way. Love is mightier in her griefs than Jupiter armed with his thunderbolts. Love is grieved for iniquity, in order that she may overcome and destroy it.

Love rejoices with the truth. Correctly speaking, the contrast requires, for popular use, that "truth" should be rendered by "good." Grieved is love with the bad; rejoiced is love with the good. This is but another side of the thought which I have just been discussing. Grieving over the bad, implies rejoicing over the good. The spirit, which can intensely mourn because of abounding evil, will also heartily rejoice because of triumphant good. Observe, it is rejoices with *the* good. It is not said with *our* good—the good which we ourselves have been able to attain or achieve—the truth we have been able to preach or to discover. But *the* good—*the* truth, come by whatsoever means, and from whatsoever quarter. A good many Christians are quite ready to rejoice with their own good—the good of their own church or party—but there is never a word of rejoicing when it is the good of some other church or party which is presented. Oftentimes, Christians can even indulge in a good deal of very unholy envying and grieving at the good of their brother Christians. Love seeketh not her own; and she is as well pleased, when the victory of truth and righteousness is won by Christians of another party, or sect, as by her own friends and allies. She calls the whole world kin; and when the light of the Christ appears in one quarter, with exceeding brightness, she gives God praise, that by so much, humanity at large has been elevated and enriched. Truth triumphant, anywhere, is Christianity the richer, everywhere. Love rejoices, that in any way humanity and Christianity are the gainers.

Here endeth St. Paul's analysis of love. The graces ascribed to Queen Charity in verse 7 have been already considered, under the, "long-suffering of love," in verse 4. It is not to be expected, that all these nine elements will be represented at their best, in any man or woman. Only one has ever worn Queen Charity's crown, with perfect grace and dignity, and none other shall ever wear it as He did. But all men and women can make the honest attempt; and it is certainly demanded of all Christians, that they do try their very best, to excel in some of these royal virtues, and to attain creditable success in them all. There is a saying, which has come down from ancient days,—" All paths lead to Rome." She was the centre of the world's life and thought, and towards her the aspirations, and the ambitions of mankind, for centuries, gravitated. That saying will never again be true in the same sense. The Carpenter of Nazareth has superseded the Queen of the Tiber. All spiritual paths lead to Him, and it shall be so for ever, and for ever. He is the sun of righteousness and love, because all virtues radiate from Him. At sunrise, and at sunset the bright orb of day casts, across the wide expanse of waters, a golden pathway leading straight to itself, as if Apollo were inviting the race of mortals, to pass by a shining corridor, to the palace of the Heavenly King. The sun of love, which fills the Christian's heaven with light, casts, across the sea of human life, the same brilliant avenue for the feet of the loyal and true to walk in. Every one of these nine elements I have been considering, is a strand, so to speak, in that glittering pathway. The Christian who can cover most strands is the most Christ-like disciple; but he who can cover one strand only, if he do his best, is none the less a disciple. "According to our several ability," is the law of the Christian, as of all, life. Let us realize how gloriously rounded his full-formed life of love is, by pondering much St. Paul's wonderful eulogy, and fulfilling with all our hearts its behests. God knows fully, and we know in part, how far short of the sublime height our best efforts have brought us; but it is encouraging to think, that a two-fold power is at work on the side of the willing and obedient mind. The honest and good heart urges the Christian onward, and upward; and the grace and loveliness of the Good Shepherd draw him upward, and onward. Rightly obeyed, and responded to, these influences can never fail. They must, and will bring towards the fullness of the stature of Christ, all who will be brought; and there is life and blessing in none other. May the Christian church realize this as she has never done yet, that her Lord's spirit within her may have freer course and be glorified. Only that is needed, to make our little earth, a heaven of the graces of love. For, wheresoever heart beats true to heart, in the full flood-tide of love's holy and blessed stream, nothing more is needed, to bring into human life the peace of God that passeth all understanding. Altering slightly memorable lines, I would have us all absorb the poet's thought:—

> Ah, my God!
> What might I not make of Thy fair world,
> Did I but love my highest, holiest here?
> It is my due to love the royal Christ;
> It surely is my profit, so to love;
> It ought to be my pleasure, and my joy.

God help us all to breathe this holy confession of faith, and to make it the holy expression of our living Christian trust, now, and for evermore.

VI.—THE SECOND CONTRAST.

"Charity never faileth; but whether there be prophecies, they shall fail: whether there be tongues, they shall cease : whether there be knowledge, it shall vanish away.
"For we know in part, and we prophesy in part.
"But when that which is perfect is come, then that which is in part shall be done away."
—Verses 8-10.

These two thoughts must be constantly before the mind of the student of this epistle, in order that he may thoroughly understand its import :

1. The outbreak and predominance of party spirit in the Corinthian Church. That spirit is apparent, in the existence of sects calling themselves by great names, in the controversy about meats and drinks, in the references to the place of women in the church and to other questions of more or less disputed interest and importance. A state of chronic strife prevailed, and the apostle wrote this letter to allay it, if possible.

2. In all the counsel which the apostle tenders to the Corinthian Christians, concerning

the matters in debate, he constantly appeals to the imminent coming-again of the Master. He says, in effect: "Why wrangle over these matters? They are not of vital importance. Even if they were, why not defer the discussion of them till the Master comes? The Lord is at hand. He will clear away all your difficulties, and settle all your controversies. One thing, however, you can do now, and do it, I beseech you, at your very best. Have charity among yourselves. Cultivate love. It will last. These other matters will all suffer change, if they be not entirely swept away, when the Lord appears. Charity will stand, however, the one great and blessed thing that shall never be shaken."

We have here what may be called the apostle's accidental, or secondary "Reason Why," for his eulogy of charity—it abides. "These other things, of which ye are making so much, as if they were essentials of Christianity," says he, "shall all vanish before the brightness of the Lord's coming. Your prophecies, or doctrines, that ye consider vital to the very existence of the church, shall then be done away; those tongues, which have so exalted their possessors over less gifted brethren, shall then cease; that knowledge, which has so puffed up some of you, shall then vanish away. One and all are but partial and temporary. Nothing better are they than human and imperfect expositions, opinions, theories. Change and decay are essential features of all human works. Only when the Perfect One returns, will the full and infallible truth be known about all things; and when the perfect is declared, the imperfect, which you have so unduly exalted, shall disappear. Not so will it be with charity. It is spirit, and it is life. It is the one thing which will abide the Master's re-appearing. Prophecies, tongues, knowledge, will all decay; but love will flourish in perpetual youth. Charity alone is the spirit of Christianity—the very heart and soul of our Holy Religion."

Most deplorably had these Corinthian Christians misconceived the meaning and end of Christianity. Like many modern Christians, they had been waxing very zealous, and losing their tempers, over questions of small practical account in the religious life. They had ranged themselves under different banners, not for spiritual discipline and development, in order that they might the better cope with the prevailing ignorance and vice; but that they might wage more successfully unholy fratricidal warfare. And so they weakened their own hands, and frustrated their own plans. They strove over things, and names, and practices; they were jealous of each other, and ambitious to excel; they suspected one another, and they freely vituperated one another. Though they strained out every gnat of differing opinion in their close coteries, they swallowed greedily the camel of a perverted Christian ideal, when they desecrated the Holy Communion into a scene of excessive eating and drinking, and degraded public worship into an arena for the display of hatred, malice, and all uncharitableness. On the very threshold of the new era, they had with wicked hands crucified and slain Queen Charity, and foully defamed her Lord and Master. "This is all wrong," the heart-broken apostle sobs. "It is an open offence against religion, and it is a deplorable blunder as well. In all your contentious zeal, you have not been seeking the good of true religion; but ye have been diligently lending your countenance and help to the promotion of irreligion. In a word, ye have been carnal, and the gospel of Christ is spiritual. Whereas Christianity is the spirit of Christ, ye have been exhibiting a spirit of which the Christ will be ashamed at His coming. For ye have been deliberately wounding Him in the house of His friends. Moreover, what a blunder all this strife and contention has been! To what Christian good have ye been discussing, and decreeing, and dividing? Is not the day of the Lord at hand? Hear ye not His golden bells? And what a sight your Corinthian Church will present to Him! Have patience, I beseech you. Seek the things that make for peace. All your problems will soon be solved by Him, who alone can solve them. All your perplexities will be cleared up. O ye rash, zealous, but indiscreet Corinthians."

These were the circumstances, and that the connection, in which St. Paul pronounced so elaborate and so exquisite a eulogy on charity. He carefully developed his ideal to meet the Corinthian troubles. He commended love as the one antidote to the anti-Christian poison of internal discord.

What a terrible blow it must have been, for those rigid sectaries, and perfervid zealots, to be told that those things for which they had been contending as for dear life, were of little account, because the great apostle regarded them as only temporary! What a blow to many modern Christians to be told, as St. Paul would certainly tell them, could he appear to-day: "Your hierarchies, they are nothing; your creeds, they are nothing; your protests of purity and orthodoxy, they are nothing. These are all passing away." Would they not rise up, and in one voice reply, with Corinthian fervour and force revived: "You are a dangerous, bold, unsettling unbeliever to suggest any such unsound doctrine. If we give up these, we may as well give up Christianity." But these are St. Paul's words to the divided Corinthian Church then, and they would be St. Paul's words to-day to the divided Canadian Church: "These are passing away. Charity alone abideth. Seek first the spirit of charity, and all other things shall be added unto you."

I. *Charity abides.* There is something in permanence which strikes very forcibly the mind of a commercial people. We all wish to get value for our money, and the article that lasts, is coveted, the most for that quality. St.

Paul takes up one and another of the things, which men valued most in Corinth at that time, and he dismisses them one by one as ephemeral. Good things they all were, no doubt; but then they were not to last, and on that account he exalts charity above them all. Now, though there are several secondary reasons to be urged on behalf of charity, which, at the first glance, most of us might consider stronger than its mere lasting power, still, looking into the matter closely, I think all other secondary reasons merge themselves in this. Nothing lives in God's universe, unless it has intrinsic power to live. That is to say, if a creature continues to hold its own on the world's broad field of battle, or if a truth can survive the gnawing tooth of time, or if a name can live in the Christian memory of mankind, on the face of it, there must be something there inherently good. Tens of thousands of men and things have come to the front, for a season, and passed away into the darkness whence they came. They had no power to live, and so they died. Many valuable inventions have, in past ages, competed for popular favour; and yet the best of them only enjoyed the popular favour until another more popular appeared. Many a book of ancient lore flashed upon a wondering world, making its author for a season the admired of all admirers, and where are their names or their works to-day? Over the last fifty years, how many books have flourished for a season and are now forgotten, except by the book-hunters? Only one book has held its own through the centuries, and to-day holds a stronger place than ever in the most intelligent minds, and that book is the Bible. The world of men and women, as well as the world of nature, treats very cavalierly anything which lacks inherent power to live. Man and nature make no real attempt to bolster up the person or thing that cannot stand alone. "Begone," is time's stern fiat, pronounced over whatever cannot of itself survive. To say, then, that charity would abide, while other things should vanish away, was to declare that it had a something, which those others lacked. Neither Paul nor Paul's Lord could keep alive anything which could not itself survive by its intrinsic merit. This power, therefore, in charity, to live, implied vital virtue and godliness.

II. *How charity abides.* The familiar word

"character," with which charity is cognate, interpreted literally, sheds a gleam of light on St. Paul's plea Character originally meant, (1) an instrument for marking, (2) the individual who marks, stamps, or engraves, and (3) the thing marked, stamped, or engraved. In Christian speech, charity exhausts the three meanings. Nothing impresses mankind like charity; no one is so skilful and so powerful to impress as the loving one; no results are so deep and so enduring as the fruits of love's work. Specially is it, the third meaning, which illustrates St. Paul's contrast. " By their fruits ye shall know my disciples," said Our Lord. Now, fruits indicate not only the quantity of life, but the quality, as well. The spiritual fruits of Christian discipleship are to be gathered, in the character. The Christian is, in fact, a character. His character is the engraving, so to speak, and its lines are cut by the Master's hand. The Christ was charity, and the Christly character is charity. In a word, the character, I repeat, is the individual, the very living self of man or woman, and that living self is charity.

Will any one then match me a thing to compare with charity for abiding power ? Take the things men value, and for which they toil and sweat like heroes, and one by one they all pass away. Name and fame—how soon do Lethe's dark waters begin to wipe out these from under the sun! Of the millions of brave men and women, who have served well their day and generation, how very few live, even by name, far less by deeds, in the recollection of humanity. Wisdom—how rapidly do the wise men of to-day, building upon the foundations laid by their predecessors, supersede, as teachers and guides, those whose wisdom was once a world's wealth and a world's wonder! And what shall I say of material things, if these other, and nobler far, are doomed to oblivion? It may be humbling, but it is stern truth all the same, that we who think we are so much to our little world, and to whom that world is so much—we, and ours are passing away, and to be superseded by others who, in their turn, will tread the path of forgetfulness, as all their fathers did. But the Christ character lives in deathless bloom. It *has* the power to live, for it *is* eternal life. The Christian will live forever, not because the Judge will say so, nor because he will be admitted to Heaven, but simply and solely because he cannot die. "God so loved the world that he gave his only begotten Son that whosoever believeth in him should have eternal life." That is charity's charter of immortality. The Christian has this life here and now; it is the life of which charity is the essence; as God lives, and Christ lives, so shall the God-like and the Christ-like live for evermore. There is no doubt about it. There can be no mistake. The thought is bound up with the very life of the Gospel:—"As I live, said Christ, so shall ye live also."

III. Here are some of the ways in which the fruits of charity abide:—

1. *In memory.* There are many events in one's history he would gladly forget. Many scenes come up in memory which we would all like to keep down. Many things charmed and thrilled our being once, which now come back upon us with a sting. Many things are to-day positively distasteful, and repulsive, which in past days were enjoyable and attractive. Life as we had it thirty, twenty, ten years ago does not abide; and, more than that, we do not wish it to abide, changed as our minds and bodies are. But the memory of some kind deed done

for another out of pure, loving interest—when that comes up, it is like the sight of a palm tree in the desert to the weary traveller. We know that refreshment is there for our jaded spirits. It never grows old or less effective, oft as it may return. It never makes us a coward to conscience, as it confronts us. It never plants a thorn in our bosom. It always brings with it, as it comes, the fragrance of " Araby the Blest."

2. *Charity abides in reward, which never disappoints, and never cloys.* Let any one take five years of life, in which he did his best to gather into his life all he could of time's pure and cultivated pleasures. He may have travelled, or studied, or visited the great art galleries of the world, or revelled in the beauties of nature, or cultivated fine taste, or built for himself a lordly pleasure-house of the finest thoughts in history, poetry, philosophy. He may have entertained his friends with an elevated grace, and been entertained. Take five years of these, all quite proper and pure, and place over against these years, just five minutes spent with a mourning widow and her weeping orphans, in trying to lighten her burden, and

brighten her future, or five minutes with a friendless wanderer, spent in saving him from despair. Tell me candidly, which brought into your being most enrichment? And which warms your spirit to-day with the sun of a sweet deep satisfaction? Does not the five minutes, cast into the balances, make the five years kick the beam? It being so, what would you take in exchange for that five minutes which has been to you for years of blessing? Could worlds buy it of you? I trow not. And the unique excellence of this blessing is, that it came without the asking. You were seeking intellectual reward when you sought out the treasures of literature and art. You sought reward in the convivialities of society. But in that sympathetic, helpful tenderness for those broken hearts, and in that saving hand you outstretched to a sinking brother, your motive was pure as the driven snow. Out of the goodness of your heart you did it, thinking only of the good service you could render to your fellow-creatures, and it lives in your being to-day a permanent spring of refreshment, while other streams are but as "gilded puddles which the beasts do cough at."

How disappointing are most, if not all, of our worldly ambitions! Where is the man who will stand up and say, that he has ever got out of his acquisitions anything like what he expected? And the truer and higher his spiritual nature, the less can it be satisfied with material things. Oftentimes, the grosser natures even, instead of getting out of these just what they expected, get a great deal they did not expect, and certainly did not desire. There are many gracious Christian souls, happy in the Christian use of a large portion of this world's good things; there are far more to whom these things bring the great worry and unhappiness of all their lives.

Here then we have a blessing that never disappoints, that never palls upon the sated spirit, that never weakens; but always strengthens in its power to make happy. This unfailing grace of love, this holy blessedness of the true human life, this undying reward of loyal service to the Christ—what can we desire more, or better for our children and friends than it? Parents have the laudable ambition to make adequate provision for those who are dependent upon them, and to die with the comfortable conviction, that those they love will never know penury and want. A very proper ambition within proper limits. But I have seen such provision become the ruin of a family of sons. I have seen boys who, if they had been left without a penny, would have built up an honourable name, and been a great blessing to society; but because they had inherited great wealth, the stewardship of which they did not realize, society came to regard them as a curse and a pest, and the discredited bearers of a worthy name. Whatever else parents can bequeath to their children, of this I am confident, that there is nothing comparable with the heritage of a noble and charitable Christian character. With that, sons and daughters will live to bless for evermore, the memory of those, to whose pious and wise upbringing, they owe all they possess. Without such a spirit as that, the best accumulations of wealth will be only as a millstone at the foot of sanguine, ingenuous youth; or as a weight of lead around the neck of the strong swimmer battling with the surges of the sea of life.

There is another reward which the Christian, after the type of St. Paul's "Loving One," enjoys, and it is to many-a-one of the utmost importance. Some good people search nervously in the scriptures, enquire at their minister, and puzzle themselves generally, to make sure of the reality of their religious faith. They desire earnestly to be assured that they have found Christ, and that the great work of conversion has been accomplished in their case. The spirit of such questioning is essentially morbid; but if an individual will so question, let him know that the life of love offers the only valid answer to his enquiries. For the man who is inspired by love finds Christ in his own soul, and the earnest of the heaven before him in the spirit of loving-kindness. Depend upon it, dearly beloved, if you do not find God and his Christ in your bosom you will never find them elsewhere. If you find them there you will find them everywhere. The reason why many good Christians are so often disappointed, in what they call "the search for God," is, that they do not look for him, first of all, where he should chiefly be sought—in the manifestations he makes of himself in their own minds and hearts. They suffer the noisy loves of the world, to drown the still small voice of the divine love in their souls—a voice that never fails to plead for the presence of God, and to soothe by the blessing of the divine fellowship—a voice that never ceases to urge them, to keep in the paths of righteousness and truth. If all anxious enquirers will follow love, they will find, every day, a growing assurance, that "Christ is in them the hope of glory."

VII.—THE THIRD CONTRAST.

"When I was a child, I spake as a child, I understood as a child, I thought as a child; but when I became a man, I put away childish things.

"For *now* we see through a glass darkly; but *then* face to face; *now* I know in part; but *then* shall I know even as also I am known."
—Verses, 11-12.

St. Paul is very strong in his contrasts, and he is very fond of them. Here we have his third contrast, within a very limited compass, to illustrate the intrinsic worth and importance of his great subject. In the *first*, he compares charity with seven well-known precious things. These are all good gifts, and yet their virtue consists in the love which inspires the mind to the right use of them. With charity in the soul of the gifted one, these are great and blessed gifts. Without charity, a man may be endowed with them all, and yet be nothing religiously in God's sight. Charity may, therefore, be truly characterized as, "the greatest thing in the world," because it can lend greatness even to what are supposed to be the greatest and best things in the world. The *second* contrast expresses the "reason why," charity is the chief good. Other gifts will fade away, or be superseded by others greater than they. In the roll of the centuries the law of progress is, " All old things pass away ; all things become new." But charity will abide, when all that seems shall suffer shock. It will never grow old ; it will ever be new. The queen of the graces, in the former contrast, was declared supreme, by reason of her intrinsic excellence ; in this, she is supreme, because of her unique permanence. Charity can endure ; therefore, charity shall endure. The *third* contrast brings up, very suggestively, a great cardinal belief of the first Christians, to which I referred incidentally in the previous discourse, and the importance of which, in interpreting the earliest Christian writings and history, can hardly be overestimated.

The Apostle, in these verses, is comparing two states of Christian life and thought ; and he illustrates the contrast between the two by means of three emblems.

1. He presents the one state as corresponding

to childhood, in which intelligence is budding only and judgment immature; and he places over against it, the state of manhood, in which intelligence is ripe and the reason strong.

2. Again, he compares the two states to the human eye—in the one, beholding an object through a dim, distorting medium, and in the other, seeing the same object, without any intervening substance, and just as it is. " *Now*, we see through a glass darkly, but *then*, face to face."

3. And lastly, he compares the two states, to partial knowledge, and full knowledge—" *Now*, I know, in part; *then*, shall I know, even as I am known."

These *states* of being are characteristic of *times* of being. The *now*, or *present*, is the child stage, the state of seeing only through talc, horn, or thin metal, the stage of imperfect knowledge of life and religion. The *then*, or *future*, is to be the manhood stage, the state of seeing things as they are, the time of coming face to face with them, the stage of full and perfect knowledge, the knowing of life and religion as the Highest will know us.

The childish stage, the *now* state, was that of

St. Paul and his Corinthian friends, at the moment of writing. Concerning the true import of our Lord's life and work, and the true mission of the Christian Church, they were all like "Children of the Mist." Observe, St. Paul includes himself in the same category as his correspondents. He says *we* see through a glass darkly. He and they were thinking weakly, and imperfectly of everything religious, as compared with what they would do, by and by. They saw nothing in true perspective. They judged of nothing quite accurately. They valued nothing at its true worth. And yet, they thought they did see very clearly, and that they were appraising very wisely, and well, everything concerning the kingdom of our Lord and Saviour. They would have been grievously insulted, had any one but Paul stigmatized their ecclesiastical and theological conclusions as childishness. St. Paul was right, however, and they were wrong, with all their dogmatism and pride of party spirit.

The future, or *then* state, of manly judgment and piercing vision, and ripe understanding, is the daily expectation of St. Paul. It is to the Second Advent he is looking for the striking and marvellous change, indicated by these suggestive and expressive emblems. "Maranatha, our Lord cometh," contained the sum of hope and consolation for St. Paul and his fellow-Christians. They referred everything to that great event. It was the testing point of their faith; the very soul of all their Christian hope; the joyous greeting with which they saluted each other in the streets. From a careful examination of New Testament references to this topic, I am convinced, that no other single article of faith, can be said to have occupied anything like the place in Christian estimation, with the belief in the immediate coming again of Our Lord in glory. So completely did it fill the Christian mind and eye, that it coloured every thought and ideal of Christianity. When the Christians were persecuted, their one consolation was, "The Lord is at hand," to execute summary vengeance on the persecutors. When they were despondent, because of the opposition of foes, or the defection of friends, their spirits revived as they prayed, "Come, Lord Jesus! Come quickly!" To the careless, or the backslider the warning voice came as a trumpet-blast, "The Lord cometh as a thief in the night." For the mourner, who consigned the remains of his dear one to the tomb, and sorrowed most of all, that the departed would not be with him to welcome the coming King, the apostle had this word of consolation, " We who are alive will not anticipate those who are fallen asleep. The dead in Christ shall rise first, and, with us also who shall remain, shall join to meet the Lord in the air." When believers mourned in hopeless sorrow, because their Pagan parents having died before the gospel sound could reach their ears, these could not share with their children in the resurrection, and joyful reception of the returning Lord —even for these St. Paul had a crumb of comfort, which suggested, after all, a happy family re-union, when he baptized them for the dead. Family life, social life, individual life, were all saturated with the influence of this gladsome hope. It was the fundamental dogma of their simple faith. The man who doubted it was an infidel of a deep dye. When some one, apparently discrediting the universal hope, enquired of St. Peter, " Where is the promise of His coming?" that fervid and impetuous apostle had no better answer than this: " Begone, thou scoffer! Thou walkest after thine own lusts."

Very appropriately does this reference to the second-coming dogma come up in connection with St. Paul's eulogy of charity. The writer is apparently driven almost distracted, by the unloving and unchristian conduct of those Corinthians. He is in despair—so bitter are their feuds, and so perilous their excesses. He is confident respecting one thing, however. When the Lord comes, the wranglers will see the error of their ways. In the brightness of the Messiah's glory they will pass a long step upwards to his spiritual fulness. In the Paronsia charity will abide; and when all these other things of which the Corinthians are so enamoured shall have disappeared, because they could not abide the Master's coming, then will they realize that charity filleth all in all. Then will they bow to kiss the feet of the queen they are now so grievously offending. He has no stronger appeal to urge than this reference to their most cherished hopes.

Alas! for the purest of mortal hopes. Brave, noble Paul was doomed to die a disappointed man. The master, whose return he so longed to see, came not to gladden his true servant's eyes. The kingdom of love was not set up by the Loving One in person on the earth, as the apostle desired and expected to see it. The childhood of the Christian Church did not pass into its manhood, nor did its blurred vision grow clear, in the first ages. It had to see, for long centuries, as through a glass darkly. After nineteen centuries have run their course, he would be a bold Christian to-day who would assert that he knows, even as he is known. The Christian community still knows only in part. That early hope so tender and so strong was not to be fulfilled—indeed, could not then, and can never be fulfilled—but St. Paul's faith in charity's price, and charity's power, has been justified in every age, and will be vindicated ever more fully, as the ages cycle onward.

The question may be asked, "How did this hope arise? How did a belief so mistaken, come to lay hold of the universal mind of the Early Church? This is how it came about. It was quite natural for St. Paul and his associates, conceiving as they did of the Kingdom of God, to transfigure their faith and hope as Jews into a commanding Christian faith and hope. From the first, the Messianic ideas of their nationality were the bread of their life. The times seemed ripe for the advent of Isaiah's, Servant of Jehovah, to vindicate his master's name and honour. On the other hand, never were the times less ripe for the acceptance of a dominion among men, in the spirit—a kingship of character—than in those days of Sadducean pride and Pharisaic severity. Their Messiah, more than ever, must be clothed in purple, and wear a jewelled crown, if he was to be the deliverer of God's ancient people. Not meeting with this pomp and majesty, in Jesus of Nazareth, the ruling classes crucified him as an impostor. His disciples believed in his Messianic office, notwithstanding his unlikely origin, and his lowly life. They had implicit faith, that he would restore the kingdom to Israel. On the very Ascension day this question absorbed all others—"Wilt thou, at this time, restore the Kingdom unto Israel?" Our Lord's reply to their simple, absorbed minds was, to say the least of it, enigmatical: "It is not for you to know the times and the seasons." That reply might be legitimately interpreted as meaning, that the time and the season were coming. When he ascended, therefore, without fulfilling their hope, what more natural than that holding these preconceived opinions, they should at once have jumped to the conclusion, that he had ascended only to descend again, in heavenly splendour, with ten thousand of his saints to confound all his, and their foes, by the breath of his mouth. The time was not come yet, but it would undoubtedly come, and they should eagerly expect it. Obviously, their Master's work was unfinished, and they could not believe that it should remain unfinished, or that another, but himself, should finish it. Thus the Jewish Messianic ideal was adopted by the Christians without material alteration. The Jews continued to look for a Messiah to come; the Christians waited with confidence for a Messiah to come again. Both clothed their Messiah in much the same attributes; both assigned to him much the same functions. Only, the Christian ideal was broader than the Jewish. The Messiah of the Jews was to be the King of Israel—Great David's Greater Son: the Christian Messiah was to be, "a light to lighten the Gentiles and the glory of his people Israel," as the broad-minded Luke puts it. It was a simple, pure, unselfish hope.

Such is the explanation of the origin, and development of a belief which exercised so important an influence on the fortunes of the Early Church, and, without due appreciation of which, it is impossible to interpret the New Testament scriptures intelligently. It was as vain an expectation as its Jewish prototype. The Lord did not return. He was to come again in spirit *only*, and he has been coming again, in that fashion, ever since he ascended, wherever he could find a church faithful enough, or a heart pure enough, to welcome him. Well was it for the Great Apostle, and for the Early Church, that the Master did not come again, in the manner they expected. Disappointed as they were, when he did not come quickly, they would have been more disappointed had he come as they desired. The veil of flesh would have intervened to obscure his beauty, and impede his power, in the second advent, as it had, in the first. If those who companied with him in closest fellowship, for three years, never realized, while he was with them, the true character of his kingdom, how should they realize it better

THE THIRD CONTRAST. 129

when he returned to dwell among them, in heavenly splendour and authority? And, if his foes were not converted by the scenes and incidents of his first advent, what hope was there that they would be converted by the second? Moreover, this personal-reign-of-Christ idea is quite foreign to the spirit of Christianity. Men and women are not to be awed into submission to the Cross of Christ, by the outward symbols of regal state and majesty. Such a submission would mean nothing, in a religious sense. The only inspiring and converting power, among moral and responsible beings, is the power of the Spirit of the Lord. For such conversion, the fleshly Christ was a hindrance before. "It is expedient," said Our Lord, "for *you* that I go away." The twelve were not to understand him otherwise; and, there is no reason to assume, that the personal Christ to-day, would succeed where the personal Christ failed before. But, in point of fact, the Saviour's going from the disciples, was the beginning of his coming to them, for the first time. When the, "Word made flesh," had ascended into the heavens, they began to realize the Son who had for ever dwelt in the bosom of the Father.

St. Paul and his fellow-christians expected, that the second coming would bring them face to face with their Lord, and that then, he and they should see eye to eye—they, knowing him and he, them, as they were known. But could the Lord have so come, the disappointed apostle and his friends would have had to sigh in tears, "still we see through a glass darkly." They would have found out, that something more than geographical nearness is needed to bring spiritual beings into true spiritual communion and affinity. It is the mind that makes its world. None the less true is it the soul that makes its own Christ. The Christ, coming in the heavens, may be nothing to an individual; the Christ, coming in the spirit, will be everything to him. The expectation in any mind of the first century, or of the nineteenth, that the Christ is about to appear, without the mind and heart of the Christ, would have been nothing more then, and it is nothing more to-day, than the gift of martyrdom without the spirit of charity. Though a man should be the very loudest in his "Maranatha," if he have not the Christ spirit, he is like one who might give his body to be burned, but yet, not having charity, he would be nothing. On the other hand, the man who has the Christ spirit, to him, his Lord has come again, though he never cried "Maranatha," just as in the man inspired by love, there is the spirit of the martyr, though he never be called to mount the scaffold or the stake.

Though this hope was destined to be disappointed, because it could not be fulfilled, for more good reasons than one, it was by no means a useless hope. It did good to the Church and it made men better. In his epistle to the Romans, St. Paul speaks of, "salvation by hope." I can quite understand how the belief in the near coming of the Master, though radically a mistake, should be fruitful of much inspiration. The man who expected the Lord of love to return at any moment, had in that hope a powerful inducement to cultivate the graces of the spirit of love, that he might welcome properly his distinguished visitor. Just as a good child, whose mother is in heaven, has one of the most powerful incentives, to cultivate the holy life, that he can have. His first ambition will be so to live, that the dear departed, if she can look from within the upper light, at her darling fighting life's hard battle, may be filled with pride and joy at his pure and noble life; and his second, that he may be able to confront that sainted one, after life's work and warfare are over, with unabashed countenance and undaunted heart, saying: "Mother, I kept thy charge."

> "Thrice blest whose lives are faithful prayers,
> Whose loves in higher loves endure;
> What souls possess themselves so pure,
> Or is there blessedness like their's?"

Ah, my friends! do not deride this early hope of the Christian Church. There is something exquisitely touching in the simple devotion with which the first Christians clung to it. An old English ballad presents the pathetic picture of a poor maiden, demented at the death of her lover in a distant land. The particular form her mania took was, undying hope. Day by day, she expected her lover to return; and so she sat by the brook, decked her hair with flowers and berries, and prepared a welcome for him, singing all the while this hopeful refrain:

> "He will return, I know him well,
> He will not leave me here to die."

This was the spirit of the Apostolic waiters

for the coming of Christ. They believed, that their dearest Lord and Master would not leave them there to die. Mistaken though they were, see what a band of heroes they became. A valuable element, all things considered, in the training of the Infant Church, this strong hope was the inspiration of many a holy, martyr life and death.

Neither should we slight the faith, or hope, of a Christian brother, though it may seem to us not only baseless, but absurd. It is not so to him; and, if his life show the good fruits of fellowship with Christ, depend upon it, that hope, or faith is a salvation to him. He would certainly be a more enlightened Christian with a larger hope or a truer hope, a broader faith or a tenderer faith; but he will be judged by the great God, according to the loyalty with which he lives true to the hope or faith he has, and not according to the hope or faith he has not.

No blame then to St. Paul and his fellow-christians, though they clung to a hope doomed to be disappointed. With the best of them, it was the pure love of the Lord that made them yearn so eagerly for his presence. It was their lot to look for him to come to them; it was their blessedness, as they looked, to go to him. Disappointed in one way, they could not be disappointed in another. While they looked for the rending skies to reveal a descending Saviour, the Saviour looked to earth and beheld many ascending saints. In this looking and longing, this hoping and rising up, they won the encomium from those who were not at all their friends—"Behold these Christians! How they love one another!"

Neither does it deteriorate, in the least, the value of the apostolic writings, that their authors wrote under the spell of this baseless hope. Had they written as we should write to-day, concerning like topics, these letters would not have been worth the paper they were written on, to the churches who received them. It is in the fact, that these documents are a simple, artless, unaffected reflection of the spirit of their time, that they are beyond all price precious, and that we shall never cease to be thankful for them. They show how holy men of God in the first century, being men, saw through a glass darkly; and they suggest that holy men of God, to the end, will be able only to see through a glass darkly. What a much-needed lesson in

Christian modesty this teaches to us, who are interpreters and expounders of the sacred Scriptures! If the holiest and the best among us will only remember, that having done all we can to clear our spiritual vision, nevertheless, at the best, we shall have to fall back upon the apostle's words—words he applied to himself, as to all his fellow-christians—"Now we see through a glass darkly"—"Now we know in part"—I am sure it will teach us toleration, and spare us that despotism of pride and arrogance, which has made so many faithful Christians oppressive dogmatists, and cruel persecutors of their brethren.

This confession of St. Paul is a fine practical exhibition of the love he had been analysing in the previous verses. He is sitting here meekly at the Master's feet, like Mary. He knows only in part; but his Lord knows all. That is love's humble, unpresuming way. He saw through a glass darkly. That is love's generous, unsuspicious way. She would not blame another for not seeing everything with her eyes. She gives all Christians credit for being as conscientious as herself. He, though specially called, and specially illumined, knew that he was in the child-stage, religiously. That is how love delights to make herself of no reputation. She will not vaunt herself, nor be puffed up. She would be treated as a child; and, simple as a child, would ever treat others. She will not think she knows everything; she will be ever desirous to learn more. Blessed are they who can believe, and by their lips give practical expression to the sentiment, so well expressed in these lines :—

> We are a stage too—not the end;
> Others will come yet our work to mend,
> And they, too, will wonder at our poor ways.
> It is God who guides the world's affairs,
> And ever it rises by winding stairs,
> Screwing its way from the less to more.

PART II.
JESUS OUR LIGHT AND LIFE.

I.—THE COMPASSIONATE GUEST.

"This beginning of miracles did Jesus in Cana of Galilee, and manifested forth his glory."

St. John ii., 11.

St. John undertakes, in this gospel, to show that Jesus is the Christ, the Son of God. Both interesting and suggestive, is his method of setting forth Emmanuel, God with us. Not by strong assertion, nor by elaborate argument so much, as by natural inference, does he portray his great subject. He declares in so many words his belief in the divinity of Our Lord; but he bases his faith mainly, on the perfect humanity he presents. He speaks, as a man to men, about one who was undoubted man, though also divine high as human mind can conceive divinity. God, the High and Holy One, to our finite comprehension, stands at an infinite distance from the creatures made in his image. We have not at any time heard his voice nor seen his shape. But, in the form of "the highest, holiest manhood," we have the divine in the human. No longer clothed in thunder, with the lightning playing around his brows, and a voice speaking terrible things, need frail man conceive of the God with whom he has to do; but in our Lord and Master, the divine comes into the human, the great Father descends very near to his lowly child, and humanity is assured that, "God in man is one, with man in God." Only through the humanity of Jesus can human beings climb to any practical idea of his divinity.

It is a great misfortune of what is called, quite improperly, religious controversy (for there is usually very little religious spirit displayed in it), that both sides of the question under debate are usually stated in extremes. No dogma of Christianity has been more keenly canvassed than the Incarnation. From the Docetae of St. John's day, who denied Our Lord's humanity, alleging that his bodily appearance was nothing but a phantom, to the Immaculate Conceptionists of our own day, who find a sinless human Jesus only by creating a sinless Mother Mary, church history is one long wild war around this subject. Many bitter words have been spoken, many savage blows struck by Christian brethren, in vindicating the true humanity, or in defending the pure divinity of the Master. And, as usual, the whole truth has been with neither side. The orthodox theorised about the divinity till they lost any sound religious conception of the humanity; and the heterodox lost the divinity, in trying to solve the problem, how divinity of character could be separated from divinity of person. St. John falls into neither blunder. While ostensibly exhibiting a divine Jesus, there is no New Testament writer who offers so sublime touches of a human Jesus. For a divine flash of true human sympathy, no better can be quoted than: "He that is without sin among you, let him first cast a stone at her." For divine simplicity and human grandeur, what episode to be compared with the feet-washing of the disciples, on the night of the betrayal? Never were sweet human interest in innocent festivity, and fine delicacy of feeling, so divinely illustrated as at the marriage banquet in Cana of Galilee. Indeed, of all Our Lord's works of beneficence, I do not hesitate to say, that, in some respects, this last holds a place peculiarly its own. Few could have resisted the pathetic silence, and the searching speech, which put to shame the accusers of the guilty woman; fewer still could have come unimpressed through that touching scene in the upper room, where the Master girded himself with a towel, and became a servant, to teach his disciples how to become masters. But very many, who would have slunk away conscience-stricken from the Lord's presence in the temple, and who must have felt the divine spell of the feet-washing, have read the story of this marriage feast, and gone away, quite unable to believe, that the emergency was at all adequate for the inauguration of a series of wonderful works of beneficence. Some good people have even felt so strongly about this episode, that they would have given all they possessed, could they have expunged it from the Scripture narrative. Nothing is so difficult, as to convince some minds, that mirth and festivity in their own place, are important factors in working out the problem of the best human life; and, moreover, that the life into which sympathy for these cannot enter is maimed and mutilated. Christian doctors never erred more grievously than when they tried to weave into the fabric of Church life, the gnostic fibre, that the flesh is the sworn foe of the spirit, the human the greatest hindrance to the development of the divine. If they were right, this world would be properly described as a vale of tears, and God's highest creature here doomed by his Creator to be stretched upon the rack from the cradle to the grave. But if that were so, for what did God give the nightingale her song, and the dragon-fly her jewels? Why did he cover the earth with loveliness and fill the heavens with light? That we should shut our eyes and ears against these blessed sights, and sounds, and drag on through life heavy-hearted, heavy-footed, and heavy-headed? I, for one, don't believe anything of the kind; and Our Blessed Lord did not believe it, when he accepted the invitation to that marriage, and did his very best lest its joy should be broken. More than that, the hosts had no notion that his presence would restrain the natural outflow of rustic hilarity, or they would not have invited him and his disciples. I treasure this incident, in my heart of hearts, as a priceless boon to the Christian Church. In its boldness and uniqueness, it is to me the gem among the Master's good deeds. It reveals a perfect manhood, as appropriately employed when speeding the mirth of a marriage banquet, as when lifting the face-cloth from the dead and bidding the slumberer awake. Indeed, I do not believe that perfect manhood is possible on any other terms; for I have yet to learn that he can heartily weep with those who weep, who cannot as heartily rejoice with those who rejoice. Most certainly Our Lord would never have been " the chiefest among ten thousand and altogether lovely," had he been unable to fulfil perfectly both functions. Had the young cowered under the severity of his look, or the gladsome been frozen into sadness in his presence, his self-selected emblem of "the Good Shepherd," would have been a misnomer. Had the young and joyous not found in him a friend to love, and to trust, the mourner a consoler, and the penitent a welcome, his influence on society would have been largely negative, and his doctrine nowise different from that of the Scribes and Pharisees. It could never have been spoken by the mixed multitude who followed him—"He teacheth with authority, and not as the scribes." Moreover, his life is to be the example for all good men and women to follow. But how could he have been our example if his sympathy had been only partial and one-sided? How could the story of a man, who was not a man in the fullest sense, be a perfect standard for mankind to aspire after? Putting controversy aside, I think every Christian will accept Our Lord as presenting all of the divine, and all of the human, which these terms can ever convey to the human intelligence: and that he is to be revered as the Son of God, as truly as he is followed as the Son of Man. As an illustration of the divinity in humanity of Our Lord and Saviour, this incident at the beginning of his ministry is invaluable. If I had ever indulged any doubt as to the true manhood of Jesus, and of the identity between my nature and his, this narrative would have dispelled it. The scene is a marriage merry-making. Jesus and His disciples are there, to offer their congratulations, and good wishes, to the youthful bride and bridegroom. There for another purpose, would have been an insult and a wrong, to the wedded pair, and their hospitable friends. As keen-eyed Pharisaic spies—moral policemen—they would have been base intruders. I scan narrowly the movements of the Lord, for he is my example, and I must learn of him. No patronizing self-importance, as if his society were a favour for which the company should be specially grateful, mantles on his countenance. More human than any of them, in his sympathy with the happiness that bounds through every bosom, is the Master; for none knew so well as he that

> "There is one
> Who makes the joy the last in every song."

Indeed, to a divine artist, who could follow the spiritual lines of that festive group, the soul of the bridegroom was not more full of a sweet and true humanity, in that hour of manhood's pride, than the soul of Jesus, as he mingled with the party, and shed abroad the sunlight of a pure, good, and friendly spirit.

In the course of the feast, an opportunity presented to test his friendship and sympathy. Among the Jews, the fruit of the vine was an article of daily consumption. As regularly as the family meal was spread, was the juice of the grape laid on the table. On this festive occasion, the supply of wine, doubtless owing to some unforeseen circumstance, was exhausted, probably at an early stage of the feast. A consternation, which unsentimental people can hardly appreciate, spread throughout the company, at a state of affairs painful in the extreme, especially to the parties more immediately concerned. How those two youthful hearts were wrung with grief, amid the joys and hopes of that auspicious season, one may imagine, but can feebly describe! Our Lord caught up, in an instant, the extreme delicacy of the situation, and entered perfectly into the desire of those perplexed and anxious hearts. Then, without a moment's hesitation, he spoke the word at which

"The conscious water saw its God and blushed."

He did not wait to be importuned, and then, like many a little, great man, proceed, with assumed reluctance, and a great air of importance, to comply. Nor did he lecture soundly the unhappy hosts, on their lamentable lack of foresight, as so many excellent people would have done, in all good conscience, and then, with the worst possible grace, relieved their embarrassment Nor did he hesitate till he had enquired, What will Mrs Grundy think, and say of me? Freely and unreservedly his whole heart went out in an act of prompt, choice generosity. No dread had he, apparently, lest the creation of a commodity, around which then, as now, the most tragic and pathetic associations clustered, should be misconstrued. He knew full well that there is no good thing (and he must have believed wine to be a good thing), which ill-balanced, or carnal natures may not abuse, and of which unfriendly lips will not speak evil. So, with a pure motive and a clear conscience, he did the deed which scattered the cloud from that wedding sky, and fulfilled, in one way, the prophetic words of Isaiah, " He carried our sorrows." At that unlikely scene, as some might judge, he struck the keynote, that was to go on sounding, till on Calvary, it should die away in the solemn accents, " It is finished." Deed of power, thus combined with spirit of love, to teach mankind, that no brighter halo can encircle a human brow than deeds of generous, spontaneous sympathy Very suggestively, come in St. John's words at the close, " and manifested forth His glory "—His glory of the human, quite as much as of the divine. The divine was there, but St. John loses sight of it, for the moment, in the glory of the kindliness and love, which rested in the bosoms of all the party. Carping sectaries might stupidly try to discredit his good deeds, by ascribing them to an evil agency ; but I will venture to say, that no one present at that marriage ever could harbor such a vile suspicion. It was the wonder of love, far more than the wonder of power, which impressed them. And it is in the power of the love, which inspired his kind deeds, that the great religious value of Our Lord's beneficent life appears. The reader of the New Testament, who gets no further than the miracle of power, is very much like a child, who listens, in blank amazement, to the traditional nursery tales of fairies and giants, who performed most fabulous deeds. But the reader, who goes behind the powerful hand, and touches the compassionate heart which electrified it, penetrates to the Holy of Holies, and meets face to face with the true Jesus, whose meat and drink it was to do his Father's business. Heart alone can attract heart ; power is heartless as a marble statue. One may dread almightiness, but he can never love it; God must be loved before he can be known. Miracle can never compete with merit for the homage of the human mind. Nicodemus came to Jesus by night, struck by the rumor of his mighty deeds, and he went as he came. Had he been impressed by the love of these, he would have come, by day, and he would have remained when he came. The Hebrews trembled at the thunderings, and the lightnings, and the dread voice from the Mount, which might not be touched; and, in a few days, they worshipped, amid great rejoicing, a golden calf. Moses went into the thick darkness, to meet the God he loved, and his face shone with the glory of the Great Unseen. The miracles of the Gospels are in reality no aid to religious faith, except as they are regarded in the light of human exhibitions of divine love. 'Tis the sublime character in them which makes these wonders, signs from heaven. It is from the Jesus of Cana, far more than from the wine of Cana, that virtue flows to heal and help us all.

These three lessons, among others, may be drawn from this thrilling incident of Our Lord's ministry.

1. Very ordinary minds, as I have already hinted, have great difficulty in justifying a deed like this, because they cannot enter into the subtle refinement of sympathy which inspired it. Others, who cannot conceive of any real

good which is not religious so-called, have greater difficulty still in comprehending, how the creation of what they call a luxury for a marriage feast, could possibly be a religious duty. But those who believe that everything which brings light and sweetness into human hearts and lives, is a good gift and a religious, have no such difficulty. They believe that the Great Lord of all is as pleased with his servant when he is drying an infant's tears, as when he is on his knees at the bedside of the departing saint. From Cana to Calvary, flows onward, in increasing volume, the stream of the Messiah's helpfulness and mercy. But its waters are as pure at the fountainhead, as at the mouth of the mighty river; and their cleansing efficacy not less genuine at Cana, though their redeeming virtue at Calvary transcends all human thought. No Christian can stand on Calvary and fail to realize, that there the most tragic and the most sublime event of the ages transpired, the most infamous crime was perpetrated, and the most meritorious life sacrificed; but it will not magnify Calvary to belittle Cana, or Bethany, or Hermon. These sacred spots have all their special inspiration, and Christianity would be infinitely the poorer, could she be robbed of any of them. Wheresoever the master was, there the aroma of his holy presence will forever linger. Whatsoever deed he did, shall ever be cherished by the faithful heart, as a deed of piety and religion. From the manger, to the cross, his entire life was permeated by one pure inspiration ; and, whether it be in deeds of usefulness, or works of mercy, or psalms of praise, a Christian finds he can serve his maker, the oil of the Saviour's consecration will distil upon his head, and make him a saintly worker. In this marriage scene I find a lesson of the sacred unity of human life. "Religion in everything, and everything in religion," is its standing maxim for all the children of men.

2. Christians should not merely tolerate, because they cannot help it, innocent joys and festivities ; but, like their Lord at Cana, they should patronize and promote these as a sacred duty. A Christian's presence ought to sanctify pleasure, and make it the more pleasurable ; it should never restrain the pure outflow of natural enjoyment. Work and play are both requisite, for the health and development of mind and body ; and the best results from both sides of

our nature, are not to be obtained, without a judicious admixture of labor and recreation. It is the duty of Christianity to seek the best for man's nature as a whole; and to that end, her sanction should be as cordial as her Lord's was, to all that can gladden, or elevate, or bless humanity. Christianity has suffered much from her attitude to innocent amusements. She has sometimes decried many innocent pleasures, and dared to allege that they were irreligious. The pleasures were practised all the same, however, but with this unfortunate result, that the young thought a great deal more of the pleasures, and a great deal less of the Church that banned them. Thus, in the degradation of amusements, the Church did not elevate her sons and daughters; while they, in their hearts, had their faith shaken in the wisdom of a mother, who could so treat her children. By so acting, the Church dropped into a double blunder, and, like an unskillful pilot, struck the very rock she was steering madly to escape. She laid her ban upon things her Lord never condemned, and by withholding her patronage, she refused to walk in the footsteps of the gracious guest at Cana's marriage feast. Thus, she left the enemy master of the field. These pure pleasures became secret vices; right things forbidden, became wrong things coveted. A hard and fast line was drawn through human life, on one side of which a man was religious, and on the other irreligious; and the black banner of the Pharisees was floated over the disciples of the Master whom their wicked hands crucified. Christianity is only now recovering from the errors of centuries; though in some quarters, which it is unnecessary to mention, the old attitude to innocent pleasures and recreations is still rigidly maintained. With the spread of broader and truer ideas of Our Lord's example, there is developing the conviction, that Christianity ought to pour her benison on all rational recreations; and exclude nothing from her active sympathy, in which a good man can interest himself, to his pleasure and profit. The young ought to be taught, both by the precept and example of their parents, and teachers, that fellowship with Christ means gladness, and not gloom, good news to their bodies, as well as to their souls, and sweetness to all that is pure as well as severity for all that is impure. Our Lord's precept and example teach nothing less;

and he who, in the Master's name, teaches another doctrine, must find his Jesus somewhere else than within the compass of the four Gospels.

3. There is an infinite charm about Our Lord's way of doing things. Without ostentation, he did his very best for that marriage party; and within the material blessing there was wrapped up a precious spiritual blessing. "Thou hast kept the best until now," said the governor of the feast—the best wine, the finest compassion. How could it be otherwise, when the motive was so pure? There is the secret of all human *best* for others; there is the explanation of all human *worst*. Wherever the pure motive is, there will be the quiet, unobtrusive, best blessing for a needy fellow-creature. Wherever the motive is impure, there will be the noisy, ostentatious, unchristian service, which does not bless, as it should, him who receives, and blesses not at all him who gives. I do not know a better blessing, many Christians urgently need to-day, than deliverance from the spell of unconscious humbug, in much of their helping others. And I can prescribe no better cure for the delusion, than Our Lord's *manner of working*, in this episode at Cana of Galilee. Un-

known, apparently, to any but the servants, he did the best good in the best way. If many men and women, who say their prayers, concluding "for Christ's sake," would just look into the springs of our Christ's activity, and learn of him, in all their so-called good doing, it would be of the greatest possible advantage to themselves.

II.—THE MIGHTY WORKER.

"I spake to thy disciples that they should cast it out ; and they were not able."
St. Mark, ix, 18.

"Master, we saw one casting out devils in thy name, and we forbade him, because he followeth not with us."
St. Mark, ix, 38.

These passages, taken from the same Gospel, and referring, perhaps, to events which happened in close proximity of time, suggest a train of highly interesting and important thought. They indicate, " power," and, " no power," in either case unlikely in the circumstances, according to our idea of things. Here is a lonely worker in the cause of suffering humanity, and working in the name of the Great Healer, though owning no visible relation to him. Who he was, or what he was ; how he worked, or why he worked, the narrative saith not. One thing only we know ; and it sheds a halo of light around this nameless worker for Jesus. He was a great success. That fact lifts him right out of the darkness of obscurity, and plants him high up on the "Hills of Light." The man, who could face devils alone, and single-handed, was no ordinary man. He, who could conquer such foes, in the name of Jesus, was, at the moment, very near in spirit to the Lord, though preferring to do his good work in isolation. Not without good reason, therefore, do I assign this noble man a first place among the Christian helpers of humanity.

Jesus was in the Mount for devotion, along with the chosen three. In his absence, the disciples were necessarily the subjects of keen critical inspection, by hostile scribes and Pharisees. While their critics were eagerly canvassing the work and teaching of the young Nazarene, and endeavoring to elicit from his associates something to fan the flame of their hostility, an opportunity seemed to offer, for the disciples to vindicate their Master's name, and cover with confusion his enemies. A distressed father, having heard of Jesus, came, leading by the hand a demoniac boy, and imploring, with all the pathos of a parent's heart, relief for the miserable sufferer. The disciples hailed the opportunity, and did their best, we may be sure, to work a cure. But they failed. They could not cast out that devil ; and their humiliation was complete, when Our Lord descended to find them in the midst of an excited populace, who were jeering at the defeat of their pretentious attempt to do a deed evidently beyond their power. They who were with the Master, and had seen so many of his mighty works, were helpless to perform a work, which one, who had enjoyed no such privileges, was performing successfully every day. Plainly, he had a power which, for the moment, at least, they lacked. Had he been there, a different story might have been recorded. Jesus would have returned to an exulting band, who, in his absence, had been able to vindicate his authority, and put his foes to shame.

One is naturally curious to know the secret of this, " power," and, " no-power." How did this nameless solitary succeed while the disciples failed ? How could one who had far less knowledge of the method of Jesus, perform cures, which those who had so much better knowledge could not perform ? What, in short, was the secret of this man's strength, and what the secret of the weakness of the disciples ? Our Lord more than suggests the explanation. He states it explicitly. When the disciples enquired: "How is it that we could not cast it out?" he replied, "This kind can go forth by nothing save by prayer." The words, "and fasting," are an obvious interpolation. This lonely worker was able to cast out devils, because he was a man of prayer. In the spirit of prayer are we to find the spring of his power. Let us see what that spirit implies. The spirit of prayer is the spirit of submission. This man was strong because he could submit; he was high in the religious sense, because he could be lowly. Our Lord himself is the best exemplar of this spirit. In the garden, where the agony of prayer is seen at its keenest, the conquest is in the soft breathing of resignation, "not my will, but thine be done." Whosoever fathoms that depth, has entered into the truest fellowship with the Lord. He has touched the height at which St. Paul's high ideal becomes possible. He can then be "strong in the Lord, and in the power of his might." It was of such a spirit that the Master said, "All things are possible to him that believeth;" and the world has yet to discover the worker who can do any genuine work in another spirit.

What demoniacal possession, meant, in Our Lord's day, nobody knows, if it meant anything different, from those exceptionally distressing and appalling forms of bodily and mental disease, with which every age has unhappily been too familiar. I do not propose to put any other meaning into the phrase, inasmuch as we know nothing, either physiologically, or psychologically, of the actual indwelling of a distinct and separate evil personality, within a human being. As I take it, "casting out devils," refers to certain desperate forms of physical, mental, or moral evil, over which this isolated worker for Jesus had such authority and power, that he was able to achieve the most distinguished success. So true was his motive, so intense his zeal, and so wise his method that, as is said of Our Lord, " virtue went out of him, and healed them all." So thoroughly had he entered into the spirit and mind of Christ, that he himself became a Christ—the anointed of the Lord, to heal, and help, and bless mankind. His life was one great prayer; for from it there rose daily the incense of true self-forgetfulness, true self surrender, true consecration to serve God and man. That is the highest ideal of prayer.

Well might Our Lord, just then, commend to the twelve the power of prayer. For had he not just descended, from a season of devotion so beatific, that in the shining garments of the divine fellowship, he seemed no longer a denizen of the earth? No experience less exalted could have sustained that lonely worker, whose hands James and John were so ready to paralyze; no power less real than the spiritual power of the Supreme could have passed him onwards from victory to victory.

You perceive, quite readily, that such power could not be the offspring of what in ordinary speech is termed, knowledge of Jesus. I do not know how much, or how little, this man knew personally of Jesus and his mode of working; but I do know, that the disciples knew far more than he could possibly know. Nevertheless, he triumphed where they failed. It seems to me that we have here an inspired worker,—one who could be inspired by the Christ, because he had the ability, and who was inspired. In such cases, it is not the quantity of knowledge that tells so much as the quality. This man had seen Jesus, watched his gracious works, and heard his blessed call. Of that I have no doubt. Then, momentarily, that sight and hearing of the Master may have struck in his pure, good soul the spark of an enthusiasm to go and do likewise. He was capable of being a mighty worker against evil, and the spirit of the Master took possession of him. No doubt the twelve were inspired. Who could have given up all to follow Jesus, had they not been inspired by the spirit of Jesus? But there is inspiration, and inspiration. There are great, pure souls who can be inspired greatly, and there are lesser souls who can only be inspired in a lesser degree. This man had a mightier power than the twelve, because he had a fuller inspiration; and he had a fuller inspiration, because he had a fuller submission in the spirit of prayer. The twelve had received the lesser inspiration, to follow Christ; he had received the greater inspiration, to go out and lead in the holy name of Christ. This lonely worker resembled more the Master himself than the disciples. The twelve were, by and by, to assume the leader's place, and to do great things among the devils; but their time was not yet. They were leaning, meanwhile, upon their Master; their strength was in him; their highest ambition, to follow his lead.

And they did follow, not knowing whither they went. Accordingly, till the time came when they should find their own strength, and be able to stand upon their own feet, and cast out devils with their own hands, they must take a second place. They could not cast out that devil, because this kind could not come forth, save at the call of that higher, fuller inspiration, which they were to receive, one day; but that day was still future.

This contrast is important, not so much for the incidents themselves, as for the living word it has for every Christian. It points out very distinctly, in what the true power of man or woman consists. It shows that neither in place, nor rank, nor in anything which represents material power, lies the secret of an individual's real strength. The disciples were near enough to the mightiest among the sons of men, and yet they were not mighty. At the moment when, by every consideration of loyalty and self-respect, they desired to succeed, theirs was humiliating failure. Whatsoever authority they had from being within the charmed circle of the Apostolate, utterly failed them at the pinch. In the hour of testing, it vanished. The name of Jesus in their lips proved of small account before the devil in possession, when they had not the power of Jesus in their souls. That power our Lord could not commit to them, except as they could receive it. Real power is always of the spiritual nature, and must be an individual's very own. Supernatural power can be apparent, only when it becomes natural power, in those who can utilize it. The teacher's power in geometry becomes the pupil's, only when the pupil has made it his very own. On that principle, this eminent worker in the name of Jesus, possessed no power that you and I cannot possess, if we touch the secret of it as he did. Therein lies for us the value and the encouragement of his success. We may be mighty casters-out of devils, if we learn in the school of prayer, that our strength lies in the charter of human dignity conferred in the first chapter of Genesis, "God made man in his image, after his likeness." To be strong in that wise is the natural ambition of every true man and woman. Such strength is the grand seal of high discipleship. They who bear it have in their bodies, like St. Paul, the marks of the Lord Jesus. Men never dispute the piety of those who are thus sealed. They accept it as promptly, and as naturally, as Jesus accepted the discipleship of that worker, though he followed not with the twelve. They may dispute the piety of some who, like the twelve, bear the name, but cannot do the works, of Jesus; and they may even go so far, as to jeer at the Christianity which has so weak apologists and defenders. But before that other they are silent. By his fruits he is known. Like the priests of Egypt, they acknowledge, " This power is of the Lord."

It is a touching conclusion, from this episode at Hermon, that seeming strength may be but weakness. To whom did men think of going, to learn of Jesus, if not to his disciples? Nevertheless, they had better have gone to the lonely worker, whom the Apostle John forbade to cast out devils. For he knew Jesus better than the twelve; because the mind that was in the Master was more truly, and more fully in him. How often has it happened since, that some mighty man outside the pale of the Christian Church, has been more powerful to enlighten sinners, and shew them Jesus, than a whole host of her choicest sons? Alas! how much, and how often, have Christians trusted to the power of their privileges,—to their sacraments, their methods, their priesthoods,—and against the great devils who were ravaging the Church and Society, they had no more real power than the apostles at the foot of Hermon. Not that they were either idle, or unwilling; for, like the twelve, they had every reason to try honestly to do their very best. But they could not. If words could have done it, or demonstrations, or organization, not a devil had been alive to-day to tell the tale. But what care the devils for words? They have nothing to fear from spasmodic seasons of devotion, which are really more physical than spiritual. They know that the blaze of Church artillery means usually nothing more than "a flash in the pan." Like Mephistopheles, in Faust, the one thing they dread is the sign of the cross, not borne aloft in the hand, but worn deep in the life. How often, alas! has the power of Christianity been but weakness, because her leaders were content, to trust in the power of authority, rather than in the power of holiness! How weak are so many Christians of pure motive to-day, against the devils of sensualism and materialism, because they can think of no better strength than the arm of flesh. Give them the firm administration of justice, repressive legislation, stringent police regulations, and they are certain the millennium is at hand. But if the man whom John and James forbade were here, he would say: "Trust in the spirit of the Lord. Trust in the development of a higher Christian sentiment among all ranks and classes. Trust in the power of righteousness, justice and charity. Then, I will guarantee the devils will be cast out. A mighty wave of genuine Christian enthusiasm will sweep the land clear, of all such unwelcome guests. For, while the devils can laugh at any amount of Christian strength on paper, they cannot brook the virtue of a true, strong Christian piety, though it be represented only by a minority of one.

There is a pregnant word here also for a most catholic toleration. Though St. John's tactics were so explicitly condemned by Our Lord, St. John has had many admirers and imitators in the same hateful work ever since. Though this apostle was privileged to lean on the Master's bosom, he had learned his spirit no better than to attempt to arrest a good work, simply because it was not done in his way. This good man was doing an undoubted good, in his own way, and he was content to labour alone, giving all the honour to Jesus. His motives were unimpeachable; but his plan was peculiar. That was enough for John and James. "He does not do the good in our way," said they, "and, therefore, he shall be stopped, because he is working in the name of Jesus. The devils may rage, if they will, but they shall not be cast out in an irregular way." Just the very language bigoted and narrow Christians are hurling against their brethren to-day. I rejoice at the emphatic, unmistakable reply of Our Lord: "Forbid him not, for he that is not against us is for us." What a broad principle of toleration is that! To how fine a point it brings the terms of Christian discipleship. Spiritual life and power are its only tests. Fellows in good work are they, knowing no rivalry, but only how to bring the greatest honor to the feet of Jesus, and to plant the richest jewels in his crown. Seeking, first of all, good and pure hearts, and leaving their heads to learn heavenly wisdom through the devotion of their spirits. Leaving methods of Christian work to the selection of each worker, and making success the sole test of every mode of operation. These are the lessons of the Master's reply ; and there is not a Church in Christendom to-day, which does not in some manner recognize their justice, and at the same time give practical denial of them. After nineteen centuries, the Christian Church has to be taken back face to face with this lonely worker of Galilee, to learn that every method Christianly pursued is sanctioned of Christ; that true fellowship with the Master, is in the consecrated life and the good work, and that success is the Master's warrant for crowning any worker with authority.

III.—THE NEIGHBOURLY JESUS.

"Who is my neighbour?"
—Luke, x, 25.

Probably the best criticism of the "Cottar's Saturday Night," ever uttered was the simple remark of a peasant maiden, who, on hearing that rustic idyll recited for the first time, spontaneously exclaimed, "I think nothing of it at all; for I have seen the same in my father's house a hundred times." It was a splendid tribute to the fidelity of the poet's description— all the more valuable that it was the unconscious compliment of an unsophisticated, candid mind. The criticism of the lawyer on the story of the good Samaritan, partook of the same spontaneous character. He had enquired in apparent puzzlement, "Who is my neighbour?" expecting Our Lord to enter into an elaborate definition of the term. But he was disappointed and disconcerted. As if hardly conscious that he had asked the question, Our Lord proceeded to unfold the tale of a suffering fellow-creature, neglected by orthodox selfishness, and saved by heterodox charity. Then, when the hearer's interest had been fully awakened, he turned almost abruptly upon him the question, "Which, now, of these three was neighbour to him that fell among the thieves?" The lawyer was thrown off his guard. Before his head had time to evade, his heart had spoken right out, "He that showed mercy on him." Here is nature's spontaneous definition of one of nature's first duties.

The Priest and the Levite had also their definition for neighbourliness; but it broke down when tested, and so proved futile. The Samaritan's was the same as the lawyer's, and he came to it in the same way—spontaneously. The Priest and the Levite reasoned themselves into duty like religious men; but the result of their reasoning was to leave a brother Jew to die untended. The Samaritan heard neither reason, nor religion, for the moment. The voice of humanity in his soul drowned every other, and inspired him to do, both for the wounded wayfarer and for himself, what reason and religion had failed to accomplish. Where these two guides had broken down ignominiously, humanity triumphed, to read to mankind forever the sad, suggestive lesson, that, while reason is good, and religion is good, a man may be very little of a man, and yet have a very considerable reputation for both.

It is very significant, that Our Lord should have made no appeal to religion in support of the doctrine of neighbourliness. He seeks a much broader basis for his teaching than many who have followed in his train. He does not say, that to be neighbourly a man must be of the Jewish religion, or of the Samaritan religion, or of any other religion. The Priest and the Levite were very religious; but, in spite of their religion, they were grossly unneighbourly. Notwithstanding their high religious rank, they were as cold and heartless as the most blatant infidel could be. On the other hand, the Samaritan was neighbourly, not because he was a religious man, but right in the teeth of his religious teaching. The best Samaritan lover of God, according to his creed, was the best Samaritan hater of the religion of his neighbours in Judea; just as among ourselves, the most approved Protestant is, by some, thought to be the most bitter Anti-Catholic demonstrator. Had he listened to the precepts of the Church fathers, he would certainly have left that poor wounded Jew to die on the Jericho road. But, like a good many Christians, his character was vastly better than his creed. He heard the still small voice of nature, and, in defiance of his Church teaching, promptly fulfilled his duty as a man. God help the Christian Church, and the Unchristian World, if thousands of Christians are not better than their creeds, and thousands of so-called unbelievers are not better than their cold negations.

I take this narrative, therefore, as in the main illustrative of three great lessons.

1. *That heart is the chief factor in the discharge of neighbourliness.* This is a most pathetic story. On that bloodiest of Judean highways Our Lord finds a miserable wayfarer —plundered, naked, wounded, dying. In the hot, parching blaze of the midday sun, life seems to be ebbing fast away. So exhausted is the unfortunate man, that he is, apparently, unable to appeal for help, to any chance passenger. Along the road from Jerusalem Our Lord brings a priest, fresh from his sacred functions

at the temple, bending his steps homeward; for Jericho is a priestly city. Surely, if, at any time, this man's heart will be compassionate, as he emerges from the sacred associations of holy scenes and holy services. But there are those who preach, and yet are castaways—their preaching hardening rather than quickening their own spiritual nature—and there are those who worship a God of love, and yet are heartless as a marble statue. This holy man, with the aroma of the holy incense still hovering around him, cannot even cross the path, to staunch a fellow-creature's wounds, or shrive his soul. He passed by on the other side.

Next, a Levite appears upon the scene. Inferior in ecclesiastical rank, he seems to be superior in pure selfishness and hard-heartedness. He crosses the path, and bends over the hapless victim. His apparent interest, however, brings no real good to the sufferer, but much harm to the spectator, who can look on such a scene of misery, unmoved. The priest could always say, that he had not seen the true state of the case. The Levite sees all, and yet leaves the unfortunate man to his fate. As he disappears in the distance, a third traveller comes into view; but there is little to be expected from one, to whom the unfortunate Jew is only the hated member of a hated race. He approaches, and looks upon the tragic scene. Quick as thought he takes in the situation. Springing from his horse, in a moment he has lifted the dying man's head, and resting it gently on his arm, is busy binding up his wounds, pouring in wine and oil. Then, taking him up with all a woman's tenderness, he seats him comfortably on his own beast, to bring him to the nearest hostelry. Placed safely among his fellow-worshippers, the Samaritan might, quite gracefully, have then left the object of his benevolence to their hospitality. Not so, however. He does nothing by halves—this good Samaritan. Mercy must have her perfect work. Handing him over to the inn-keeper, he deposits a sum for the sick man's maintenance, and becomes responsible for any further charges. Such a fullness of neighbourly grace was in his soul.

The radical distinction between the unneighbourliness of the two ecclesiastics, and the neighbourliness of the Samaritan lay in the principles which they respectively followed. The clergy reasoned with that prudent caution so

dear to the official mind :—" Here is a miserable
" victim, and I am so sorry for him. But what
" can one person do in such an emergency, and
" in this lonesome place ? Perhaps the robbers
" are near, awaiting another victim. I have a
" wife and children, and they should be my
" first care. It is not quite safe for me to linger
" here. This is a duty very important, but it
" calls for the help of several benefactors. After
" all, the poor, speechless, sufferer may be fatally
" wounded. Were it not a kindness to leave
" him to die in peace ?" And, as each recounted
in his home, that night, the incidents of the
day, there would be no lack of cheap sympathy
for the poor man, and the fervent hope would
be earnestly expressed that some other passenger, only *half as willing*, but *twice as able*, had
rendered the necessary aid. Perchance some
tender maiden may have whispered in her
father's ear, that in another family there might
be a vacant chair, and loving hearts wrung with
agonizing suspense for the safety of one whose
dear footsteps lingered long. But if such im-
proper thoughts were obtruded on the peace of
either of these good, kind husbands and fathers,
the stock sedatives of pious mutterings about

"the friend of the friendless," "the shield of the stranger," "the deliverer of the oppressed," would be judiciously administered to restore his equanimity. So ready is the ordinary type of humankind to argue itself out of the most abominable selfishness, into calm complacency. All these arguments, and some more besides, were equally at the service of this good layman. It had not been his business to theorize about neighbourliness, and tell plainly to other people how very neighbourly they should be. Fortunately for Christianity, his simple mind could not be so easily driven into the refuge of specious and plausible excuses. Obeying the generous impulse of his soul, he saw in the injured wayfarer only a man and a brother. The royal law of love inspired him to do to another what he should, most of all, have desired that other to do to him, had their places been changed. And as he laid his head on his pillow that night, his rest was all the sweeter, that he had no need to forge apologies for the conduct of the day, or compound salves for an accusing, troubled spirit. In his bosom he had the priceless jewel of a conscience without offence, and, though he knew it not, he had the treasure of grateful hearts, who mingled his name in their morning and evening prayers. His heart's answer had won for him a golden crown, and the head's answer had crowned the Priest and the Levite with shame and contempt. And when this first of Christian philanthropists came to hear the roll-call of eternity, he could answer with a readier alacrity ; for there were those ready to stand up for him before the great Judge, and plead, " Lord, he did it unto one of the least of these, thy brethren."

Some one hearing me may be cherishing a lurking sympathy for the respectable Priest and Levite, who followed the dictates of a prudent mind. Ordinary minds believe thoroughly, in reasoning long and well, especially when they are asked to do some urgent but trying service for others. " I will think of it," is the stereotyped phrase of those who never think at all, and never mean to think. Reasoning is the glory of reasonable beings ; but if reason is to be one's supreme guide in everything, 1 am afraid the record of humanity will be but a very poor affair. Tried by cold reason, every martyr who went bravely to the stake, every patriot who fell bearing a brand against the tyrant, every missionary who gave his bones to whiten on Afric's burning plains, was a misguided man—a restless, adventurous spirit, who could not take care of "the great Number One." That is how reason would make havoc of history, and reduce the Christian life to a round of scheming and planning, how to gather to ourselves the most, and how to sacrifice the least. But right in the face of all selfish squirming, this parable stands out bold and uncompromising. There is no evading the drift of its teaching. No one has ever read it, without recognizing its sublimity. Wherever this gospel is preached, splendid monuments on every side testify to the fame of the Good Samaritan. While the world stands, institutions of benevolence and philanthropy will be the eloquent testimony which the human soul will delight to bear, to the triumphs of charity over selfishness, the conquests of the melting heart over the reasoning head.

2. *This parable discloses Our Lord's faith in human nature.* Very hard things are often said about our poor human nature. We don't need anybody to tell us how wayward, how selfish, how heartless, men, aye, and women even, can be. Nevertheless, after the very worst has been

told, there is a good deal to be said for erring, faulty human-kind. One could hardly say of a brilliant deed of goodness, like the Samaritan's, or of the life sacrificed to rescue a fellow-creature from destruction, that all such tokens of a nobler nature are but as filthy rags. History testifies abundantly, that human nature is susceptible of fine touches of genuine nobility, and heroic sacrifice. That Scottish engineer, on the steamship City of Paris, who, at the risk of his life, dashed into a cloud of steam, to stop the engine, lest horror should be added to horror; and Enoch Arden, the rough sailor lad, who

"Thrice had plucked a life
From the dread sweep of the down-streaming seas,"

are heroes, whose deeds shed undying glory upon our common humanity. Our Blessed Lord constantly assumed the sublime possibilities of human character. He invariably credited the good-doer with his goodness, just as truly as he discredited the evil-doer, by reason of his badness. He believed in human nature. His mission was to teach men how to throw off the fetters of selfishness, and to be free in the glorious liberty of sacrifice. He never encouraged anyone to contemn human nature, nor to ignore it. He had faith in the germ of inherent goodness, which exists even in the most abandoned sinner, and his gospel is the charter of emancipation, from that slavery of misdirected passion and devotion, which had so defaced the character, and defamed the reputation, of many of God's highest creatures here below.

The lawyer, in the narrative, may have expected that the new prophet had some special law of neighbourliness to unfold, superior to the old Mosaic law. Not so, however. Our Lord was no destroyer of the old truth. He came, like all the great masters, to confirm the old, by evolving its deeper meanings, and exhibiting its wider application to human needs. Those who would justly appreciate his teaching, must not only have a large hope for humanity, but a deep faith in its powers and possibilities, as well. They must begin every healthy movement, for the good of the individual, in the fullest alliance with his better nature. They must believe, that in the soul of the most obdurate sinner there is a seed of goodness, if only it can be got at—a spring of heavenly origin, if it can only be tapped. Many a good man has failed utterly to raise a sinful one, because, while he had the

gospel lever, he did not take into his reckoning the gospel fulcrum in the sinner's nature, on which to operate. No man ever yet reformed another, who did not make this the first word, and the last, of all his philanthropic efforts,— "Brother, reform thyself." Our Lord's gospel to the lawyer, on this occasion, and to you, dearly beloved, in these pews, is just this :—
" Be a man ! Give free scope for the play of
" the noble impulses of thy better nature. The
" God of love made man to love ; and if you
" would be true to your creation, obey the sym-
" pathetic throbbings of your heart, as this
" great soul did. Head and heart must be fel-
" low-workers ; for the heart that loves deeply
" should love wisely. But in neighbourliness,
" heart must be first in command, and head her
" faithful lieutenant. This is the old gospel of
" brotherliness, and it is the new gospel. It
" was the gospel of Amos, and Isaiah, and all
" the prophets ; it will be the gospel of every
" good and helpful soul, while the world stands.
" Go thou and do likewise."

3. *Religion is genuine and efficient only when it is electrified by the battery of a full-charged human kindness.* Some of the fathers

used to speak of the good deeds of heretics, as being only evil, because they were performed by men whose heads were unsound, concerning the dogmas of the Church. Some of those, who like to be called fathers still, hold very much the same opinion. Our Lord, you perceive, does not make the dying Jew inquire, concerning the soundness of his would-be benefactor, about religious times and seasons, or offerings and sacrifices, before accepting his good offices. He finds him sound on charity, and that suffices for the time. Neither does Our Lord say, what his own opinion is, of the religious soundness of the Priest and the Levite. We know what he thought about their ideas of duty to a suffering brother. I have not the slightest doubt that St. John accurately represented his Master's sentiments when he wrote: "If a man love not his brother whom he hath seen, how can he love the Father whom he hath not seen?" That is the statement of practical piety on high authority. St. James corroborates his brother's opinion, by actually defining religion thus; "Pure religion, and undefiled before God and the Father is this, to visit the fatherless and widows in their affliction, and to keep himself unspotted from the world." With heads full of the talk about God, which went for very little, the hearts of the Priest and the Levite were sadly lacking in true and generous feelings for man. Their piety did nothing for the dying Jew. Can it have done very much for themselves? The Samaritan, on the other hand, was worse than an unbeliever in Jewish opinion. Nevertheless, he responded to the voice of nature, as if it were the voice of God, showing mercy, and that so graciously, that the splendid act of beneficence was enhanced tenfold by the splendour of the grace of doing it. Do I need to enquire, with whom you would like to enter the world of spirits? With the orthodox Priest, or the heterodox Samaritan? Do I need to ask, with which thought you would like to lay your head on your dying pillow? To recall opportunities for supplying need, or soothing sorrow, or saving a soul, or resting a weary one, suffered to pass unembraced? Or to reflect on the poor ministered to to by a kindly hand, or a heavy burden shared with a heavy heart, or tender words coming like a cordial to a fever-racked frame, or blessed light brought into souls darkened and ready to perish? I do not need to suggest the answer. Your own hearts have already anticipated me. Need I say which is the most religious retrospect? I would not like to say that the Priest and the Levite were irreligious men, though their conduct, on the occasion referred to, was decidedly irreligious. At the same time, a religious ideal, which had so little to say for itself when tested, was surely a very faulty thing indeed. I hope that none of us will ever cherish such a miserably defective conception of duty to God, and God's creatures. If we do, we shall certainly deny ourselves many a choice blessing, and rob our souls of the sweet refreshment, which spontaneous generosity always brings down from heaven above. Moreover, we shall lay up for ourselves a heritage of woe, to embitter and sadden our latter days. Well had it been for the Priest and the Levite had they been done with the omissions of that evil day, when they had slept off its fatigues; or could they have forgotten its incidents. Though they might try to forget their heartless conduct, it could never forget, nor forgive them. They were never again the same men, after they had selfishly passed that scene of misery. They had, in their brother's misfortunes, a grand opportunity to be themselves richly blessed in helping another. The opportunity declined, however, that which would have blessed, came back constantly to curse. Better a thousand times, to have changed places with the maltreated traveller, than to have had the heart to look upon his miseries, and to pass complacently on their way. Better a thousand times to be Lazarus with his rags and his sores, than Dives with his purple and fine linen, and a nature so unneighbourly that only the torments of Hades could purge away its unbrotherliness. Better a thousand times any trial or privation, than the terrible fate of a nature beat hard as adamant by the hammer of selfishness, through shutting its ear to the cry of the wretched, or clenching fast its hand against the poor, or damming up the flow of the milk of human-kindness. Such a soul is alone, in the most awful sense of the term; for it can find no friend in earth or heaven. There is no wrong a man can do himself more tragic, than to deliberately crucify the divinity within him, by denying himself the rich endowments of love.

Who is my neighbour? puzzled the lawyer,

because he asked it in the wrong quarter. It is a question which will puzzle everybody who asks it at another. No man can answer it for his brother; every man must answer it for himself. It is a question to be put in the inmost shrine of our being, where God and we are the only witnesses. It should be put in the spirit of love, and not in the spirit of law. For law will put it thus: "Who have claims on my neighbourly thoughts and feelings? In fact, how few neighbours have I?" Love will put it thus: "Am I neighbourly? In fact, how many can I possibly include within the sacred name of neighbour?" Law will always limit the circle. Love will always try to make the circle boundless as the horizon. If ye have heard with the hearing ear, and the sensitive heart, ye will go forth to-day to make more than ever, love, and not law, your Vade Mecum of neighbourliness.

IV.—THE GLAD MASTER.

"Lord, even the devils are subject unto us in thy name."
—St. Luke, x, 17.

Never since the world began was such marvellous success achieved, by means so very unlikely. Interpret these words as you please, they are the record of sublime triumph. The greatest moral, social, and religious difficulties had been overcome; the most hostile foes subdued. And by whom? And by what means? By agents as unpretending, and as uninfluential as ever trod this earth, and by no arts, nor symbols of awe or power, nor words of terror and authority. Alexander, Cæsar, Charlemagne, spread the fame of their might, amid the nations, and founded great empires, by dint of their own genius, supported by the robust virtue, and cold steel of their battalions. They came, they saw, and they conquered. At their nod the world trembled. But how ill their triumphs compare with the conquests of the

Seventy! These warriors had much in their favour—military genius, national prestige, the pomp and pageantry of war. The Seventy had nothing on their side, but a lowly, inoffensive spirit, and a true faith in their Master's teaching, as they comprehended it; while arrayed against them, were all the influences which men usually trust in.

The time, was against them. Jesus was on his last journey southward. His foes now dared to be openly hostile, and even old friends were dropping away. Long before, the Samaritans had besought him to tarry with them; now, they rudely repulse him, as he proposes to take the direct route for the capital, through Samaria, and he has in consequence to make a long detour to the eastward. This was the moment he selected, to send the Seventy into the Samaritan country, bearing his message of peace and good-will to men. Well might he forewarn the missionaries as they departed, "Behold, I send you forth as lambs in the midst of wolves."

Fortune, was against them. They were told to rely for supplies on the good-feeling of those among whom they went. A purse was to form no part of their travelling equipment. If they commended their mission by labouring in the spirit of the Master, they should not lack hospitality; if they did not so commend it, no amount of treasure could command success. At the moment, he had seized the opportunity to teach his disciples how to behave among unfriendly people; and they were to have free scope to show how well, or how ill, they had learned the lesson. When the villagers, I have referred to above, refused to permit him and his company to pass the frontier into Samaria, James and John, like many of their successors since, deemed that flaming fire from heaven was the only fit messenger of offended justice. Our Lord was of no such mind. Turning meekly to the bystanders, he uttered the suggestive remark, "The Son of Man is not come to destroy men's lives, but to save them." If they went forth in the spirit of these words, they should lack no good thing.

Further, appearances were against them. They were to carry no extra raiment, and to be content with the sandals of the common people.

Social custom, even, was to be against them. The last of their marching orders was not the least important. They were to waste no time in useless salutation; but, like business men to whom time is money, they were to proceed vigorously with their enterprise, turning aside to practice no trifling formalities. Among a people so formal and punctilious such an omission, or rather innovation, could not commend, if it did not hinder, the apostles of a new doctrine.

Such is the simple story of the sending forth of the Seventy, with the circumstances under which the greatest mission ever committed to man was inaugurated. A scene more impressive in its simplicity, or more suggestive of a divine method in religious life and work, one can hardly imagine.

1. Observe the naturalness of the arrangement. Our Lord, finding that his Galilean followers were a goodly company, determined to utilize their loyalty to himself, in the interest of others. Accordingly, he selected seventy to proceed on a missionary expedition into Samaria, going two and two. The twelve had gone on a similar expedition many months before; but they were restricted exclusively to Jewish work. The new missioners were detailed for purely Samaritan work. And what prophetic commis-

sion did they receive? None. Each man was to go forth, and tell the story of Jesus, and his love, and truth, in his own way. No written documents had they to preach from, nor church methods to work in, nor holy sacraments to celebrate. Simply, the story of Jesus, his word and his work, told just as it struck the individual mind, in its simplicity and beauty.

2. Those humble missionaries exhibited an obedience sublime in its simplicity. They were Jews, and they were starting out to work among a people, to hold intercourse with whom, they had hitherto regarded as a dishonor to their name and disloyalty to their religion, if not a sin against God. It required a very strong sense of conviction and duty to condescend to that step. Besides, the Samaritans had always repaid Jewish national scorn and contempt with the usual ecclesiastical rancour; and it called for conviction, not to say courage, of the highest order, to face the ordeal, which was certainly in store for them. This aspect of the mission must have been as unique in that age, as if Hindoo Brahmins of to-day were sent forth with orders to care nothing for caste, and associate freely, and even eat, with abhorred pariahs and sudras.

The Seventy were to join without hesitation, or reserve, in the household life of the hated Samaritans, and eat with them at their tables. Such a triumph of the purely religious spirit over the ecclesiastical, stands unparalleled in the history of missions. Only the firmest belief in the character of Jesus, and in his good work, allied to the purest desire that others, for their good, should share that belief, could have carried them through.

3. What a sublimely simple faith our Lord had in the power of genuine religious truth! He took-in the situation perfectly, in all its bearings. He knew, how vast is the influence of early association, over even the best minds. He discounted fully the hostility, peculiarly deep and rancorous, of ecclesiastical zeal, and how ready bitter feeling is, to excite bitter feeling, and the intolerant word, the intolerant rejoinder. Nevertheless, he had such perfect confidence, in the power of simple truth, in simple lips and lives, that he was willing to stake the success of his cause, and his reputation as the Christ, on the result.

4. Our Lord displayed great faith in the latent fairness and goodness of human nature. Those

simple missionaries could not possibly be successful, unless their earnest words struck an echo in the souls of the Samaritans. Their inspiration could not be shared by Samaritans, unless the Samaritans were capable of being inspired. Had our Lord had any doubt on that point, he would have employed other agents than those seventy simple, loving souls. Whether we consider our Lord's confidence in his truth, to find its way to the most bigoted Samaritan hearts, or his confidence in the Samaritans' readiness, to respond to its simple appeal, simply put, the conclusion is alike striking and remarkable.

5. Observe the business-like way in which all things were ordered and the work undertaken. The grand enterprise was of vast importance, and all means available should be employed to win success, or at least to deserve it. The missionaries were to be without resources, lest they should be less active, or less prudent, or less zealous than they might. They were to go without encumbrance of superfluous clothing; and they were to go as poor, simple men, commending the gospel of a poor, simple teacher. There is no hint in the narrative, that

the goodness of the cause might justify any methods, however disorderly or ill-adapted, but everything to encourage orderliness and prudence in Christian, as in all work.

Such was the humble missionary enterprise of our Lord's last days; and such the equipment of the agents by whom this brilliant result was achieved. How simple and humble the means, compared with the greatness of the end! How inadequate, your typical ecclesiastical organizer of to-day would say! How impossible for such means alone to effect so signal a triumph, say those who know nothing of the power of religious truth unadorned, yet adorned the most! No doubt, the result was astounding, all things considered ; but to us mainly, as a striking testimony to the power of simple piety, and earnestness in Christian lives, and to the living force of a genuine and fitting message. Theirs, was only the power of a noble childlike devotion, and of an honest and full heart. These peasants were not scholars; they were not Christian theorists; they had no book knowledge to speak of. They could speak only of that which they knew, and testify to that which they had seen. Only that and nothing more. They were sent to represent the Great Teacher, and they could only do it in his way. His teaching consisted of a few simple precepts about doing justice and judgment, charity in thought and act, brotherly love, and the divine fatherhood. He condemned all formality in religion, and advocated the liberty of the spirit, in opposition to the slavery of the letter. That was the sum of his teaching. He did not set himself to expound the sacred books, best qualified though he was to do so. He had no formulated creed to prescribe, as the test of discipleship. He had no new ceremonial regulations to enjoin, and he had nothing ill to say of the Mosaic institutions. He never aimed at making a party in the State, nor a sect in the Church. He took no name for his following; he organized no society. His works were the reflex of his teaching, as opportunity offered. Whatever precept he taught in word, he was prompt to exemplify in act.

The work before the Seventy, therefore, was very different from what we might, at the first glance, suppose. They had been attracted to the fellowship of Jesus, by a certain magnetic influence, and they had nothing to tell the

Samaritans, but just what he was to them. Each might have a somewhat different story to tell, because each had his own way of regarding things; but they were one in unlimited devotion to their leader. He was their all in all. No better proof could they have given of their devotion, than by undertaking a mission so unpromising, and beset with difficulties peculiar to it; but so thoroughly had they become branches in the true vine that, like the Light Cavalry at Balaclava, at his command, it was

"Their's not to make reply,
Their's not to reason why,
Their's but to do and die."

Never did simple devotion reap such a rich harvest. In due time, the elated missionaries returned, and reported with exultation, "The very devils were subject to us in thy name." Apparently, not a man among them had failed, or grown discouraged. It was an unanimous report; and it filled with rejoicing the Lord, and the apostolic company. On hearing it, the Master broke out into that magnificent rapture of thanksgiving, so striking, because almost unique in the narrative of his ministry: "I thank Thee, O Father, Lord of Heaven and

Earth, that thou didst hide these things from the wise and prudent, and didst reveal them unto babes." They were babes in knowledge, comparatively speaking, those early disciples; and it was because they were babes in simplicity, that they had power to do great things for God and for man, and to prevail. It is the babe spirit, that is always the strong spirit in religion; and it is the spirit of the so-called wise and prudent, which, though strong in theory, as in the Pharisees, is too often weak as water, and cannot excel. Not that Christianity lays any embargo on the cultivation of wisdom and prudence, both excellent qualities in any individual; but it is not your babes in Christianity who are artificial and theoretical, whose heads are full of schemes, and whose tongues are always ready to fight in the ranks of wordy controversy. Your babes may be able often to give a very poor account, by their lips, of the faith that is in them; they may never have seen, through and through, one of the answers in any of the catechisms; they may know nothing of the history and development of Christian doctrine. But, thank God, the gates of the Kingdom of Heaven are not shut against all who are not theologians. These babes are religious and nothing else; their strength is in their character, and religion owns no home but character. Their faith in Jesus is the fruit of the spirit of Jesus in them. Their power to commend Jesus is the very same, though in a lesser degree, as the power of Jesus to commend himself. And their triumphs for Jesus are of the same kind, as his triumphs were in the days of his ministry. They conquer, not by might nor by power—indeed, they cannot conquer on these terms—because true religion can never assume the sword, and become aggressive. They conquer, not by demonstrations of a whipped-up enthusiasm; for, like their ancestors, the Seventy, they steal away quietly to their good work, and sound no trumpet before them. They conquer, not by brazen-browed intolerance, and loud sounding proclamations of purity and power. They leave these tactics to the sons of thunder, who know not what manner of spirit they are of. They conquer, by letting their light shine; never by flaring their light wildly about, to the offence and damage of their friends and brother-Christians. And even the devils are subject to them in Christ's name; that is, the most perverse and the most vicious, the most bigoted and prejudiced, the very embodiments of evil or intolerance, or prejudice, cannot resist the wisdom and power with which they speak, nor miss the aroma of the heavenly incense that rises from their lives. Oh! for some great developments, in these days, of the power of the Seventy! Oh! for more of that simple fidelity to Christ, which knows little, it may be, but lives out, and loves, all it knows! Oh! for more of the power of religion, in artless, simple guise, such as it was in those first missionaries, to save us in this age, from the bondage of names, and things, and shibboleths, and theories, which never yet made a man religious, but many a time, have seduced the unwary into the net of rank Pharisaism. " Except ye become as little children," said Jesus, on another occasion, " ye cannot see the kingdom of God." In other words, unless ye become simple, natural, straightforward, honest, tender in sympathy, and transparently true, ye cannot enter into that religious affinity with the Christ, which, in the sixth beatitude, is termed, " seeing God."

The Seventy had nothing to convert Samaria with, but the spirit of Christian childhood, which had been created in the society of the Christ. They received no miraculous gifts, so far as this narrative bears. This mission stands forth, therefore, as a type and model for all who would conquer evil, either within them or without them, in the name of the Lord. These Samaritans were conquered by the meekness of the missionaries, and the demon of party hate was exorcised by the spirit of charity. The demon of the letter, which had well nigh killed out religion, by divorcing it from common life, fled howling away before the preachers of a living Saviour, whose motto was, "Spirit and Truth." The demon of selfishness, which had ruptured so terribly brotherly ties, and forbidden brotherly-kindness, and dammed up the stream of brotherly sympathy, was swept away, like the frail parapet by the spring freshet, when the sluices of sympathy, compassion, and tenderness were opened by the apostles of the Nazarene. Before our Lord's day, these demons ranged the earth, "like roaring lions, seeking whom they might devour," and epoch after epoch had been drenched, with the torrents of blood they had shed. Well might the nations personify evil in him, whom they called the prince of this world.

But Messiah, the Prince, showed how an end should be put to his sovereignty ; for grandly has "the incarnation of all the virtues," been welcomed by men of every nation and clime, as King of Kings, and Lord of Lords. Nevertheless devils have many lives, and they die hard. In a general way, it is easy to trace in society the discrediting of the spirit of selfishness before the spirit of Christ. One, who cannot be suspected of any desire to favor Christianity, the great Napoleon, bears his testimony to that fact. He was no weak-headed hireling, or prating special pleader ; and yet, in conversation with a companion on lonely St. Helena, he uttered these remarkable words: "The heroes of antiquity and myself founded great empires upon force. Jesus alone founded his empire upon love ; and to this very day, millions would die for him. The soul, charmed with the beauty of the gospel, is no longer its own ; God possesses it entirely ; he directs its thoughts and faculties ; it is his. What a proof of the divinity of Jesus Christ! Yes, in this absolute sovereignty he has but one aim—the spiritual perfection of the individual, the purification of his conscience, his union with what is true, the salvation of his soul. Men wonder at the conquests of Alexander, but here is a conqueror who draws men to himself for their highest good; who unites to himself, incorporates into himself, not a nation, but the whole human race."

The general influence of Christianity, I need not say, is only the aggregate of the personal influence of particular Christians; and the battle of Christianity is only to be won along the line, by the victory of the individual. To this great battle we, who are wise and prudent, are individually called. The devils will be subject to us, if we have caught up the mind of our Lord like those simple Seventy, and if we bid them go, by lips which can testify what good things he has done for them, and what a good thing he is to them, in the fullness of his grace and truth. The devils of oppression and misery will depart before our rendering of Christian justice; the devils of class strife and civil feud will flee away before the face of Christian fraternity; the devils of profanity and ungodliness will be expelled by the spirit of true piety and holy reverence; the devils of anarchy and lawlessness will go down before the authority of righteousness and peace in friendly alliance;

and the devils of intemperance and unholy passion will be unable to hold up their heads, when self-sacrifice and self-denial rule in the hearts of those, who have called themselves by the name of Christ.

James Russell Lowell touched a chord, with a master hand, when, some little time ago, he said : "The Republic has gone on far too long on the principle, ' I am as good as you,' and she must now begin on the other principle, 'you are as good as I.'" These two principles illustrate, most forcibly, the respective principles of superstition and religion, of selfishness and sacrifice. Going on the principle of superstition and selfishness, the old world sickened and died, slain by its own hand. "I am as good as you," filled the earth with "demons and chimeras dire," whose chief employment it was to prey upon their authors. Christianity struck the note of fraternity, and pride gave place to humility, when the apostles went forth to declare to all men, "you are as good as I." The demons heard the note, and trembled. The Jewish demon made a show of fight, and, with cruel hands, crucified the Great Author of the new principle. But a legion of demons could not slay the prophetic word, though the prophet fell. Once spoken, it must stand forever, sounding like the blast of a silver trumpet throughout the ages. It was the note of those seventy peasant preachers who went into narrow Samaria; it was the inspiration of their successful work; it was the secret of their splendid report. It is the true Christian word, which alone can bring help into any heart, and light into any life. Let a man go to another with the proud challenge, "I am as good as you," and that other will take much pains to show, to his own satisfaction, at least, that he is much better than his challenger. Henceforward, these two will not be brothers. Let him go, however, with the kindly counsel, "you are as good as I," and from that day these two are friends. The seed of brotherhood has been sown ; and it will bear its blessed fruit, as it did in Samaria. Well were it for our Christian civilisation, if this principle were universally recognized. Then should we see an end to sectarian strife ; the difficult problem of the employer and the employed would have some chance of a solution ; and the social inequalities of society's own creation would be on the fair way for being redressed. Till that principle seize the soul of society, however, our present difficulties, wrongs, and anxieties will continue and increase. Only, when men recognize that every man, woman and child has the right to live, and be happy in the world into which they have been born, and that the well-being and happiness of their fellows ought to have a place in, every Christian soul, and become a factor in promoting the happiness of society—only then will the Christian Church rise to the level of these simple missionaries, and her people learn to look, not on their own things only, but also on the things of others. That is the simple panacea for the ills of our Christian civilization. The Christian soul and conscience must realize, that the natural rights of man are sacred, and that there can be no stable society where these rights are tampered with, either by the rich or the poor, the lordly or the lowly. It has been through practical denial of the sanctity of these rights, that the demons of selfishness have often worked such wicked havoc, and that the best men and women, of our day are perplexed and puzzled, at the social troubles already upon us, and the greater troubles in store. God help the Christian community to be wise and faithful; to face the coming crisis in the spirit of Lowell's motto. Nothing but the true spirit of brotherliness will bring Christendom safely through.

V.—IN THE MOUNT.

"And every man went to his own house."
—St. John, vii, 53.
"Jesus went to the Mount of Olives."
—St. John, viii, 1.

The individual who divided this gospel into chapters and verses, made a most unhappy mistake, when he broke off the seventh chapter at the 53rd verse, and began the eighth chapter with a remark, which is the natural conclusion to the day's history related in the seventh chapter. At the close of day, the parties, who had been disputing, separated, and took their several ways. The partisans of the hierarchy returned to their homes ; the young Nazarene betook himself to a lonely retreat in the Mount of Olives. The first verse of chapter viii is, therefore, the proper conclusion of chapter vii. : the second verse, is the natural opening to the narrative of a new day's life and work.

These violently separated verses, brought together into the same chapter, suggest a striking contrast in our Lord's history, which their separation in our authorized version rather conceals from the casual reader. As I have shown, they have the closest connection, both in fact and in suggestion. When put into separate chapters, however, the connection in fact disappears, and the lesson of the contrast is lost. Putting them together, I think we shall find that they exhibit a picture of the Gospel most pathetic and suggestive. Those who made the original division into chapters and verses did not see the picture, and so they tore the verses asunder and the picture dissolved.

I. *The Contrast,* — "*Every man went to his own house ; Jesus went unto the Mount of Olives.*" That was a day of much anxious toil and worry in the life of Jesus. The scene was the Temple courts, where among the crowds of worshippers, high and low, literate and illiterate, rich and poor, the Master seemed to have one of the grandest opportunities of his ministry. Humble countryman was there, ready in the simplicity of his soul to give the young teacher a fair hearing. Many such were impressed, and exclaimed, " Of a truth this is the prophet ;"

and others, "This is the Christ." But there were learned Rabbis in the crowd, and robed Priests, and phylacteried Pharisees, alarmed that the peasantry should be captivated by the common-sense and naturalness of our Lord and his teaching. They raised captious shouts of opposition ; they plied all the arts of the skilled ecclesiastic. "Shall Christ come out of Galilee?" they said, as if it was of any consequence where the teacher came from, if he had the word of truth in his lips. "Out upon this rude "Galilean. Hath not the Scripture said, 'Christ "'cometh of the seed of David, and out of the "'town of Bethlehem, where David was?' A "prophet of Nazareth is, on the face of things, "an impostor. He must be dealt with as a "fraud. Let our officers arrest him, and let him "be brought to trial as a pretender." But the officers could not. Their sympathies were with Jesus and not with their masters. "Never man "spake like this man," was their blunt, but candid confession why they did not apprehend him.

Our Lord was gratified at the good feeling of the common people. It was a valuable tribute to the living power of his simple gospel. But he burned to make converts among the educated classes and the priestly order. The peasantry were soon to return to their homes, and the common people of Jerusalem were not likely to be of much account, when the day of trial came. But the priests and influential church-people were always there, and if he could win their adhesion it would be an immense help to the good cause. The natural leaders of the people should lead in all great movements. Moreover, apart from every other consideration, it was of all things important, that the teachers of the people should be leaders of the people in duty, and devotion to God and man. They had a tremendous responsibility ; theirs was a glorious, but grave, stewardship. He saw that they were blind leaders of a blind people. He would save them, if he could, from their false position and from the terrible remorse of an enlightened conscience, which sooner or later would show them things as they were. He would save the people from a religious service cold, and hard, and unsatisfying. He would give life to the message of enlightened priest and scribe. He would give consolation, and hope, and a Father in heaven, to the toiling, tried, and weary poor. So our Lord bore with the malice and cavilling of the upper religious classes, reasoned calmly with the disputatious, and meekly reviled not again when the narrow-minded called him a pestilent blasphemer. His one thought was how to do them good, and he was willing to bear all things, and to be all things to all men, if by any means he could save some.

It was in that noble and self-sacrificing mission that this day had been spent. The results were various, but little satisfactory. Accordingly, at nightfall, he retired—not to rest, nor to complacent congratulation, nor to indignant thoughts at the hard treatment with which his good and kind offices had been met. He gave his foes credit for sincerity ; and his retirement to mountain solitude was to reconsider his plans, to endeavor to find a more acceptable way of commending his truth, to seek new energy in prayer, to find a heavenly refreshment in his heavenly Father's love. He was to be the Saviour of the world ; and the salvation of the world lay ever on his spirit. He could not go, where his mission was not before his mind, in all its vast importance. He was to bear the world's sins and sorrows, and this was one way of doing it—retiring alone to the Mount of Olives.

Oh, my dear friends! if we could break in upon the privacy of our Redeemer, and peer into that lonely oratory within Olivet's shadows, what a spectacle were that to melt the hardest human heart! To see the pure, the peerless, the holy One there, alone with God, agonizing in tenderest pity for those who had no pity upon themselves, thinking not of sleep, for the sake of those in whose bosoms he longed to plant a single seed of heavenly truth and love. That is the one side of the picture. And what of the other? What of those who had disputed, and cavilled, and menaced, and plotted all that day, in the name of God and Holy Church? "Every man went to his own home." While Jesus was sobbing within the olive shade under the silent stars "O Jerusalem, Jerusalem, how often would I have gathered thee as a hen gathereth her chickens, and ye would not," they were in the midst of their domestic joys—sipping the nectar of life's pleasures—thinking little and speaking less of the young Galilean teacher whom they had withstood. They were men strong in their official position, settled in their religious convictions, calm in their religious hopes, unchanging in their religious dislikes.

Why should they concern themselves, or disturb their home bliss, by the shadow of the Carpenter of Nazareth? And so one played with his children, another wrote a letter, a third entertained his friends. Chatting gaily, as the wine circulated, the conversation may have turned, for a little, to Jesus. But beyond the casual remark that he had been silenced, or that he was likely soon to be, one cannot conceive of a social gathering giving him anything but the slightest attention. Thus they spent the evening hours, and then—slept. Though they had committed great sin that day, for they had uttered bitter and angry words, they had hardened their hearts against the truth, they had conceived malicious and vengeful thoughts against an innocent person, they slept the sleep of the just. It was Jesus who should have slept, had he had his deserts; it was they who should have found sleep forsake their wearied eyelids, could they have seen themselves as the Holy One saw them.

2. *This contrast is characteristic of the life of Jesus.* This was no lonely episode in the life of Jesus. His whole life stands out, contrasted with the lives of those who surrounded

him, like these two texts. Nothing perhaps could better illustrate the transcendent superiority of a true, pure, noble soul. While ordinary men were falling back on their comforts and enjoyments, betaking themselves into the privacy of their own affairs and interests, in short, caring for themselves and theirs alone, the entire life of Jesus was characterized by forgetfulness of self and mindfulness of others. The one absorbing feature of his ministry was watching for, caring for, praying for, others. His meat and drink, he declares, was to seek and to save, the lost. While ecclesiastics were struggling for party and power, and congratulating themselves that their disgraceful tactics were serving their own interests, he was tolerating even them, and, with no end of his own to serve, spending himself to promote their supreme good. Though he spake as never man spake, and though in his character and method there was an authority that neither priest, nor scribe, nor zealot could command, he had no prouder boast than to proclaim himself "the preacher to the poor." It was to do all that better that he retired from society to Nature's, and God's companionship. While others slept, he was sleepless; while others rested, he was active. It was *himself* he gave, and not *his* merely, for the salvation of the world. A Scottish poet, now living, of considerable fame and ability, published some years ago a striking poem called "The Self-Exiled." The idea of the poem is that of a pure soul at the gate of heaven, looking within the golden city, but declining to enter and enjoy its reposeful bliss, and the reason she gives is this:—

>For I must go
>>Across the gulf where the guilty dead
>>>Lie in their woe.
>I come where there is no night, she said,
>>To go away
>And help, if I yet may help, the dead
>>That have no day.

And when the angels all are silent, St. Peter says:

>Can you love the Lord who died for you,
>>And leave the place,
>Where his glory is all disclosed to view,
>>And tender grace?

But she hesitates not a moment to reply:

>Did he not hang on the cursed tree,
>>And bear its shame,
>And clasp to his heart, for love of me,
>>My guilt and blame?—

> Should I be liker, nearer him,
> Forgetting this,
> Singing all day with the seraphim
> In selfish bliss?

And then there comes at the close a brilliant, and daring flash of genius, when the poet represents our Lord as saying to the pure, self-exiled one:

> We will go seek, and save the lost,
> If they will hear;
> They who are worst, but need me most,
> And all are dear.

Now, I have quoted these lines, of a distinguished Free Church minister, to give me the opportunity of saying, that if we had not the historical Christ of my text we should never have had such a sublime poetic conception, fanciful though it be. If we had not a Saviour who preferred the cross to the crown, and the working coat to the imperial purple, the world had never been filled with the light of saints, confessors, heroes and workers, who, following Jesus at a long interval in entire consecration to a holy mission, have been the crown and pillar of our humanity. If we had not the sublime Jesus, living only to help others, what should we have to shame selfish men out of their selfishness, and the easy, stay-at-home people out of their idleness, and the ambitious vain out of their vanity? Had we not a Christ to illustrate the royal law of love, and teach, that love's losing is love's finding, and love's dying, her living,—one whose doctrine and whose life present the strongest contrast to the doctrine and life of other men — then humanity had been the poorest thing in God's creation, its very dignity being its disgrace.

3. *The exhibition of this contrast in common life.* This contrast is set before every Christian, and he has to choose which side of it his life shall exhibit. Shall we go to our own home, or to the mount? In other words, shall we lead selfish or serviceable lives? Shall we be formalists, or spiritualists in the proper sense? Shall we live for what is called our interests, or shall we live for others? Prudence, policy, modesty even, counsel us to go to our own home. They bid us seek the easy, the popular, the pleasant path through life. The enemies of Jesus made a choice, and that was their selection. But Jesus could not go home. The sorrows and the sins of the world would not let him go home; and there

must always be those in his church who are ready to go, in his spirit, to the mount. The world is still bleeding, lost, and dying. Who will go? Who will leave a life of ease and set their faces to the hard, cruel facts, and make the world better, and lift the world up? They will be the anointed of the Lord.

Dearly beloved! in whatsoever position we are, the call comes to us, and, what is more, the call *can* be obeyed. No need to forsake society, with its loves, its duties, its obligations, its responsibilities, to go to the mount, as Jesus went. No need to be an ascetic and live among men, only to frown down everything human, in order to go with Jesus to the mount. No need to wear a hair shirt, or an iron chain, in order to bear in our souls the marks of the cross. Jesus lived among men, and his foes urged that as an objection to his commission. "He was a man gluttonous and a winebibber," they asserted; "the friend of publicans and sinners." He went to the mount for the night; but the morning found him again among the temple worshippers. The one thing he had, and the one thing needful for us, is a thoughtful, zealous, consecrated spirit—a mind that grasps the great purpose of life, and by piety and prayer strives to fulfil it—a will loyal to the truth and light of God, and that knows no other desire, but to do ever that which will please him.

Need I say that for such a spirit there can never be defeat. What may seem defeat may be the grandest victory. Men called our Lord's ministry a failure. They said he had gone to the mount, as well as to the cross, in vain. But the history of these centuries has another tale to tell. And so will it be with every faithful disciple of his. Keep it as an article of your creed, " there can be no failure to the good and wise." But men judge everything a failure which cannot be tried by their tests and declared a success. And yet how little genuine success would be left for the historian to record, on these terms. A godly mother prays over her infant son, and dedicates him to God. That son becomes Thomas Scott, the commentator, whose influence, under God, arrests John Newton, the wicked, reckless captain of a slave-ship, and gives to Christian praise some of the most popular hymns in our language, such as "How Sweet the Name of Jesus Sounds," and "Approach, My Soul, the Mercy Seat." That good mother never saw the success which her piety and her prayers had won. The world's scales have no weights small enough to find her worth. But John Newton, an eminent saint of God, casts his crown before the throne to-day, and praises the good lady who did her humble part with all her might. To rear her boy "a consecrated man," was her mission, and she fulfilled it gloriously.

But whatsoever be your lot and whatsoever your mission, go to the mount with Jesus as you may. Your spiritual life needs that refreshing stimulus. The writer of the 39th Psalm tells us how he caught up the inspiration for that noble song. "My heart was hot within me; while I mused, the fire burned; then spake I with my tongue." His burning heart sent him also to the mount; there he meditated, and, when the moment came, he returned to break forth into song, and sing help for tried, weary, souls, through all time. There is no other way of it but to go the mount—the holy place, where, as Tennyson so well puts it, "God-in-Man is one with Man-in-God." There is no lightening for care but in the mount; there is no light for our darkness but in the divine fellowship; there is no strength for our weakness but in the divine ministry; there is no balm for our souls but in the fruit of Olivet. To the mount, then, let us go day by day. We need its blessed refreshment. We cannot live without its consecrating dew.

Oftentimes, we stand in marvel at the extraordinary labours of some good, earnest, Christian soul. How unwearied his efforts, how persistent his purpose, how unconquerable his energy, how bright the glow of his zeal. We wonder how human strength and will can go through it. Ah! there is our mistake—it is not human strength. Our hero has been in the mount. He is bound to the oar, not by fetters of fate, but by the silken cords of choice. He needs must labor and pray for the well-being of others. Realize, more and more, the preciousness of life in the mount. Seek it; prize it; make it the life of your life, the joy of your joy, the source of all your spiritual conquest.

VI.—THE AGONIZED MESSIAH.

"A place called Gethsemane."
—St. Matt. xxvi., 36.

Hebrew names, like the names of all primitive peoples, had originally a direct reference to the circumstances out of which they sprang. There was nothing meaningless, or haphazard in the first names. If their story could be written out, it would be found the most perfect, and the most fascinating narrative of the world's childhood. Special personal characteristics, family joys and sorrows, social habits and customs, local crises and disasters, primeval thoughts and ambitions, sublime natural phenomena—these would all be preserved in the young world's word-history, like an insect imbedded in a mass of translucent amber.

The place called, Gethsemane, is not to be more particularly identified, than as situated on the Mount of Olives, somewhere in the vicinity of the brook Cedron. The exact spot, however, is of little consequence; but the association of

Gethsemane and Olivet is divinely suggestive. The Mount of Olives owes its name to the groves of olive trees, which, at one time, adorned its slopes; and Gethsemane is the House of the Oil-press. Both natural and necessary was the association. The olive groves and the olive press should be conveniently contiguous, in the interests of the large and valuable oil industry, which formed so important an element in the commerce of the East.

That there was any significance intended by our Lord, in the lonely spot selected for devotion, on the night of the betrayal, and which was destined to be the scene of that terrible historic agony, which seems to fill up the mystery of all human suffering, I do not suppose. At that season it was a deserted spot, and therefore specially convenient for the solitary devotion of a sorely tried spirit, on the eve of a great catastrophe. Nevertheless, there is a mine of suggestiveness in the fact, that between the circumstances of the Master and the uses of the place, there is a deep symbolic fitness. For, in the place where the spiritual sorrows of the Christ culminated in

"That mysterious woe,
Which wrung his frame at every pore,"

the careful husbandman was accustomed to collect his olives, that, in the oil-press, they might give out all their virtue, to become a priceless blessing to the old and young, the sickly and the strong, the lowly and the lordly. There, under the pressure of many weights, the precious olives were made to yield up all they had to give in blessing to mankind. So, in the same spot, the Messiah was crushed to the very dust under the burden of cares and trials, only to shed upon humanity priceless virtue. In that awful paroxysm of bodily anguish, those blood-clots on his brow, and, in the more terrible paroxysm of spiritual anguish, that great human cry, "Father, if it be possible, let this cup pass from me," embody a load of misery and woe such as none other ever bore. Gethsemane presents the sublime spectacle of a pure, good soul

> "Breasting the blows of circumstance,
> And grappling with his evil star."

Like the patriarch by the Jabbok, the Son of Man is in the grip of a great spiritual need, and also, like the patriarch, he is to come forth victorious, realizing that the greatest spiritual force and the truest spiritual freedom, grow out of the spirit of sublime submission expressed in the prayer, " Not my will but thine be done." As the Master rejoined " the sleepy three," he came with the power of a heavenly calm in his soul, and the light of a divine faith in his eye. Neither the infamous kiss of Judas nor the jibes of hostile Pharisees, the thorns of the rude soldiery nor the agonies of the bitter cross, could, for one instant, ruffle that peace, or dim the lustre of that faith. To Gethsemane the sore-bestead, and troubled spirit ever goes, first of all, to

> "Know how sublime a thing it is
> To suffer and be strong."

It is the Gethsemane-pressed Jesus who comes into the life of the stricken and desolate one, whispering as he comes, " Courage, brother, do not falter. At evening time it shall be light." Jesus in Gethsemane is a spring of heavenly virtue, at which weary men and women ever drink, and derive new vigor, to fight life's battle, and toil on under the burden of life's cares. From those olive shades, a great multitude which no man can number, have gone forth inspired by a new life, to dare and to do anything in the name of our Christ.

1. Among the sources of the Gethsemane agony was, the sense of cruel wrong. Our Blessed Lord felt that agony keenly. He was the faithful and true prophet of his people, and his mission was his life. Throughout his brief ministry, he had never a single thought, that had not for its inspiration the glory of his people Israel. How had his pure, good offices been met? By the most obstinate, unprincipled, and malignant opposition of the pious people of his day. They insulted him, they suspected his motives, they maligned his beneficence, they accused him of a "master conspiracy," against the souls and the bodies of men. Impostor, blasphemer, devil, were some of the epithets they applied to this strong apostle of truth, benevolence, and righteousness. His own towns-folk, his relatives, the priests of God, were against him. Can you imagine a set of circumstances more depressing for a pure and pious nature? It was bad enough to have his kind words and good deeds flung back contemptuously in his face; but it was infinitely worse to be told that he was playing a dark

game, from the basest motives, and that all his professions of piety and religion were but the climax of his diabolic policy. It was surely monstrously absurd, to stigmatize the Master as a bold destroyer of the law and the prophets, and, generally, as the enemy of all righteousness. Nevertheless, that was the grave charge, which godly priests and pious rabbis, in all gravity, alleged against the only prophet, who for centuries had been able to inspire the law and the prophets with life. Marvellous inconsistency! Deplorable blindness! Pathetic illustration of the maxim which Christians also have unfortunately too often verified, "None are so blind as those who will not see."

2. Inconceivably crushing, though the sense of cruel wrong was, to the pure good spirit of the Master, there was another burden, less oppressive to ordinary human nature perhaps, but still more depressing to his finely-strung emotional nature. At the grave of Lazarus, Jesus wept. The scene was an exceedingly touching one. There, were the weeping sisters mourning for their dead, with the sorrow of utter desolation. Around, stood the motley crowd of thoughtless sympathisers. Some were there be-

cause they desired to do the proper thing; the gushing sympathiser was there, for whom a funeral has quite a fascination; and the sincere, sober sympathiser, who, like our Lord, entered, in some measure, into the sorrow of the disconsolate Mary and her sister Martha. But there were others there, who watched with keen, untiring eye the every movement of the young Galilean. They were of those on account of whom Jesus withdrew into retirement some short time before. It was of them the disciples spoke when they said, "Master, the Jews of late sought to stone thee; and goest thou thither again?" Sorrowing like a brother with the weeping sisters, our Lord sorrowed far more for those perverse, cruel persecutors, who had no answer for the truth, but only the threat to kill the teacher. There they were, an organized conspiracy against the Gospel, posting on in their moral and spiritual blindness, to the most disastrous fate that ever can come to men or nations. Only a pure and noble soul can appreciate the fatal loss of those who will clasp darkness to their bosoms, saying, "Darkness, be thou my light." Try to realize, for instance, what the loss is to be born an Indian of the plains, as compared with the lot of the civilized child. To have savagery for refinement, brutal ignorance for modern culture, the most degraded superstition for enlightened Christianity, low tastes and vile pleasures for social, moral and intellectual elevation. No educated and refined Christian can contemplate such a degraded human state, contrasted with the higher civilization, without recognizing the terrible loss of those unfortunates, who, having the possibilities within them of so grand a life, are doomed by fate to grovel like swine. That has always seemed to me to be an unanswerable argument for foreign missions. Would that it were urged more earnestly from platform and pulpit! But that loss is as nothing compared with the loss of those who are in the light, and yet walk as in darkness; those who are born among civilising and Christian influences, and yet choose to lead a barbaric life; those who, under the waving folds of the banner of the Cross, hug their selfishness; those who, in a day of intelligent, reasonable religion, will be unreasonable and superstitious; those who, while professing to follow the Good Shepherd, are driven into the kingdom of Heaven by the knotted cords of divine vengeance, rather than drawn by the magnetism of the uplifted Christ. Nobody of fine thought and feeling can reflect on the terrible loss and damage to all that is best in them which those incur, who so belie their manhood and turn the possibilities of the angel into the deformities of the demon. How, then, must the high and holy Jesus have been grieved at such a spectacle, looking as he did from a plane so much higher than ours, and seeing with a vision which could pierce to the very heart of things! If our highest and holiest cannot contemplate such a terrible loss, without being seized with the consuming desire to roll away the burden from their unfortunate brothers and sisters, by how much the more must Jesus of Nazareth have been wounded by the transgressions of his countrymen, and bruised by their iniquities, committed in the darkness of spiritual death, during the brief space in which he taught and toiled in their streets. Moreover, this gifted teacher and prophet knew very well what all this blindness and perversity, this rejection of the truth, and this devotion to falsehood must end in. He could look adown the vistas of the years, and forecast only shame and suffering, for the unhappy dupes and those who duped them. As confidently as if it were, he could foretel the inevitable future from the infallible past, and, as he took in at one wide glance all the dread consequences, socially, nationally, religiously to those who had committed themselves obstinately to the wrong path, none but God and himself could know what he endured in his sublime humanity, under the pressure of a weight so stupendous.

3. A third element in the pressure of Gethsemane's load was the pressure of the vices and miseries which met him at every turn. We know what it is for a pure, compassionate man or woman to read the daily catalogue of crime and vice, which the morning papers spread before society, and to reflect upon the untold suffering and woe brought upon innocent victims, through the faults and follies of others. Tender, sympathetic hearts have borne a cross of sorrow for other's sins and sorrows, always growing heavier through the years till they found out a way by which to attack and wipe out some glaring evil, or redress some glaring wrong. How many humane hearts did the cry of the slave pierce through and through, as

with a sword, ere the day of emancipation crowned a half century of noble, generous endeavour! How many fine Christian spirits were torn and crushed by the tale of degradation among the women and children in the factories of Christian England, till Mrs. Browning's "Cry of the Children," electrified an awakening nation, and rang the death-knell of that atrocious inhumanity. How many noble Christian souls are almost driven to despair of the "conquest of the Cross," by the shocking revelations of crime in high places, by the gigantic frauds that appal ordinary minds, and by the gross materialism, yea, animalism, which ramifies modern society, and which foreshadow, for the English-speaking race on both sides of the Atlantic, a dark day of reckoning. Now, what must it have been for the Divine Son, in his ineffable sensitiveness to vice and wrong, to have had borne on his ear, from every side, the cry of the outraged, the wail of the oppressed, the many-tongued burden of man's inhumanity to man. To know all that, and to bear it on his tender heart, in his perfect fellow-feeling with our common humanity, much as we try to realize it, involves an intensity of feeling we can never fathom. Our Master bore all that in its harrowing and crushing detail. Nothing escaped him. Everything pressed on him with infinite weight. Do you wonder, then, that he sweat blood-clots, or that he seemed oftentimes to be straitened in spirit? Do you wonder that, time and again, the vast human craving for sympathy took possession of him, and that, in the sense of crucifixion-isolation he cried, " My God, my God, why hast Thou forsaken me ? "

I might touch upon other elements of this great Gethsemane load. But this day's service (the Holy Communion) is very practical in its meaning and aims. We take our places at the Holy Table, seeking practical help in the battle of life; and all topics which do not partake of a strictly practical character should be avoided. The three points, referred to, are eminently practical, and I do not propose to go beyond them. They touch our lives at many points. We all suffer under the injustice, or selfishness of others; we all bear, as our Lord did, vicarious trial and suffering in the contemplation of the world's sins and sorrows. Furthermore, we all struggle along, many a time, under the load of a burden our Lord could not bear—the burden of penitence for things done, which ought not to have been done, and for things left undone which we should have done. We have all, from time to time, to seek our Gethsemane, under the same pressure of great spiritual need, when we can only agonize with sweat-bedewed face and throbbing brow, groaning out in our penitence, "Father, if it be possible, let this cup pass from me." It must, therefore, be good for us, to contemplate, at such a season, the conflict of the sorely-burdened Jesus, if perchance we may learn the secret of his devotion, and enter into the fellowship of his sufferings. Such contemplation, faithfully pursued, must bring us back to active life and duty, knowing better how to bear our trials, and how to pray in trial; how to acquire increased spiritual energy, and how to conquer the flesh by the spirit of the Lord.

The conflict is over; and Jesus has won the calmness and composure which are the very wine of life. The cup could not, in the nature of things, pass from him. The burden was there, and he must continue to bear it But in communion with the Highest, there came into his life a better blessing, than the withdrawal of the cup, or the lifting of the burden. Short-sighted mortals think there can be nothing better than to have every care and sorrow lifted, and every stone of stumbling, and every rock of offence, swept from the path of the faithful. A mouth continually filled with praise is their ideal of the religious life, and not a bosom filled with groanings unutterable. But it is the law of our growth to suffer, and to suffer long. Accordingly, Gethsemanes are planted for us along our weeping way; and if we know the spirit of Him whom we profess to follow, we shall wisely betake ourselves to their solitary altars, that we may learn there, in submission to the will of God, a composed strength, by virtue of which we shall be able to face resolutely every foe of God and truth, even though, like the Master, we may find only cruel death as the reward of our loyalty and courage.

Have I justified the symbolic fitness I pointed out at the beginning of this discourse, between the place called Gethsemane, and the circumstances of him who made it the scene of his last devotions? Have you seen in the olive-press a not-too-far-fetched simile of the highest, holiest manhood growing perfect in sufferings? Then see in it also the symbol of common experience. Recognize in Gethsemane a meeting-place, between the Great Master and all who have named his name. You can tread no other path than he has trodden before you. It is because of this consciousness of identity in life and spirit with him that the faithful hie to his table to appreciate the privilege the more, and to grow truer, freer, holier, while they feed upon him, as the very bread of their life.

We have considered the pressure of Gethsemane; but what of its power? Calm, as from the couch of sweet repose, the Lord met the armed band, which, guided by his trusted disciple, was on the way to arrest him, at the very moment when he was rapt in praying agony in the garden. It was a shocking outrage, to apprehend as a criminal, a law-abiding and worthy citizen. Jesus felt a strong sense of wrong; but the kiss of the traitor, for pure baseness, threw the arrest of the priests into the shade. Still, calmly and tenderly, he bore all that perfidious friend, or bitter foe could do. Calmly did he submit, amid hootings and scorning, to be dragged to the palace of the high-priest ; and, when the loud-protesting devotee of yesterday swore a rude denial of his Master at a little servant maid, though his heart was breaking for the swearer, he had only a look of infinite pity for his sin. Calmly he confronted imperial pomp and corruption at Pilate's bar, and testified for conscience as the world has never yet appreciated. Then, when scourging and insult and mockery were exhausted, and petty hate and religious spite had done their very worst and very best, these bland words of infinite mercy were his only retort to it all, " Father, forgive them ; for they know not what they do." Gethsemane and Calvary must be linked together, to reveal the full history of a soul's conflict and conquest. It is the best answer to the caviller at the alleged value of devotion, or to the questioner of the efficacy of prayer, or to the protester who claims that he can get along without either, to point them to the Grand Master in submission, victorious, in prayer, almighty, and through the pressure of a load such as none of woman born ever bore, giving forth a virtue, which has raised him to the height sublime ; and before whom every knee shall bow, and every tongue confess that he is Lord, to the glory of God the Father.

VII. "THE REJECTED OF GADARA."

"They besought him that he would depart out of their coasts."
—Matt. viii, 34

This request of the Gadarenes indicates the effect produced on the popular mind, by the presence among them of our Blessed Lord, in power. It is, as I take it, a typical illustration of the impression created on the human mind by an act of great power, viewed simply as such, and without consideration of the motive principle behind the power. A poor demoniac had been cured of the most distressful malady which can afflict a human being, and the district delivered from one who had for years been its dread and its disgust. But these good offices had been attended by a disastrous circumstance. When the demoniac was restored to reason, the last frenzy of his madness seems to have been so wild and demonstrative, as to startle a herd of swine feeding close by. These animals breaking away in a mad panic from the control of their herds, stampeded headlong down the steep hill-side into the waters of the lake, and were drowned. This fatality involved a serious loss to the owners; and dreading, lest the sojourn among them of one, whose arrival had been associated with so great a commercial disaster, should lead to further and greater loss, they unanimously besought him to depart out of their coasts.

From their point of view it was a most natural request. These Gadarenes regarded this wonder-worker as the repository merely of a mighty, preternatural power. That power, they judged, had been already exerted to their great prejudice; and, like shrewd business men, they were not to be exposed to loss and damage, a second time, if they could help it. Doubtless, their idea was erroneous. There could be no necessary connection between the power which so graciously delivered the demoniac, and the unfortunate destruction of their property. To assume such a connection, was to make the Master, at one and the same moment, benevolent, and malevolent. Moreover, they had before their eyes, in the recovered demoniac, an undoubted trophy of the triumph of good over evil. The new-comer must have been a good
16

man, to do so great a good. Nevertheless, their minds were full of the one thing, and they were not to be reasoned with. They could think only of the business calamity which had befallen them; and in it they lost sight of the obvious blessing to the wild maniac, who had been so long the pest of the neighbourhood. Jesus was to them, for the moment, the incarnation simply of tremendous power, and from the demoniac to his deliverer seemed but to pass from one alternative of power to another; in fact, was to escape from under the shadow of a power which could burst assunder iron fetters, only to pass under the shadow of a power greater far. In their consternation, they saw nothing but a change of powers. They could only shrink away trembling, therefore, from a presence fraught with great actual damage; and, with how much future mischief, who could forecast? So far, these Gadarenes were quite logical. Their premises being granted, the conclusion could not be denied. If power only was represented by the Prophet of Nazareth, then he could never be a welcome guest in Gadara, or, for that part of it, anywhere else.

But I am not to linger over the facts of this

episode. I have only taken it, to illustrate a mode of presenting our Lord and his authority, once highly popular, but now happily passing away, and to suggest a more excellent method. The old apologists used to rest their main argument, for the divinity of Christ, on the preternatural events which are recorded of him. They laboured to prove that he worked real miracles, so that they might find in his divine works, the surest evidence for his divine rank. Their theory was this:—"Jesus Christ performed a brilliant series of actions beyond the power of ordinary men. He performed them in the full blaze of the midday sun, in the streets, in the public places, in the presence of friends, before immense crowds, under the eager and malicious gaze of enemies. Moreover, there is no natural way of explaining these wonders. Therefore, doing supernatural works, and by his own authority, he has proved himself to be divine." Such was the argument of the old apologists, and they carried their method to perfection. They never were really answered by the other side. Nevertheless, the principle on which they rested could only be considered satisfactory, in an age better pleased to trace the divine in the extraordinary, than in the common, in disorder and convulsion, than in scenes of peace and beauty. We are not to judge our fathers harshly, nor minimise the value of the heritage which they have transmitted to us. Nevertheless, we cannot fail to perceive, that in resting their case almost exclusively on the *power* of the miracles, and almost ignoring the *character* which inspired them, our ancestors really reversed the proper order of things, and attempted to perform the impossible. They thought the human soul could be made to worship power, and that in his omnipotence, the church had the kernel of truth concerning the person of Christ. It was a delusion, however. There is only one thing which human nature can love and adore, and that is, merit. The Gadarenes were really more logical than our ancestral defenders of the faith. Before Jesus, as a great power represented in the calamity to their swine, they could only cry out, like St. Peter on a similar occasion, "Depart from us." Could they have looked a little deeper than the brute power of the miracle, so to speak, they would doubtless have found in the spiritual power which directed it, a sure foothold for devotion; but stopping short where they did, their prayer was the logical outcome of their belief. But the old apologists deliberately tried to strike the spark of love, by the iron of logic, on the flint of power; and the result was a Jesus very much like the Elohim of Jewish history—a being of vast power which overshadowed all his other attributes.

The more excellent method, into which the church has been growing steadily during this century, is to centre interest in the wonder of love, rather than in the wonder of power—in short, so to exalt the love which attracts, that the power which repels may be cast into the background. It is to stamp the miracles as magnificent testimonies to a holy cause more by the sublime merit they illustrate, than by the childish amazement they excite. God is in them, but far less in the power that controls the insane, or heals the sick, or makes the crystal fountain blush into rosy wine, than in the still small voice of compassion and tenderness, which woos and wins, to the submission of love.

This view of our Lord's miracles is sustained by the whole tenor of the New Testament narrative. Though he did wonderful things, there is nothing to show, that the people generally shrank from his presence as from some mysterious, powerful Magus. On the contrary, the simplest and the gentlest natures clung to him with child-like fondness. Multitudes flocked to him, drawn by the pure kindliness and goodness of his works, and never dreaming that his mighty power could ever be exerted, save for beneficent ends. Even his foes, who, on their own showing, recognized in his works a preternatural power, never seem to have entertained the suspicion, that those works of mercy might become works of vengeance, against those who were plotting his destruction. The railers around the cross admitted, that he saved others; but wondered that he did not save himself. And thousands of good Christians have, oftentimes since, cherished the same wonder. Their Messiah is one who can rule the nations with a rod of iron, and break them in pieces as a potter's vessel. That is frail man's symbol of authority. But our Jesus never seeks so to rule; he never can draw the glittering sword nor wield the jewelled sceptre. He is the great phenomenal ruler of history. His ambition, was to rule in men's hearts; and the way, in which his fellow-men gathered round him shows that he succeeded.

The miracle of character was greater far than any miracle of power. Many came to him drawn by the fame of his power; those who stayed when they came, were held by the loveliness of his character.

In point of fact, whatever power our Lord possessed was constantly controlled, directed, or restrained by his character. The sublime self-restraint, which he practised, habitually, in very trying circumstances, is, to me, the greatest miracle of his ministry. It is much easier, for ordinary human nature, to obey the call of compassion, and perform good and kind deeds, if it has the power, than to restrain itself when character is to be vindicated, or calumny refuted. Only a mind of the finest fibre can remain self-restrained under insult and wrong, and bear it all meekly for the sake of some good cause. Our Lord possessed that marvellous self-restraint. The motto of his ministry was this: "The Son of Man came to seek and to save the lost." " Be ye wise as serpents and harmless as doves," was his counsel to the twelve. He never wantonly provoked opposition, nor heedlessly courted a bitter word. For opposition and raillery, plotting and treachery, he had only patient meekness. Malice he met with mild rebuke; for the traitor's foul kiss he had only, "Friend, wherefore art thou come?" The cross, with all its suffering and shame, could only wring from him, "Father, forgive them; they know not what they do." Had righteous indignation flared up in his bosom, to blast with the lightnings of heaven those guilty defamers and persecutors, our poor human nature had applauded him to the echo. But had he yielded to this very natural temptation, his work had been a ruin to-day. He would have been honored as a great prophet and martyr; he would not have been worshipped as the Saviour of the World. He would not have stood before admiring mankind, in the glory of a splendid self-restraint utterly unparalleled in the history of our race. Our noblest, and our highest would have given him the first place among the sons of men; they would never have exalted him to the virgin heights of divine purity, the one pure soul, at whose feet the nations are destined to worship, in ever-growing devotion. If our Lord's spontaneous readiness to good-doing was a true mark of his divine nature, much more so was his perfect restraint from vengeance, under circumstances of extreme provocation.

Once only did his restraining power falter, if I may be allowed the expression; and that episode reveals not the weakness of his character, but the strength of his compassion. The occasion, was the healing of the poor woman with the issue. In her modesty she approached him from the rear, whispering to herself, "Oh! if I can but touch the hem of his garment, I shall be cured." "Blessed among women be thou, Veronica, who didst thus creep up stealthily to thy Lord! Thou hast been one of the great benefactresses of thy race. For thou hast lifted the veil to disclose how deep was the common faith in thy Lord's ability to save, and how sweet the attractions of his grace. Thou hast shown how naturally he moved among his people,

A kindly man among his kind.

Better blessing still, hast thou bequeathed to us. For thee was it reserved, to discover the only weak point in the Messiah of the World. Thy faithful touch drew from him those blessed and suggestive words : " Who touched me ? Somebody hath touched me; for I perceive that virtue is gone out of me." To thee, oh! poor, shamefaced sufferer, was it first given to find out, that thy Lord was weak, only in restraining himself from helping and blessing men. Thou didst trust in his character, and thou wast not disappointed."

The manner of our Lord's working is a valuable aid to faith. The sacred writers relate, that he performed his greatest works, with the artlessness and naturalness of a child. From the deep repose of "tired nature's sweet restorer, balmy sleep," he rises calmly to speak, "Peace!" to the raging billows, and the untamed spirit of the storm cowers meekly at his feet. No Ajax he, defying the lightning, but the simple, unaffected Son of God, doing as a matter of course his Father's business. In the home of Jairus, he is offended by the hireling outgush of wild lamentation; but melted by the silent sorrow of the broken-hearted parents. Taking the hand of the dead, he speaks the quiet, strong word, "Maid, arise!"; and the great deed is done. The whole story, from beginning to end, is as natural as possible. He gives, as if there were nothing remarkable in the gift; the parents receive their child, from the dead, as if she had

come into the room, to receive a morning kiss.
All through the gospels, it is the same perfect
simplicity. Our Lord never takes any pains to
proclaim his power; he never works ostentatiously. He does take pains to avoid publicity,
and the inconvenient popularity of the wonderworker. His best works are performed in the
most ordinary way; he is never so calm as
when he is conferring the grandest favors.

The miracles of Our Lord, in the sense I have
indicated, are a valuable branch of the Christian
evidences. In any other sense, they must, I
fear, be an evidential delusion, and they may
often be a religious snare. As illustrations of
power merely, they actually put the thoughtful
reader in a stand-off attitude, towards him at
whose feet he would lay the offering of his life.
To the uncultured reader, on the other hand,
they suggest a faith, which is no faith. The
preternatural is not to be excised from the
gospels, without violence to every canon of literary criticism. Miracle is in our Lord's life, in
his speech, in his character. Though the miraculous be excised from his works, there will be as
great difficulty with his character, or with his
teaching. Our Lord had great faith in the

power of character, and he never showed that he had faith in the power of works. He utterly refused to give a sign, to prove his Messiahship. No converts were made to his following by the miracles. The strength of Christianity must, therefore, lie in the character it presents, and in the type of character it produces. Man must love the highest when he sees it; and if those who decline to accept Christianity because of the miraculous in the gospels were to begin with the character of the Master, I am persuaded that they could not remain in the attitude of those benighted Gadarenes. Rather would they find growing up in them, as they realized the Christ character, the creed of St. Thomas, when the living Lord appeared to him, "My Lord and my God." They would realize, in the personal, spiritual fellowship of Christ, that their difficulties were really least where they thought them greatest. A divine character would become to them the very bread of their life, and they would not desire to live or die away from such heavenly nutriment.

PART III.
"WE SEE AS WE ARE."

What a light hath fallen upon the men and women of this century! What bibles of divine knowledge have been unfolded for their enlightenment! More truly, perhaps, than could ever be said of the children, of a past generation, must it be written of the children of to-day, "the lines have fallen unto them in pleasant places, and they have a goodly heritage."

1. There is the Bible of Nature, in which, as in a mirror, is reflected the face of the Great Creator. Speaking comparatively, the "Book of Nature," may be said to be the prize awarded to the persevering industry and research, of the students of the nineteenth century. For, though poets had often sung of nature's grandeur, from the days of the Hebrew psalmists downward, through every era; and, though wise men had gazed in marvel at nature's grace and loveliness, and pondered long and deeply what it all meant, it was reserved for the men of genius of

our time, to lift the veil from her face and reveal to admiring mortals the laws by which all life is evolved and perfected, in the working of the Divine Creator Spirit. What inspiration for the reverent spirit, in the secrets of nature thus far disclosed to the gaze of the men and women of this epoch!

2. The Bible of History has also its vast stores of wisdom to reveal. "The philosophy of history," is a phrase with which society has become familiar, only in these last days. Historians have, in recent times, been able to trace the story of the human race physiologically, psychologically, and morally, with as much accuracy, as a naturalist traces the evolution of a plant. "God in history," has become as great a reality to nineteenth century Christians, as the "God of revelation," was to our ancestors.

3. Science also has her wondrous Bible. Nothing, in the history of our planet, has more grandly revealed the glory of him who is "wonderful in counsel and excellent in working," like the prolific scientific research of this century. It is a stupid blunder of uncultured minds, to regard scientific progress as the great modern attempt of ungodly men, to banish Deity from

the earth. Scientists have, in point of fact, helped to bring the Deity very near to us, presenting him in new relations, and more engaging aspects. Vastly have they magnified his glory, by pointing out his footprints everywhere, within us and around. How can we ever be thankful enough, for the enlargement of our knowledge of God's workings and of God's ways, of God's goodness and of God's discipline, through the labors of our wise men of science?

4. It may even be said that this century has given us a new Bible of Sacred Story; it can certainly be said that it has given us back the Old Bible, by making it more than it has been for centuries, "a living Word of God." The researches of scholars, the march of explorers, the discoveries of geographers, and the industry of historians have shed floods of light on every page of the old, old story. Truer conceptions of its inspiration have immeasurably enhanced its spiritual importance, and broadened its sure foundations; till now that which had actually become, in some quarters, a reverenced wonder merely, or like a fetich to an African, is on the way to become again what it was three centuries ago—a living power, in living men. To the scholars
17

and critics of the last half-century are we indebted, it may be said, for giving us back the Bible, again to be our light and life.

Am I not justified, therefore, in extolling the good fortune of the generation, at whose feet those treasures of wisdom and knowlege have been laid? "All truth leads to God," is the proud message of science and scholarship in our bright, Christian day. Rightly regarded, every fountain of human knowledge empties itself into the great river of truth, which rises from, and returns to, the great throne of the Eternal; and it cannot but be the pious duty of every dweller by the sacred stream, to guard loyally its limpid waters, that they may be for life and salvation to all the generations of men. How we shall best prize and utilize our goodly heritage, to the glory of God and our own well-being, is not difficult to perceive. "Unto the pure all things are pure; but unto them that are defiled and unbelieving, is nothing pure; but even their mind and conscience is defiled," is a great truth of St. Paul, which Carlyle and Emerson, and many more, have translated into current speech. The soul finds in everything without it, only what it brings. The eye sees only, what it can see. Man gets out of God and His universe, only what he can take. The soul makes its own world. We see as we are. The beautiful in art, or nature is for the soul, which is itself beautiful. The sublime in our Father's vast home is for those only, whose natures are elevated enough to touch it. With us all does it lie, either to make that home a "Holy of Holies," or, a "Chamber of Horrors." The light within must make the loveliness without. The soul, that has received power to become a son of God will find God everywhere. I propose to roam about in this great thought, as it applies (I) to Nature, (II) to Man, (III) to God.

I.—IN NATURE.

"His work is glorious."
—Psalm iii., 3.

Man sees in nature just as he is, that is, just as *he can* see. Nature to any one is just what he makes it. Nature gives to any one only what he can take. It is a bible of God, or it is not, according to the light and spirit with which it is studied. How grand the teaching of this bible may become, the most heedless may in some sense appreciate, as he looks out to-day upon a world bathed in glorious spring sunshine, and studded with the myriad beauties of spreading leaf, and opening flower, and fragrant blossom. A friend once said to Turner, "I never see those wondrous sunsets which you put upon the canvas." "Don't you wish you could, though?" replied the great artist. Those wondrous effects were there, open to everyone, but only he, who had the divine gift, could see them. A gentleman once came up to me, in an

Edinburgh drawing-room, at an evening assembly, and said, " I believe this room is a marvel of fine taste in its decoration—what are the leading colours ? You know, I am colour-blind, and these walls are to me all a leaden gray." Just so it ever is.

> " The poem hangs on the berry bush
> When comes the poet's eye—
> The street is one long masquerade
> When Shakespeare passes by."

Many a Spanish mariner had perseverance and hardihood equal to a Columbus ; but only one Spaniard saw the great Western Continent beyond the wave, with the certainty of a divine intuition. No one but a botanist can see the thousand and one beauties which line a summer morning's walk. Everywhere, his eye is finding some humble specimen of rich plant life, which the unskilled eye never rests upon. A young man observes a strange scratching on a rocky hillside, and his penetrative glance gives birth to the theory of glacial action in the remote history of this planet, which electrifies the geologists of half a century ago, and is today the only explanation for many striking geological phenomena. A single bone was enough for Cuvier to build up a huge animal extinct long before historic times; and the subsequent discovery of more complete remains proved the accuracy of the great anatomist's forecast. Newton, sitting under an apple tree in the Fall, struck the theory of gravitation, by which countless phenomena in nature, previously inexplicable, have since been adequately accounted for. These all saw as they were. Their habits of thought and observation enabled them to receive the new thought, and to strike the new observation. As Our Lord said, "To him that hath shall be given." Like every new discovery, the results which these thoughtful ones achieved, reiterated the grand, simple, inspiring law, "Men see in proportion to what men are. Every past sight counts into new visions." The great pure mind sees the great pure, Creator in the fact and life of his creation ; the little mind sees only the fact. Moses penetrated to the divine ways as in Horeb solitude, .

> "He felt the power
> Of nature, and already was prepared
> By his intense conceptions, to receive
> Deeply the lesson, deep of love, which he
> Whom nature, by whatever means, has taught
> To feel intensely, cannot but receive."

Then, as the lesson expanded in his soul, by daily meditation among his fleecy charge, there came to him the supreme hour of visitation from the living God ; and

> " Rapt into still communion, that transcends
> The imperfect offices of prayer and praise,
> His mind was a thanksgiving to the power
> That made him : it was blessedness and love."

Thus, like a true child of nature, who had read her bible well, when Israel was hopeless and helpless, fickle and perverse, the one day chanting lusty hosannas, and the next repining at her lot, and worshipping a golden calf to mend it, her great leader could go into the thick darkness, fearing neither the lightning's glare, nor the thunder's roll, and return with a heavenly glow on his face, and a heavenly strength in his life. His elevated soul could come into touch with the Deity above the facts, and be filled with reverence and worship. The poor, low-minded Israelites could but wonder, and stare stupidly at the acts of God—the one day beside themselves with childish glee, because of the manna, and the next, despairing with childish petulance, because flesh was not rained upon them from the skies.

A great English scientist, of whom many hard things have been spoken by religious teachers, while lecturing at Manchester some years ago on a bit of crystal, uttered these memorable words :—" I have seen these things (the experiments), hundreds of times, but I never look at them without profound wonder. And I would add, that I have stood in the spring-time, and looked upon the sprouting foliage, the grass, and the flowers, and the general joy of opening life; and, in my ignorance of it all, I have asked myself whether there is no power, being, or thing in the universe, whose knowledge of that of which I am so ignorant, is greater than mine. I have asked myself, can it be possible that man's knowledge is the greatest knowledge, that man's life is the highest life ?" In that reverential awe and wonder, in that reaching out of the spirit to a power above and beyond human, I do not say you have the highest religious expression, but I do say, that in it you have an element of religion, which may include greatly more than either the scientific man suspects, or the theologian scouts. Of this I am sure, that the man who can commune through nature with the Great Spirit of the universe, in rapturous admiration of his working, or in melting thankfulness for his beneficence, or in silent adoration at his majesty, has in his spirit a link of sympathy with the Master, whose teaching is permeated with a profound sense of all natural grace and beauty. Nature was, to his pure soul, a baptismal font, in which he found, as often as he could, rich refreshment and vigour. To Nature's wild care he committed himself during those forty days of preparation for his ministry. On Nature's bosom he reposed time and again, in mountain solitude, when surging crowd, or nagging scribe, or crafty Pharisee vexed and jaded him: for he knew,

"That nature's heart beats strong among the hills."

There, mortal toil and burden were transfigured; and thence, he came forth ready, and resolute, to face every foe, and die the death of the cross. It was in the gloomy recesses of the hill-side garden, that angel balm refreshed his weary head, and angel hand up-bound his broken spirit. And when he would lead up his followers to a higher plane than that miserable arena of jealousy, and hate, and evil tongues, he pointed to the happy sparrows as they chirruped in their glee, not one of whom is forgotten by God, or to the grateful lilies in their virgin purity and calm unconsciousness, filling the air with fragrance and flooding the soul with charm—he took these, and tried to lift his disciples with him, to the simple truth and the simpler trust of the true sons of God. Again, when he would bring hope to their desponding minds, and the assurance of final triumph for his holy mission, he pointed to the sprouting corn, and the springing mustard, and consecrated these forever, as true emblems of the slow, but sure, and lawful progress of the Kingdom of God. Once more, when he would breathe a word of tender farewell, which the hearers should never forget while memory survived, his great mind was not so distracted with the present, or the coming miseries, that he could be oblivious to the rich, Spring beauty and promise of the vine-clad slopes of Jerusalem. "I am the vine," said he, on the way to Gethsemane, "and ye are the branches;" and after that, he needed not to speak the encouraging promise, "Lo! I am with you alway even unto the end of the world." Their hearts enshrined the emblem, their lips often recalled the aspect of external nature on that sad, memorable night; and when St. John came to put together, long after, his reminiscences of the Master, the vine parable of the night of the betrayal must hold a prominent place.

Ah my brothers and sisters! how much rich, fresh blessing do we miss, when we fail to follow our Lord into nature, with the devout spirit, which lifts us from nature up to nature's God! Oftentimes, when tried and disappointed among crooked, faithless fellow men, how pure the refreshment and solace in

> "That nature which never did betray
> The heart that loved her."

When, in the work and worry of daily toil and duty, with nerve and muscle at extreme tension, one is fairly fagged out, how welcome is the call, to him whose ear can catch the blessed sound

> "Go forth under the open sky and list
> To Nature's teachings;"

And if when our hearts are hot and restless panting after the material rewards of life, and never getting soul satisfaction out of them, we cast ourselves into nature's holy calm and let our spirits catch something of her thousand and one beauties—then we learn an answer for the poet's question,

"Who can paint like nature? Can imagination boast
Amid its gay creations, hues like hers?"

Indeed it is the one prescription of the wise physician, which never fails to cure, if cure there can be—rest and quiet in some fair rural scene. Christians know, like Elijah at Horeb, that the still, small voice of whispering hope and peace, never rises so sweetly, nor so clearly, as in the haunts where soul of man and soul of the universe meet in holy communion.

Looking as we now do to the bright summer time already upon us with sanguine spirits ; and trusting that the change from town to country, and from work to play, will do for us again the vigorous good it has so often done before, it must be a religous duty to look forward, and to go forward, in the spirit of earnest piety. The devout Christian is sure to be as devout, under the blue vault of nature's great temple, and by the bank of the gently flowing river, as within the most magnificent cathedral pile or on the altar steps of the holiest shrine. He will see his God in the green meadows sparkling with a thousand gems, and in the blooming orchards alive with the hum of busy bees, in the vast vistas of the forest primeval, and by the pebbly shore of the mighty ocean. The divine voice will stir his soul in the melody of the grove, or on the wide waste of waters. The frisking of happy lambkins in their new found life, or the gambolings of great sea monsters spouting in their play, will alike suggest the great creating and protecting care of Him, whose footprints are to be traced on the surging seas, as well as on the stable land. If man can be religious, he shall be religious, whether he look out upon the marvels of the divine handiwork from the deck of an ocean steamer, or be impressed by the indwelling of the spirit of the Lord in the lowly life of one greatly beloved.

To all of us the teachings of the book of nature—the sweet influences of nature's ever-changing but ever-lovely moods—bring their message in a greater or lesser degree. To some, for obvious reasons, their teachings may be less suggestive than to others. But to the young, considering their great educational advantages, there should be a growing affinity with the spirit of the great God stirring in his works. They should see, with clearer vision than their fathers did, into the bursting, teeming life around them. They should find fellowship with the Highest in his lovely, grand and imposing creations. If light could do it, no age should ever have had a deeply reverent and religious youth like ours. Is it so with our young? Are the results commensurate with the privileges, ? Is there, think you, that seeing of the beautiful in holiday season, and that going behind the beautiful in nature to the Great Lord of beauty, which we are entitled to expect? I hope in some sense it is so; I believe that this spirit will yearly become more a characteristic of the youth of this continent. In some quarters, however, there are painful illustrations, among the young-who-know-more, of the spirit of irreverance and irreligion. Such a tendency, however slight, is greatly to be deplored: but the zealous propagators of a Christianity without-much-knowledge, have had much to do with the creation of a party of those-who-know without Christianity. Time will cure this eccentricity; for it is as impossible for one who knows nature's laws, and appreciates her excellencies, to be irreverent, and I may add irreligious, as it is for the hunting dog, not to point in the hunting field to the game.

A much more painful and ominous phase of social life, is the tendency to carry the spirit of town life into the country. Instead of seeking in nature, a corrective to the uneasy and restless life of the city, too often is the same restlessness apparent and the same deliberate attempt to convert pleasure into a toil. This spirit of incessant whirl, of feverish restlessness which is so marked a feature of American society, is most repugnant to those who would obtain rest and refreshment in rustic quiet and beauty. It has come to this, that even the Holy Sabbath does not afford an hour's sober thought, or profitable reading, for multitudes of young people. Hundreds of young men start their working life on Monday morning, more tired than when they quitted it on Saturday evening. They have been to the country ; but nature's blessed medicine of holy calm and repose, which comes as the best reviver to the toiling, busy sons of men, they have not known. I suppose the Sunday quiet and rest which I advocate would be called tiresome—

lonesome is the word—to some of our gilded youth. So much the worse for their spiritual nature, if it is so. Such youths only profane nature's sacred temple. Her loveliest shrines are polluted by their unhallowed feet. They dishonour the Lord of the Sabbath; and they do it, most of all, by robbing their own spiritual nature of that which is its rightful due. He was no religious poet who said it, and yet his word is no less true :—

> "To sit on rocks, to muse o'er flood and fell,
> To slowly trace the forest's shady scene—
> This is not solitude; 'tis but to hold converse
> With nature's charms, and view her stores.
> But midst the crowd, the hum, the shock of men,
> To hear, to see, to feel, and to possess,
> And roam along the world's tired denizen,
> With none to bless us, none whom we can bless,
> This is to be alone; this, this is solitude."

"We see as we are," is a great monitor. It constantly admonishes us to think more purely, love more freely, and live more saintly, so that we may project upon nature something of our candour and of our truth. From her rich, fresh, true life, we shall then draw richer, fresher vigour for our daily life. We shall then go to nature as to a familiar friend, in whose society we find a spring of many delights: we shall bathe our spirits in the fountain of her simplicity and loveliness; and she shall inspire us with such a high ideal, that it will put to shame the paltry meannesses, the petty jealousies, the unworthy rivalries that so stain the whitest shield among us. Then shall we realize that we are never less alone than in solitude, and we shall return to society to feel that we are never so lonesome, as among the madding crowd of selfish, mammon-loving men.

II.—IN MAN.

"What is man?"
—Job vii., 17.

Current thought about man, his being and his destiny, may be classified, speaking roughly, as pessimism and optimism. The pessimist sees nothing good in humanity in its past, its present, or its future. Born in sin, living in sin, dying in sin, is very much his brief summary of human existence. In society, he sees the spirit of the age gradually but steadily deteriorating. Selfishness, he will tell you, is rampant; vice respectable, and vice disreputable abound; the misery and suffering among the poorest of the poor in great Christian cities, who are compelled to herd together like the beasts, have never been surpassed in the darkest ages, or among the most barbarous peoples; the spirit of Christianity is dead; the Church is a mockery and a sham, for from her soul has fled the spirit of the Master—the characteristics of sacrifice and humility. There is no hope for humanity.

The former days were better than these, and these are better than those that are to follow. "I give up the human race," says he. "Mankind is on the down-grade, and to ruin is it rushing. We shall want another deluge to sweep away the race of hopelessly discredited mortals, and give humanity a new start. There might be reason to hope, if we could begin anew but, as things are, the outlook is dark as Erebus." That is what your pessimist sees, in man. He sees as he is.

The optimist believes in a great future for our race. He sees many symptoms of advance. He will tell you, with emphasis—the former days were not better than these, but worse. Christian living is by no means what it should be, he knows; but Christian civilization is a healthy plant, whose roots have struck deep and wide, and its leaves are for the healing of the nations. Want and wrong, despair and vice, a foul animalism, and a fouler mammon, degrade and blight, poison and dehumanize creatures who bear the image divine, to an extent absolutely appalling, he admits ; but he can recognize, as well, signs of a hearty philanthropy, which convince him, that in no previous age, have so many hearts mourned over human sins and wrongs, nor so many humane minds been strung-up to high tension, to devise wisely, how to purge away the one, and right the other, nor busy hands been so diligent to write, in ineffaceable characters, all over the globe, "The Lord reigneth. Let the earth be glad." Oftentimes, the results are quite incommensurate with the efforts put forth; but the growing honest purpose abroad, to give a higher tone to legislation, to redress class abuses, and abolish class disabilities and class privileges, to adjust the rights of minorities and majorities, and generally to give to society a broader and more equitable basis, above all, the rapid extension of enlightened ideas of the Christian religion, as the grand panacea for all the ills of the world—these hopeful signs of a brighter day for humanity, which are more or less apparent in all civilized lands, the optimist points to, with confidence, as tokens of a rising and not of a falling fortune for society. He has hope in mankind; he has faith in its destiny.

The optimist and the pessimist will continue to represent roughly, in the future, as they have done in the past, the great body of students, who have believed in the maxim, "The highest study of mankind is man." These terms indicate, with sufficient clearness, the two great streams of thought, which, with varying fortunes, have flowed through the historic ages. The great questions, about which optimist and pessimist have waged fierce and angry warfare, are these: What is man? Whence is he? Whither is he bound? Did he begin as an angel, and descend to the demon? Or did he begin as a child, and has he been growing ever since towards manhood? Is humanity, as it is, a degradation? or, is it a development? Is it gradually sinking away from God? or, is it steadily rising to God? These questions concern us all very much, and it is of the utmost importance that we should be on the right side. For the peculiar tone of our practical religion will depend entirely upon the answer we give. If we answer them on the pessimistic side, we shall have a religious sentiment gloomy and morose, yea despáiring; for we shall have no future for the human race here, and less for the hereafter. Our hands will be paralyzed against all good doing, our hearts will not go out freely to our brethren, our minds will not be stimulated to do their best on behalf either of ourselves, or others. Should we answer them on the optimistic side, light and hope will be the characteristics of our religious thought, and others will find cheerfulness and encouragement in the spiritual influence we shall shed abroad. We shall have a bright prospect for our race, surpassing anything that has yet been realized, and, for the future life, unlimited possibilities toward the fullness of grace and truth of our Lord and Master.

Our Lord was an optimist. His soul was full of faith in the upward progress of humanity. His kingdom of God, to illustrate which he laid so many emblems under contribution, from first to last expresses advancement as the law of every subject of that kingdom, and of the kingdom in its entirety. "Onward and upward," was the motto of the Christian's Good Shepherd. He believed implicitly in the divine image in every man, defaced and broken though he often found it to be; but still capable of elevation and restoration to form and beauty. When he took those little children up in his arms and blessed them, he saw in the home and in the school an angel-garden—the arena on which were to be reared and educated the future denizens of the heavenly home. On those unhappy victims of demoniac possession, he cast an eye of infinite tenderness, as he contrasted what they might have been to society and religion, with what they were in their unhappy and miserable plight. The leper, with his tainted life, was seen by his pure eye, in all the tragic pathos of his outcast lot; and he could not withhold the cleansing tide to purify his polluted frame, and restore him to home and friends again. Saddest sight of all to his true, good spirit, was the wretched victim of his own misguided folly or passion—the moral-lepers of society. He realized the terrible loss involved in their sinful, perverse life. He saw them as a loss to the society on which they preyed like vultures. He saw what a loss their waywardness was to themselves, in the unhappiness they carried about in their bosoms, and in the rebellious spirit which shrivelled up their better nature. Moreover, he knew what a loss they were to the Great Father, whom they had so grievously wronged, and whose heart still yearned for their repentance—grieved not only at what they had become, but far more at the thought of what they might have been. And as the blessed Jesus took up these thoughts, in one great pang of yearning love, he exclaimed, most affectionately, "Come unto me, and I will give you rest." On one occasion, certain of his followers returned from a missionary tour, radiant with success. "Even the very devils were subject unto us, through thy name," was their jubilant report. Then Jesus rejoiced in spirit, and broke out into an ecstasy of thankfulness. For what, think you? That the number of his followers had been augmented by so many more? That is how the commercial spirit measures missionary success. For a truer, deeper reason far, did Jesus rejoice in spirit. He rejoiced because his hope of humanity was being fulfilled. Men were receiving power to become sons of God. The fetters had been broken; the oppressed had been set free. The liberated were henceforth to be helpers and lights to their fellow-men; in the new-found joy of freedom, they were each to be fountains of spiritual life and refreshment, and God's spiritual universe was to be permanently and incomputably enriched.

It was because our Lord had faith in, and hope

for, humanity, that he came to save it at the pinch. It was that faith, which sustained him amidst weariness, and worry, and insult, and scorn. He saw in men and women, such vast possibilities for good to the world and glory to their God, that toil, and trial, and agony, and crucifixion were as nothing, in his estimation, compared with the importance of the high commission entrusted to him. That was why he never gave up as hopeless, the most vicious or the most hardened sinner; that he made one last great effort of love, to save the traitor from his fate; and that for Pharisees and Sadducees he had only patient toleration and winning persuasion. It was his abounding faith, in that moral and spiritual height to which humanity might rise, that inspired his sublime self-surrender. It was the sense of strong contrast, between what the best and the worst were, and what both the best and the worst might and should have been, which unsealed the springs of his divine pity, and laid upon his pure soul the burden of their sins and sorrows. The great, strong Son of God himself, he saw the sonship actual and possible in all others, even in the guilty mob who were to clamour for his blood, and over whom he exclaimed, in an agony of infinite tenderness, " How often would I have gathered thee, as a hen gathereth her chickens under her wings." His ear, divinely attuned to the soul's deepest desires, he could hear the great cry for help and succour ringing through all the earnest struggles upward of the oppressed, ever since the world began. The streets were to him full of souls, not bodies merely; and from each there seemed to come the mute appeal for light, and life, and salvation. Himself, the best, he thought the best of others; he saw the best in others. And so, just because God stands to us for the best of all, is it an infinite consolation and dignity for the penitent soul to reflect, that none thinks so much of him as his Heavenly Father. Through the ignorance, the degradation, and the sin, the pure eye pierces to the live, deep soul within—to that slumbering embryo, in which humanity, and civilization, and eternal life lie folded up.

> The Christ sees white in Judas' heart,
> And loves his traitor well;
> The God, to angel his new heaven,
> Explores his lowest hell.

Now, it is this optimistic spirit, passing down

through Christian lives and works, that has saved and is saving the world for Christ. The pessimist sees only brutalism, selfishness, treachery, rascality, in man; talks about converts to Christianity as hypocrites, and mission agencies as a delusion, and loudly protests, that, so far as he can see, things are going from bad to worse. Holding these opinions, he cannot be expected to open his hand on behalf of those against whom his heart is shut. Missionary and reformatory schemes of philanthropic enterprise find in him no patron. The dark shadow of his dark creed, sits like a nightmare on his spirit. He cannot help a humanity in which he has lost confidence. He sees as he is. But the optimist is the soul and strength of all good agencies, for the amelioration of his fellowmen. Looking at wide heathendom, with its manifold vile idolatries, and degrading superstitions, he reflects on the great good possible to those unenlightened millions, in the Christian religion, and, through them, to the spiritual development of the human race at large ; and he gives his treasure, and, if need be, himself, to penetrate the dark places of the earth with the " Light of the World." Who entered the prison, and converted it from being the mere den in which were caged the wild beasts of society, behind bolted doors and barred windows, into a grand reform school? The philanthropic optimist. Who first taught the criminal, that he is a man with a soul and a conscience capable of doing God service, and that he is, moreover, dear to the good soul who can follow him into his cell, for the dear Master's sake, whose love would never let the guiltiest go ? The Christian optimist. Who first taught the sacredness of the human being in body, soul, and spirit, and sent forth his apostles, to preach the gospel of a sound mind in a sound body as man's highest, noblest state? Christ, the optimist. This century has seen some of the greatest triumphs of religious optimism. Men now see more to respect in the criminal and the unfortunate than ever before; and simply because they have been realizing the vast blessing of life, and its wide possibilities. Respecting themselves more, by realizing their dignity as Our Lord realized it, they have learned to respect all others, who share in the dignity of the divine image. Strange, that though it is nineteen centuries since Our Lord taught that doctrine, so sublime and yet so simple, it is only now, that society is awakening to the wisdom, and the piety of hoping the best and doing the best, for every human life. Society is rapidly coming to perceive, with new eyes, man—God's noblest work—because society has begun to realize, in some greater measure, her own true place and power, Society is ascending in the Christian scale, and she is giving the best proof of it, by setting herself, with might and main, to raise those whom she had formerly regarded as hopelessly sunk. True, little has yet been done, comparatively speaking. Only a beginning has been made. Nevertheless, that little is the earnest of great things to come, for Emerson's lines express a thought, which is the inspiration of countless benefactors and saviours of suffering and sinning humanity:—

> " Let me go where'er I will,
> I hear a sky-born music still;
> 'Tis not in the high stars alone,
> Nor in the redbreast's mellow tone,
> Nor in the cups of budding flowers,
> Nor in the bow that smiles in showers,—
> But in the mud and scum of things,
> *There* alway, alway something sings.

Light is a composite thing in the spiritual, as

well as in the physical world. As there are many minds, so there are many lights. The Christian religion wisely recognizes every light as a light of God, and its standing call to all its disciples is that of the Master to the twelve, "Let your light shine." All can help to minister a ray of light to the sheaf of Christianity's rays, that is gladdening, and is still to gladden, far more, the nations. The dawn broke nineteen centuries ago, and the sun of the truth is climbing steadily up the heavens. As never before, is there abroad to-day a widespread hopefulness for humanity's future, on the earth, or off the earth. Never before were helping hands held out so generously, because never before did charity's heart beat so truly, to those men, classes, and races, who seem the farthest down among their brethren. There is hope in the atmosphere of our Church life, which presents a striking contrast to the gloomy forebodings and theorizings of a century ago; and blessed are they who can be encouraged, by its invigorating breath, to stand in the Master's place—to believe in mankind, and give themselves to promote the incoming of the brighter day. No better proof need anyone desire that he has caught up something of the true Christian spirit, than the growth in him of this Christ-like optimism; for it is just the elevation of ideal, which the gospel of the blessed God has brought to him, that has inspired him, to try to elevate the minds, and sweeten the lives of others. And as he gives himself to do this great good for his less fortunate fellow-men, he begins to realize, almost for the first time, how precious the Messiah is to himself. Thus his giving is his gaining, while the withholding of the pessimist is his own impoverishment. In the Christly life of such an one, there is presented a wondrous triumph of divine grace. The soul has risen with Christ, whenever it is seized with the mighty passion to raise others also; and the higher it rises, the stronger will be the passion to rise still higher, till, in his perfect light, the disciple is lost in the Master. That heart has been educated in the school of Christ, which, as it passes along life's troubled highways, sends out tendrils of sympathy and help to the maimed and broken, the unfortunate and the sinful sharers in its common nature. That man lives very near to the Master, who can see an element of good and a seed of hope, in the most hide-bound Pharisee, who is so good in his own eyes, that he must needs treat as a personal enemy, all who will not frame their lips to lisp his shibboleth, and march in time and step with him. "We see, as we are." And, when a Christian can see, with spontaneous sympathy, some good thing even in the vilest, and will not deny mercy even to the greatest criminal, and can pray for new light even for the bigot who would burn him at the stake if he could—that man is not far from the Kingdom of God.

This is the Christianity for which the world is panting to-day—the Christianity that comes home to men's minds, strong in the faith of a glorious future before humankind, and that will gird itself, when it comes, to lend to that future all the help it can. Such a Christianity will take hold, and keep hold, when it has it, of the most selfish, materialistic, and degraded. It will work as great wonders in the nineteenth century as are recorded of primitive Christianity. To learned and ignorant alike, will it appeal with power, by reason of its sweet reasonableness; for it will be wise in the wisdom that cometh from above, "which is first pure, then peaceable, gentle, easy to be entreated, without partiality and without hypocrisy." Such a Christianity, when once it has seized the mind of the Churches, will be like the coming again of the Christ—so simple, beautiful, and true will be its message of love and mercy.

Who will give themselves to help-in "the Christ, that is to be?" Who will meditate and pray, till the divine afflatus comes, and sends them forth full-armed with the weapons of the spirit? If the blessed day is ever to come, my brothers! and sisters! bear in mind that it will only come quickly, by the combined thought, and prayer, and consecration of the faithful. In this sense we can all pray with a meaning other than apocalyptic—Come, Lord Jesus! Come quickly! Come, in the inspiration of thy chosen ones! Come, in the mind that can call every man brother, because it can see, in every man, the likeness of God! Come, in the power to disclose that likeness, in native beauty, to the most depraved nature! Come, Lord Jesus! Come quickly!

III.—IN GOD.

" Thou thoughtest that I was altogether
Such an one as thyself."
—Psalm l., 21.

Some one has said:—In the beginning of Scripture, we read, that God said, "Let us make man in our image, after our likeness;" and, all through history, man has been saying, "Let us make God in our image, after our likeness." How apt the observation is, let the gods many of paganism, and the gods many of Christianity, testify. Men see as they are, and not otherwise. They see nature with eyes clear, or dim, just as the light within is anything or nothing; they see their fellowmen, according as their insight into human life and character is true and human, or false and inhuman. And they clothe their God in the attributes, exaggerated it may be, which make up what they are in themselves spiritually and morally. They read, in fact, into their idea of Deity very much what they are in themselves. In the barbaric ages man, cruel, savage,

relentless, vindictive, found the justification of
his savagery in his religion. His deities were
simply magnified copies of his own personality,
who patronized cruelty and bloodshed, and
gloated over the broken hearts of weeping
mothers offering at their bloody shrines the
fruit of their body, for the sin of their soul
These deities were inspired, by all the tribal and
race hatreds, and prejudices, which were the
very breath of their devotees' lives. As men
rose in the scale of civilization, their image in
the heavens took on new beauty. He became a
moral governor among the nations, as in Judaism; but still he was, speaking generally, little
more than a national God, bound to glorify his
chosen people, and to shatter all their and his
foes, like as a potter shivers the dishonoured
vessel. Even when a flash seemed to enter into
poetic, or prophetic soul, of a divine fatherhood,
that tender and suggestive ideal seldom went
beyond the national relationship of Jehovah and
Israel. Jehovah was the father of his people
Israel, and Israel was his goodly child. At the
fulness of the time, the God of the thundercloud and the storm was transfigured into the
God of love and mercy; the God of bloody sacri-

fices, into the God of pity and compassion; the tribal or racial God, into the Father of men. Our Blessed Lord saw God in the light of his divine sonship, and the era of the Little Child dawned upon our planet. But society is not to be born again in a day. The Light of the World has a long battle to wage with the spirit of the darkness. To begin with, it seemed as if the attempt of the light to penetrate the darkness of the ancient world must fail, and when the crucifixion gloom wrapt humanity in the thick folds of disgrace, and shame, the hope of the Messiah vanished. But death, to the good and the true, is but the beginning of their life in the best sense. The warm rays of the Sun of Truth may beat long on the iceberg of error, and the mass seem not a whit diminished. Nevertheless, the heat is telling all the same; and the ice-mountain will collapse, sooner or later, honey-combed through and through. Christianity has had a varied fortune. Many Christians, far from taking the Christ as their divine ideal, have imitated too often their pagan ancestors, by clothing their God in the poor garments of their own very imperfect thought. In their ignorance, or pride, or selfishness, they have oftentimes read into Holy Scripture attributes of the divine character, such as they wished to find there; and presented the results to their fellowmen, with an assurance, as if they had been in the throne of Heaven, and learned the essence of eternal truth. Thus various and diverse Christian ideals of the Supreme Being have overrun the earth; till now there are, in reality, as many Gods Christian as there were Gods pagan in Ancient Rome. For man can conceive of God only as he idealises, and live as he supposes the divine life to be. It is an apt illustration of this thought, though it is couched in rather strong language, the remark of John Wesley, in the heat of theological controversy, to his friend and brother preacher, George Whitefield: "George! your God is my devil." That is only a forcible expression of the wide diversity of religious ideal, which may exist among Christians who are allied in the prosecution of a great work, but who conceive of the same God differently. It is a painful exhibition, of the too common infirmity which afflicts so many Christians, who consider it to be a religious duty to treat as personal enemies those who have formed theological conceptions of the deity different from theirs.

"We see as we are," is the explanation of all the controversies which have prevailed in the Christian ages, and which have been so fruitful of broken hearts and wasted lives. To that source do we owe all the internal persecutions, which have so destroyed the brotherhood of Jesus. More than all the swords of its assailants, the sectarian feuds of Christendom have weakened the power of the Church, and rendered her helpless to stem the tide of error and selfishness Simply, because sincere and zealous men saw in the Christian's God only what they could see, considering their training, temper, and devotion to the letter, they denied to others the right they claimed for themselves. Time and again has the holy name of God and of his Christ been trailed through the mire, by Christians who claimed it to be a Christian duty to hate their fellow Christians, and do their best to render futile what others believed to be a great and glorious work. Shrink from the conclusions as we may, the fact remains that the many Christian sects and parties have, from the first, lived and acted, as if they were worshippers of different Gods, each hostile to the other, and inspiring their respective devotees to wage against each other a war of extermination. They have been really the representatives of different gods, as truly as the combatants at the seige of Troy were believed to be the bodily representatives of the spiritual forces warring in the sky above them. I know how all this is explained away as the pessimistic croakings of a cynical spirit. I know how the various sects delude themselves into the belief that with certain small drawbacks, their rivalry is a good thing for the cause of Christ; and how zealous sectaries, by statistical, and especially by financial statements, try to make the world believe that their delusion is a fact. Nevertheless, I adhere to the assertion I have made. It is delightful to hear from public platforms the broad Catholic sentiment, "Our differences are nothing to our agreements. We differ over non-essentials of Christianity only, and we are at one about the essentials." And I believe a spirit of unity is developing among the more thoughtful and unobtrusive of the laity, especially. But when we descend to common life and work, the spirit of jealousy, assumption, and unfriendliness displayed by too many, who speak for the Churches and lead in their work, is exceedingly discouraging to those who believe in the grand " unity of spirit in the bond of peace," which, I may say, was the only religious unity St. Paul knew of or desired. It cannot be that the God of keen, rival ecclesiastics and theologians, is the same when these good men are so intent to shed each other's blood, to speak metaphorically, though the combatants hesitate to assume the responsibility of saying so. Athanasius and Arius might think or say what they pleased, but the scenes at the Council of Nice are much more easily justified, if it be supposed that the parties were struggling for the supremacy of a true God over a false God. No ingenuity can ever make the God of Augustine, who has doomed the vast majority of the human race to

"Be cast as rubbish to the void,"

the same with the God of the gospels, whose kingdom is a home, and its laws, fatherly tenderness, compassion and mercy. Those Christians who, in the 16th century, kindled Autos-da-fè, all our Europe, most certainly believed that the God of the Catholic Church could not possibly be the God of the heretics, and the heretics were very much of the same opinion. The martyrs for liberty of conscience, one and all, said to their persecutors, " If your God commands you to take our lives, because we cannot think as you do, then he is not the God we can deem worthy to be adored ; " while the persecutors retorted triumphantly, " If your God suffers you to rebel against what we call the divine authority of his Church, he cannot be the true God."

Passing from history, common life presents the operation of the same law in every-day experience. I need hardly say that, in this discourse, I have not meant to speak of God as changing or changeable. God, the infinitely good and gracious, is, and must ever be, the same loving father. His heart has ever been the same towards the creatures made in his image, and his hand has ever been the same helper to man in all the crises of history. It is the ever-changing man, and not the never-changing God, whom I have tried to present. How changing, yea, erratic, Christian man is, the various and conflicting conceptions of him who is so expressively called, "The Bread of Life," which have been held at different times, are a sadly suggestive commentary. The "great salvation," God's good message of light and peace, has been made, a thousand times, an apple of discord in homes and communities. The "person of Christ," a sweet subject, about which no rude word should ever have been uttered, has oftentimes been as the red flag of the matadore in the bull-fight, to the flaring eyes of eager antagonists. The psalmist saw more deeply into this problem than some of us when he sang—

"The Lord hath recompensed me according to my righteousness,
According to the cleanness of my hands in his eyesight.
With the merciful thou wilt show thyself merciful;
With the perfect man thou wilt show thyself perfect;
With the pure thou wilt show thyself pure;
And with the perverse thou wilt show thyself froward."

In other words, "We see as we are."

Let me attempt to illustrate what different people may see in God, just because they see as they are.

1. What does the suspicious, distrustful person make God to be? Such an one has no faith

in his fellow-men. He takes everyone, more or less, for a rogue. He suspects that every man has his price, and that selfishness is the ruling passion in man and woman. One may say, But what has that to do with a man's religion? Much everyway, I answer. We see just as we are. St. John's words come to us as the verdict of common sense, as well as of Scripture, "If a man love not the brother whom he hath seen, how can he love the Father whom he hath not seen?" The suspicious man suspects his God as he suspects his brother. He projects upon the divine character, his own character; and suspicion must therefore be a leading feature in the character of his deity. His God is a suspicious being, never trusting his creatures, but always distrusting them, and the suspicious deity has no friends.

2. What is the God of the selfish man like? The selfish man's highest ideal of life is to gather to himself and for himself the very most and the very best he knows. Outside the circle of his own interests he never wishes to go. His idea of God must be subservient to his idea of self. He cannot share with another any common blessing. His God

must be brought within the circle of his selfishness and kept there. His religion must be simply a branch of his selfishness—a thing of "all take," and "no give." Can his God be the God who so loved the world that he gave his only begotten Son to die for it, and whose better blessedness it is to give rather than to receive?

3. What is the God of the hard, unforgiving man? A stern Shylock, forever unbending as adamant, in his clamor for "the pound of flesh." A lynx-eyed Argus, unceasingly scanning human action, and noting the evil and the good, especially the evil. An inflexible Nemesis, with thunder-wrapt brow and flashing eyes, knowing only condign woe for broken laws. Such is the God of the unmerciful. Unforgiving and unforgetful himself, his mind cannot conceive a forgetting and forgiving God He sees as he is, and there is nothing to him in a God who wears "nobility's true badge—mercy." Without a moment's hesitation, and without a thrill of pity, he can consign his best friend to a hopeless future, and think he glorifies the divine justice thereby. Pity the man who can be content with such a conception of God. Pity the man

who can so misconceive the religion of Christ as to be incapable of understanding that

> " Who will not mercy unto others show,
> How can he mercy ever hope to have ? "

4. What about the God of the superstitious? His God is perpetually his foe, and never his friend. He cannot help being a slave, in the service of such a deity. His one ambition is to appease his wrath, or court his favour. He must keep on good terms with a God so vengeful, that he may escape the punishment and receive the reward. How far all that is from the Christian ideal I need not waste words to say.

5. A grand, gentlemanly deity is the God of the mammon-worshipper. Majesty and dignity are in his every step. Almightiness encompasses his way. Marvellous display, imposing grandeur impresses his devotees. His robe—the rainbow; his crown—a circlet of stars; his chariot—the wind; his horses—the fiery coursers of the sun. What more magnificent and effective than such a God! But nothing attractive, nothing loveable about him. Everything awe-inspiring, elegant, impressive. Such

is the deity of him, who weighs everybody and everything in the golden scales of mammon— an exaggerated millionaire, simply, with all the pride and the pomposity, the contempt for man, and the forgetfulness of love, which make the ungodly mammon worshipper the most hateful of mankind.

Contrast with these religious ideals, or, more strictly speaking, these irreligious ideals, the God of the Gospels—the God of the simple, true, and pure heart. His God is a being whom he clothes with supreme moral and spiritual characteristics—One whom he adores for what he is, and for that alone—sublime goodness, tender compassion, righteous justice, far-reaching mercy, and unwearied good-doing. The Christ—the highest and the best he can conceive—he takes as his type of the divine. He is pure; he sees the pure one, therefore, as he is. He is brotherly; and he sees the fatherly, and motherly in God, for he sees. as he is. He is loyal to the good, and he cannot help trusting ever more and more in the good which is,

"The source and end of all,"

for he sees, as he is. He loves God, and he

wraps in the divine embrace all who will find rest and peace in a higher life; for he sees as he is. He is patient and prayerful with the erring; for he recognises the possibilities of restoration for the sinner to the divine image, however degraded he be. His God is the good shepherd following the lost sheep out into the wilderness, the wise husbandman refusing to rush in wildly to pluck up the tares which an enemy hath sown in his wheat field, the yearning parent going out eagerly to meet the returning prodigal and anticipating his penitence and his pleading in the glorious glow of his merciful joy. These are the very highest attributes, of the highest and fairest earth has ever seen. These are some of the lights of the Exalted One in whom all fullness dwells. So the simple Christian clothes his God in that garment of salvation, and he walks side by side with him on the earth, in the spirit of him who said, "I and the Father are One." He adorns his deity, with every grace and virtue, and as he adores at his feet, he is himself richly adorned.

It must be most essential, therefore, for every one to think out for himself and make his very own, a clear, commendable ideal of God. The Great Supreme cannot be God, to any human soul, until such an ideal has been created. The Apostle was right, when he talked to the Galatians of the necessity for Christ to be formed in them. God must be formed in his servants, if they are to serve him. They must have something of his spirit. Religion is a thing to be enjoyed; and it alone can lend the truest enjoyment to life. But we must have a God who is our very own before we can be religious. In our blessed Lord, we have that ideal grandly embodied; and it must be the first duty of every true man and woman to realise the Master's ideal and embody it in active life

Specially important is this thought in the education of the young. The Christ must be the great instructor of youth. Our children are to grow in favor with God and man as he did; and they must grow in his way. What was his way? He was a reverent hearer and an earnest enquirer. He sat at the feet of the teachers of his people, and reverently learned what they could teach him, about God. But the God of the Rabbis had to become his God; and he knew no way of reaching the divine fellowship except by earnestly questioning both his teachers and himself. There is no other path to knowledge of any kind. Mere memory knowledge comes and goes with perplexing easiness. Jesus could not grow spiritually on what educationists call, cram. Whatever he acquired of religious knowledge was a clear gain to his spiritual nature, for it became part and parcel of his very self. "Experimental," is the word which describes his religious growth. Our youth should be trained on the same lines. The utmost care must be taken, that, from the first, only correct impressions of Our Heavenly Father should be made upon their young natures—impressions which will deepen with their growth, and become more apparent with their strength. How many men and women around us are standing illustrations of a vicious early training! They have no religious faith, because they never were led to believe in God. What they were taught as faith, they have been glad to abandon, because it could be nothing but unbelief in them. The God of their childhood stands self-condemned, because he cannot hold them in their manhood So they turn rashly round and declare, "There is no God." Any state of mind more deplorable I cannot imagine. A godless life, in God's universe, must be a friendless life. A thoughtless child of the Great Father, cannot be a guiltless child in Christian lands. Friendlessness is a misery, and thoughtlessness is a sin. That is the fate of him whose life has in it no light from Heaven ; and for that fate alas ! too often have mindless parents and blind teachers been responsible. The young mind is delicately sensitive to religious influences, and early impressions live when later impressions vanish. What an honourable and responsible place parents and teachers have, for developing the native seed of religion in humanity! And what a failure like theirs, if they twist and distort the young plant, till by and by the Great All-Seeing One cannot recognise the work of his hands. Surely, the best to be hoped for in such a case is, that the man should doubt, and then abandon the error of his youth ; and the worst to be dreaded is, that he should unthinkingly hold firmly to a belief which is no belief, and never know the fine, free, tender fellowship of a loving fatherly God.

How desirable that the Christian ideal should

be divinely human and attractive, for the sake
of the outside world, which knows not the truth
and life as they are in Jesus. Christians stand
sponsor for those unhappy individuals; and woe
be to Christian man or woman, who fails in
that sponsorship. Can it be denied, that degraded Christian Gods, or rather Christian conceptions of God, have oftentimes had more to
do with the repugnance of those outside the
pale of the Christian church than any other
single influence whatever? The world desires
a God whom it can respect, revere, adore—a
God who appeals to the whole man with all
the force of veritable goodness and truth—and
if it cannot have such a God it will not bow its
neck to the easy yoke of religion. For the world
without, as well as for the world within the
churches, the Christian ideal of God should be
the Christ and the Christ only.

"We see as we are," is a profound and fertile
thought. Our nature is like a glass in which
are to be reflected the lineaments of our God. If
the surface of the mirror be clean, by reason of
our purity and truth, the face of the God of the
gospels will be seen distinctly. No one can
doubt what we are, when they behold in us

the countenance of the Christ. God in the Bible, may be little to society, God in nature may be less, and God in humanity the least of all; but God in us, the life and the faith of Christ, will bring men to glorify him. May we desire ever more faithfully to reflect the sheen of the divine glory. May we give ourselves, with increasing fervour, to cleanse us from all unrighteousness, that Christ may be to us as he is. May we yield ourselves, ever more implicitly, to the charm of his spirit, that we may know the loving-kindness of God which is better than life. "We see, as we are." May it be our lasting ambition to be ever the best, that we may see at the best, nature, man, and God our Father. Then shall we fulfil the purpose of Our Creator and bear the image of him, whom, though invisible, we love.

PART IV.
THE SEASONS.

Nothing ever stirs the soul of man, savage or civilized, like the phenomena of nature. Whether in her beautiful and graceful moods, or in her magnificent but terrible displays, or in her marvellous and mighty changes, Mother Nature leaves on the human spirit impressions that never fade away.

Man never realizes his helplessness more truly than when he stands, horror-stricken, before the mad sweep of the hurricane, as it dashes down the proud monuments of his ingenuity and power, and spreads fell devastation across half a continent. He never knows his littleness so impressively as when Apollo looses the ice-fields of winter, and sends them careering along, resistless as the forked lightning, to smite down the glory of all human skill, and to arrest for a moment the mighty St. Lawrence, saying to its proud waters, "Thus far shalt thou go, and no farther."

is m ost striking and suggestive, travellers

tell us, to watch the effects of unusual natural phenomena on the savage mind. A total eclipse of the sun, for example, is apprehended by the South Africans with the utmost consternation. They seem to regard that impressive spectacle in the light of a life-and-death struggle between two great deities—Light and Darkness, or, as the Persians personify them, Ormuzd and Ahriman. They watch, with feelings akin to horror, the gradual obscuration of the sun's disc; and when the shadow is fullest, sharing in the solemn silence, which at that moment spreads over universal nature, they gaze, in blank dismay, at the threatened extinction of the blessed orb of day. But the moment the shadow begins to pass off, they think the tide of battle has turned in favor of their good god; and, breaking out into demonstrations of the wildest joy, they beat their tom-toms with deafening energy, and indulge in shouts and gestures expressive of the liveliest gratitude. Once again they believe their good sun-god has triumphed, over his and their implacable foe, and secured for his devotees a continuance of the precious things brought forth by light and heat.

I envy not the man who, standing on a spur of the great Mont Blanc, and contemplating the sea of Alpine crests and valleys which stretch before him far as the eye can reach, does not exclaim in devout rapture, as he lifts his eyes to heaven, "What a God thou art!"; or him who, under Niagara's thundering roll, or beside the mad frenzy of her whirlpool rapids, is not awed into adoration at the might and majesty of Nature; or him who can look out unmoved at the magnificent pyrotechnic effects of a Canadian thunderstorm, and catch not the majesty of the Great Unseen, as the levin bolt descends at his feet, and simultaneous lightning flash and thunder roar petrify his soul with horror. Well might the ancients personify the great forces and voices of nature; and hear in the thunder that appalled them a word of God, as well as see in the lightning that shivered the oak, a feat of his almighty power.

Quite as impressive to the thoughtful mind —probably more so, indeed—are the regular changes of the seasons, though we may be less conscious of their potent spell. They steal upon us imperceptibly almost, in the hum and bustle of busy life; and, as they come, they go.

Nevertheless, the very silence and subtlety of their operations are but the earnest of their sublime, almighty influence. All God's great forces are silent and secret, but they are exceeding sure.

I.—THE ROSSIGNOL AND THE ANEMONE.

" Lo! the winter is past; the flowers appear on the earth;
the time of the singing of birds is come."

Cant. ii., 11-12.

To-day, we stand amid the symbols of one of the great natural changes of the year—the bright season of spring hopes. Let us listen to its cheery voices, and imbibe its fresh breezes. Once again, in the roll of the months, winter has been won from his icy throne, by the genial wooing of the spring. The death-like monotony, that so long brooded over the land, has been broken. Already the rossignol and the blood-root have harbingered the spring ; and, in a few days, lovely blossom will follow swelling bud, with a rapidity peculiar to our climate. Throughout the long winter the leafless grove, and snow-bound waste have been dumb. Their minstrels had forgotten their melody, or gone to a more hospitable clime, to enjoy perpetual summer. Now spring is here, and she is sounding the keynote of nature's concert season. In a brief space, every note of her diapason will come forth, rich and full-throated, from wood and field, and sky. All nature will be jubilant with grateful mirth. And shall man be silent? Shall God's highest creature stand uninspired, in the busy springtime, and unmoved by its soft influences? Shall the snowdrop bow her head meekly at the great Creator's feet? and the larch hang out her feathery tassels to his glory? Shall the skylark carry her matin song up to heaven's gate? and the thrush pipe her gladdest music in her vesper hymn? Shall the lambkins frolic on sunny braes, in all the glee of new-found life? and the beast of the wilderness bound in sportive revelry, at the coming of the spring? And shall man, so richly gifted to appreciate the goodness and grace of he Great Creator—shall man alone, be unimpressed, while every living thing is vocal with its tribute of thankfulness? That we may join in the universal chorus of gladness and hopefulness, which fills the springtide, let us listen to the voices of external nature, and behold her wondrous transformation scene.

The most obvious lesson of the spring is, *preparation*

"Spring unlocks the flowers to paint the laughing soil."

Every thing on which the eye rests speaks of preparation. The opening bud sings, " I am making ready for the full leaf and flower of the bright summertime, and the fruit of purple autumn." For months past, the sap has been busy among the roots. Having nothing to do in the upper air it has been actively mining in the bowels of the earth, and enlarging the area of its operations. Last summer the sap was so busy spreading shade for our streets that it had no time, so to speak, to spread out its root supply to meet the increased demand of the branches. But winter gave the much-needed leisure, and for the extended growth of the past, as well as for the still greater leafage of another summer, a vast quantity of additional root machinery is now in full working order. As we look upon the bare trees, in winter, they are suggestive only of death; but nature knows no intermission in life or work. Unseen processes have been most active, in preparation for the spring; and upon that magazine of preparation, so to speak, do we plant our hopes of a future rich in the bounties of Heaven.

As we note with hopefulness the bursting buds around us, it is an easy and a short step, from the vegetable kingdom without us, to the moral and spiritual within. Sound and well-developed Christian thought and character are not things of a day. Neither are they to be looked for and appreciated only when the harvest of life comes, and the disciple is about to be gathered, like ripe grain, into the heavenly granary. These also are the work of all the seasons. There is the winter of deep, hard, secret exercisings—times of anxiety and doubt, of sorrow and affliction; the spring also of radiant enthusiasm—of pure, fresh emotion, of sparkling intelligence, and buoyant faith that can storm the very heavens; then the summer-time of fragrant graces, maturing vigor, robust courage and unclouded trustfulness; and, at last comes the golden autumn, the best of all the seasons, for it bears the sheaves of good and noble Christian result both within us and without, to the glory of our Lord and King.

Nature's seasons come and go according to "laws that never can be broken." With these we may not intermeddle. But spiritual seasons are under man's own control. He has the power to say whether he shall have a spring of diligent preparation for future glory, and reward, or no. If he says, "No," or, if he omit to say, "Yes," which is very much the same thing, then it shall be exactly as he desires. Spiritual buds have to swell, and burst, and spread out into the fair leaves of promise, just like the chestnut buds in the spring, if any really good thing is to appear in Christian character which can bless the individual or the world. But the sap makes the spring-time for the maple, and the earnest will makes the spring-time of the soul. Moreover, just as the sap of the tree is manufactured deep down in the soil, by the honest, energetic activity of the roots, gathering in from every side ; so the will of man is stimulated, and directed solely, by the truth, which study and experience have made his very own. Spiritual preparation, on its human side, is nothing more, therefore, than the result obtained by the diligent exercise of the whole man gathering into himself the highest good, in loyalty to the spirit of God in him. His faculties are the rootlets, and his circumstances, opportunities, and duties are the soil, in which the plant of righteousness is sustained in health and vigor, and steadily unfolds towards the perfection of its being. Is that all? your devotee to forms, and rites, and theories may say. One who had never seen the ocean, but who had heard much of its immensity and majesty, on being brought to the sea shore said, "And is that all?" "Yes," said his companion, "that is all." But, What an *all*! So to our devotee, we say, "What an *all* is the scope of a single life, in its powers for knowing God, and in its capacities for enjoying God's fellowship, in its opportunities for spiritual culture, and in its seasons of spiritual discipline! The roots of the tree exhaust the strength of the soil, that they may do their best in building up trunk and branch, and leaf and fruit. In like manner, the whole man is to do his best to exhaust every means of moral and religious light, and strength, that he may do his best for his character in all its gifts and graces. That is our reasonable service, and it is a stupendous *all*.

Marvellous are the artifices adopted by the roots to do their utmost for the plant. No servants are so faithful as they. Invariably do they seek out the best soil available, and they will dip down or come towards the surface, go forward or double upon themselves, yea even penetrate into the cleft of the rock, that perchance they may do their duty better. What a lesson in faithfulness those thread-like rootlets teach man! What reproachful glances they have for the best of us! Had we half the fidelity of the roots, we should have fewer ill-spent, or slothful Sundays standing against us on the tablets of conscience, no dust-covered bibles to tell the tale of our unpreparedness, no slighted or despised sacraments to wound our blessed Saviour in the house of his friends, no abandoned oratory once hallowed by the tears and fragrant with the prayers of a simple devotion, no spirit of the Lord grieved at pious thoughts quenched, and good feelings suppressed, and noble aspirations arrested, and goodly promise blighted. Were we as true as the roots, conscience could not call any of us a coward. We should be spared many a crimson blush, and many a remorseful pang; many a bitter tear and many a sore heart. "Go then, ye Christian men and women, consider the roots and be wise. They have no guide, overseer, nor ruler; yet they lay up their store in winter and find their reward in summer. They never falter in duty, nor grow weary in well doing. They never prove faithless to their charge, nor belie the terms of their existence. They abuse nothing; they put to good use, everything. They slumber not at their post; they forsake none of their legitimate functions. Intensely practical are they, moreover, as well as faithful. The power of selecting implies the power of rejecting. The rootlet that can choose rich soil and moist, in preference to poor soil and dry, exhibits a genius thoroughly utilitarian. It takes to that, and to that only, out of which it can make true profit. The dry soil may be very fine, but it is dry, and therefore useless; so it must be avoided. The rocky soil presents difficulties that are not to be courted, if a fine deep loam is at hand. Here also the roots have a teaching which Christians may well lay to heart. Religion ought to be regarded, as first and last, a practical thing. Outside common life you may have a thing called ecclesiasticism, or a thing called theology, but you cannot have the thing called religion. Spiritual food for certain minds may be found in both, but for the vast majority of Christians who give their minds to these subjects keenly, and enthusiastically, I have no hesitation in saying, that they prove a snare. Instead of finding in such things a help to increased spiritual power, by which the force of selfishness may be subdued, and the spirit of sacrifice given full scope to be glorified, I fear that the tendency is very constant, to substitute shadows for realities, and to confound forms and theories with spirit and truth. I feel strongly convinced that if, like the roots, Christians generally made a wise selection—feeding their spiritual nature by means of the highest and best aids and influences—the highest and most useful truths only—they should be able to define much better the term, religion, and to limit the terms ecclesiasticism and theology to their rightful sphere—the great sphere of the non-essential. There is not an intelligent Christian in this city to-day who will not admit my claim ; and yet, there are very few, who need no warning word, against the delusion of trying to feed their souls with that which is not bread. Jesus Christ is the "Bread of Life." In him there is everything to adorn the purest, to elevate the meanest, to broaden the most selfish ; for to every son and daughter of Adam he is the Great Saviour.

What gospel could be simpler than that? Nevertheless it is very significant, and withal very saddening, that so many Christians will take the most elaborate modes of partaking of his life-sustenance, and wander in by-paths in their search for his fellowship, and think that *his* will can bring them to his feet, but *their own* wills have nothing to do in the matter. These Christians will make religion everything but practical—everything but the simple and honest submission of their spirits to the spirit of the Master. The roots know better than that. They know their food, and they go to it straight as an arrow in its flight; the shortest way with them is the best. Most Christians say they know their spiritual food: but they don't go straight to it as if they did. Then the roots in the spring-time are never satisfied. They are so bent on making every bud, and blossom, and leaf as perfect as they can, all things considered, that they can never get enough, nor do enough to fulfil their charge. Most Christians are very easily satisfied in the matter of religious food. They have a kind of regulation amount of worship, or of devotion, or of religious reading; and what with the necessary cares of business, the urgent claims of society, and other things besides, they plead that they cannot be expected to give time, or attention to anything more. They can take extra supplies of pleasure, or extra seasons of gaiety, often at the risk of health and happiness; but the extra season of devotion, or the fresh opportunity for self-denial to promote some good work, or of meditation for the quickening of holy aspiration, well, they don't desire to be rude, but they would much rather be excused. Where were the fresh verdure, and bright blossoming of the spring, did nature behave so very unwisely?

In all the processes of vegetation steadiness is a standing law. No half work to-day with the intention of doing extra work to-morrow. Nothing in nature so very human as that. Everything up to time; no procrastination. Punctuality and regularity, are the invariable habits of a plant. No hurry, no excitement, no jostling down there in the silent but terribly active world of the spring. To do men and women justice, they profit much by the lessons of the roots in the performance of many duties. They transact business on such principles; and in other departments of human activity they are controlled by such principles. But when we come to the culture of the spiritual nature, to the promotion of all that can make a man, what do we find? Honest business men, honest masters, honest servants, by the popular standard; but unfaithful men, by the divine standard.

It is one of the devices of modern society, to atone for unsteadiness and irregularity of religious growth, and compensate for months of spiritual idleness and torpor, by special seasons of set religious effort and demonstration. This is the last resort of selfishness and superstition. Those periodical revivals, and annual weeks of prayer, and conferences on the state of religion and morals, never seem to reach the seat of the evil; for, in a brief space, there is as great a demand by the same persons, for another season of the same thing. The reason why, is very obvious to every thoughtful person. The cure for all the ills of the Church, and of the State, is personal effort in the progress of holiness. Christians must be wise, as well as honest, and earnest in this matter. Growth in religion means growth on natural, common-sense principles—growth on the principles of the spring-tide life, breaking forth into beauty all around our feet—regular growth, little by little, every day.

Further, while the spring looks forward to autumn, it is toiling might and main for to-day. On that account only, is it a preparation for the harvest. How many Christians concentrate their thoughts on the hereafter, under the erroneous impression, that life and character are quite inferior considerations, compared with the great matter of theoretical inclusion within what is called " the scheme of redemption." The monk flees from the world, the nun tortures her body, and the Protestant is gloomy and severe, doing their best to drive the sweetness out of earth, that they may infuse a deeper sweetness into heaven. Some, on the other hand, postpone serious religious thoughts to late life, and, meanwhile, sow their wild oats, firmly resolving to pull up some day and be saints. These are, one and all, delusions of selfishness, as unworthy as possible of reasonable beings. Our Master came to save men, and to bear the cross among men; and mankind is only to be converted to love and truth, by his servants serving in the midst of the world's sins and sorrows, battling bravely with the one, and soothing tenderly the other. Jesus came to sweeten the bitter waters of earth, and his gospel reveals a perfect character; but it does not unfold a perfect scheme. The beatitudes speak of a divine stature, which ought to be every true man's ambition. Jesus saved the guiltiest, and will save guilty men and women to the end; but it is a frightful presumption to begin with, and a terrible loss, in any case, to end with, when a man sets himself to glorify selfishness in the spring, in the delusive hope that, in the autumn of life, he can make amends to God and man, by an age of pietism for a youth of folly. The thing is not to be done. God and nature protest against it. Though God's mercy can reach the most obdurate, even at the eleventh hour, is it not the heavy burden of such an one's doleful dirge, that he never can have mercy on himself for the sin, and folly, and unmanliness in which he squandered the precious moments of his youth and prime? The moral and spiritual effects of evil, or folly, are not to be cast off like an old garment; nor, with the knowledge of pardon, does there follow the sense of peace. The spring must be well and wisely spent if the fall is to be rich, with the fruits of glad content, and pious restfulness, in the abiding fellowship of the Highest.

May we all ponder well the lessons of this spring-tide. Our hearts are all light, and our spirits buoyant, on this lovely May day. Well is it that they should be so. Who should be joyful, if not the Christian ? And where, if not in the House of God, on a glorious day, brimful of the season's hope and promise? God grant that the light of this beautiful day, which is bathing in radiance God's beautiful world, may be but the symbol of a brilliance greater far beaming from the Light of the World, and filling our whole being. May our inspiration, from this day forth, be Jesus, the Alpha and the Omega of every good life and work, and our aspiration ; to covet earnestly the best gifts, that we may lay them at his feet, whom to adore, with all humility, is our highest duty, and grandest privilege.

II.—THE OAK AND THE LEAF.

" We are like the oak whose leaf fadeth."
—Isaiah, i., 30.

This is a fall sermon. "The Fall," well describes the season to which it gives the name. It is the season of the falling leaf—of faded summer greenery and beauty. It is a season of many and mixed suggestions. The falling leaf speaks of decay, but the tiny, waxy bud behind it, is the earnest of a spring life to come, when nature shall have awakened from her long winter sleep. The naked orchards, and swept stubble fields, harmonize with leaden skies, and chill November's blast; but the swelling barns and the garnered fruits fill the farmer's life with food and gladness. Autumn chills and damps forecast stern winter, trying and full of risks for the old especially; but to the youthful and gay they herald the near vision of crisp sunny days, and glorious auroral nights, of home pleasures and social glee. Shall I say, that to our Canadian youth, the winter brings the brightest, and the best recreations of all the year? Thus, happily, are the light and shade blended, in the circle of our common life; the grave and the gay in nature. Thus, grateful and helpful is the story of the changing seasons, to the life of old and young, the gladsome and the sober.

As we stand to-day among the fallen leaves, and behold the naked trees that a week or two ago were resplendent, in the rich crimson and gold of our Canadian autumn, ours is not the grasshopper's dull song of woe. Glad thanksgiving is in our hearts tempered by a streak of pensive thought—spring hopefulness, as well as fall regrets for the gone glad summer-time. God is good. He mingles our cup of blessing only that it may be more blessed.

There are few more beautiful objects in nature, than a fine tree clad in its June drapery; and few less attractive, than a tree stript bare, to brave the winter's storm and cold. The foliage-decked tree is a thing of rich, rounded life and loveliness; the naked tree of hard, bare, death-like monotony. Notwithstanding, the rich verdure is only for a season, while the stark, death-like sameness is the nursling of many a wintry storm and many a hot summer glare. The oak remains, though the leaf goes; the tree lives on, though its beauty vanishes in the fall. In the tree, therefore, a fit emblem is annually presented of the permanent and the transient, in human life and experience. In man, as in the tree, there is the abiding and the changing. God searches and tries him, just as nature in the fall, searches and tries the fleeting drapery of the grove. Whatever is true in him abides, and defies the fieriest test, just as the gnarled oak resists successfully, both the blow of the hurricane and the grip of the ice-king. Whatever is false, goes in the day of testing, like the yellowing leaf, at the first snell gust of October cold.

1. *The oak and the leaf as emblems of human life.* Nature's great aim is to cherish and develop the permanent. I use the term comparatively; for nothing in the wide world is permanent. Accordingly, she utilises, whatever she needs, to promote her object, and casts it away when she is done with it. The summer leaf is of no use in winter so she lets it go. Indeed, the life of the tree depends upon the leaf

going; so nature ruthlessly strips it bare at the right time. The beauty and grace of the transient must yield to the necessity of the permanent—the robust life of the tree must be promoted, no matter what becomes of the spreading leaf.

Just so is it in human life. The higher or spiritual life is the man; the body, in all its functions and relations, is only an accessory, in the development of the real man. Essential is the body in its own place, just as the leaf is essential at its own time. But just as the leafage of the tree in one summer, gives place to a fuller life and leafage in the next, so the transient in healthy human life is ever giving place to the enrichment of the permanent. The outward man must perish; but the inward man is renewed day by day. The spiritual life remains like the oak; the bodily sustenance, the discipline, the culture are like the leaf ever changing. The great spirit of life aims at making the highest and best spirits, that is, the highest and best men and women, to be the enduring memorials of his handiwork—immortals, whom he would make perfect as the Great Father. So he utilises every element of an individual's environment—his circumstances, his associates, his business and education—to promote his great purpose; just as the spirit of the spring breaks open the buds of the tree to the summer's warmth, and covers it with fragrant blossoms, that there may be a more abundant life, in the monarch of the forest. He sacrifices beauty oftentimes to usefulness, pleasure to profit, the gain of this life to the treasures of the future. A household tree stript of all its blossoms, and, standing like an oak in the fall spreading out its naked arms to heaven, may be the agonising means by which the tide of a bereaved widow's life may reach the high-water mark. The many days of weakness or watching, of suffering or anxiety which strip life of its outward joys, and rob it even of the pleasures of hope, may be the only method to subdue the fire of temper, or purge the impurity of thought, or unseal the fountains of tenderness, or teach mercy to an erring brother even till seventy times seven; and when any of these good fruits ensue, the fading of the leaf has been the growth of the oak. The life of self-indulgence may bring a man into the fate of Lot—the fires of Sodom behind him and the worse fire of an injured conscience within him—standing a miserable fugitive, saved by the skin of his teeth, and an aching memory his only earthly possession. Nevertheless, it has a thousand times been, only then, that like the prodigal by the swine-trough, he could think of his Father's house, and of the blessed ministries that await him there. For the dear life of the oak of a nobler life, the coveted and admired leaf of sensual delights had to wither and die.

These are lessons we are slow to lay to heart; perhaps, it may be well-nigh impossible almost for some of us to lay them to heart, till they touch our nature deep down. The leaf has such attractions; the drapery of life so fascinates the eye and captivates the soul. We would like the leaf to remain even if it killed the tree. We would sacrifice, and many often deliberately sacrifice, the oak, which is their life, that they may enjoy uninterruptedly the leaf which passes away. There is great ignorance abroad in society, concerning the simplest laws of our spiritual being. It would seem as if the majority believed that the leaf should remain, and that the oak should perish. It is undoubtedly the one concern with too many—to care everything for the externals of life, and nothing for the chief end of our existence—the character god-like and divine.

2. *It is of the utmost importance to keep constantly in view, the distinction between the permanent and the transient, in our work, our life, our religion.*

Its importance in our life. What is there in life like the oak, and what like the leaf? Only the true in life has any permanence. Only that which goes to give peace, to enrich our spiritual nature, and to bind us to the love and service of our fellow-men is an abiding possession. The writer of the epistle to the Hebrews speaks of certain Christians, who had suffered grievous persecution, and spoiling of their goods; but so far from regarding their lot as desperate, he adds, that they were calm and reposeful, because they had in themselves, a better possession. What was permanent in Jesus Christ? Only what was true and personal. And as every thing in him was true and personal he will live for ever in the life of mankind, with a splendour to which time shall only add lustre. The only thing which has immortality is personality: and personality is the spiritual life. Just as the tree has a definite point, to which nature will develop it by her subtle processes, so the individual man, developing by the laws of his being, has a definite point towards which he is making. That point, I need hardly say, is the stature of his Lord. Whatever of the Christ-like, therefore, is unfolding, or has unfolded, in any character, that is permanent. Whatever, on the other hand, is not Christ-like, that must go like the fading leaf, or like the hay, straw, and stubble of St Paul's parable. My dear friends! do we realise this? Do we clearly comprehend, that only that one reality can abide to our credit and renown? Of all that we wish for, or strive for, or gain, only that which we have wished for, or striven for, or gained of the likeness to Christ will go with us and abide, at the loosing of the silver cord, and the breaking of the golden bowl. Of all we prize, and, it may be, pique ourselves on possessing, of wealth, or wisdom, or fame, nothing will count at the gate of Heaven, but the Christ-character. Only that is real, only that is genuine, only that can live for ever and ever.

b. *So is it with our work.* Every day of our lives we are doing something that we hope will last, either for our own good, or for the good of others. That is a laudable ambition, by which we should all pray to be more and more inspired. But only one kind of work can live, to any man's good or glory; and that is, the work performed out of an honest and good motive. For even though the work may fail, the worker shall be blessed. But your scheming, and dishonest worker, whose motto is, " Money—money only," never means to do good work, and never by any chance does it. To carry out his principle as far as it will go, " Money without work," would be a better motto. Such a worker stands alone, a very Ishmaelite, in God's creation. He finds no companionship in nature's rich domain. All her workers are busy at honest work. Whether it be the coral insect building up islands of the main, or the humble bee framing most wonderful cells for her precious treasure, or the beaver engineering his dam, or the horse ploughing in the furrow—everywhere, it is the same good and faithful service rendered to the Creator. How much of your work and mind will stand nature's test? The old cathedrals, dotiug the old world with shrines, at which modern architects can only gaze, in admiration, and try to copy, were all of them the honest work of men who put into these magnificent piles a bit of their own personality. The character of the men who builded can be read in the work of their hands. They were proud to work and they had pride in doing good work ; they built for future ages, for they believed in the permanence of honest work. And to-day we, who are as unoriginal as they were original, and copyists where they were creators—we cannot withhold our tribute of gratitude from the dead workers, who yet live, and preach to us by their works. There is no other law of work. The character must sanctify the hand, and give its creations immortality. We must go within, to seek for the Christly character, and then we shall find the Christly worker. Fathers and mothers can teach their children no better motto for their entire life-work than this: " Christly in spirit; Christ-like in work." That is surely an improvement on the motto of the many : "Christlike in church ; devil-like at work." That is the motto of the respectable dollar-worshipper of this nineteenth century, who thinks it a *safe* thing, at least, to own a pew in a fashionable church. Let me entreat you, however humble your calling, and however mean your work, ever to aspire to do good work, which will deserve to last, because it will embody a bit of your own personality—a portion of your very self. Then your "giving-out will be really a taking-in; your effort expended on good work will be so much given to build up the Christ-like in you. Never mind though you may not reach the millionaire's throne. He cannot take his throne with him, no more than the drapery of the summer-time can be built into the woody fibre of the tree. The humblest here may carry a better possession into the spirit-world than he will carry—excellent Christian man though he be. Keep clear this distinction, between work that is part of one's life and which makes life, and work which is only show, only dress, and like the fading leaf to live only for a season.

c. *Equally important is this distinction in religion.* Here, very emphatically, must the counsel be given, "distinguish between the permanent and the transient"—between the fair form of religion and its, too often, tawdry adornment—between the living truth and spirit, and the dead form and body. That the counsel is not by any means superfluous, let the frequent examples of Christians confounding the fading leaf in religion with the enduring oak—religion the thing, with religion the spirit —abundantly corroborate. Strictly speaking, religion means the tie which binds man to his Maker. It must, therefore, be a spiritual bond; and it will be strong or weak, just in proportion as the spirit is Godlike, and has power, therefore, to hold by God. The spiritual in religion is the essential, the real, the permanent, the oak. Forms of thought, forms of worship, books, things, names, are not essential, and must be transient. They are to religion what the leaf is to the tree, as a drapery. That is quite simple —so simple that a child can grasp it

Nevertheless, the living hold of that simple truth is the grand want of Christendom to-day. The first article of the Christian religion is, "Christianity a spirit." That was the beginning and the ending of our Lord's teaching. Notwithstanding, the vast majority of Christian people, and Christian Churches, live in practical denial of it. The spirit, which is the only reality in Christianity, is being sacrificed every day to the unreal and the unessential; to things that are passing away as surely as the fading leaf in the autumn. Every age has had its own dress for religion, its own forms, its own things: and yet the blind and daring impiety is being perpetrated daily, by sincere men and women, of crucifying the *eternal* spirit for the sake of the *passing* body. The crucifiers of Jesus did no more; blind bigotry and prejudice can do no more. An eastern legend tells of a holy man, who presented to a peasant a cocoon, at the same time charging him to keep it safely, because it contained an angel. The peasant returned home, proud of his new-found treasure, and carefully guarded that which he fondly hoped should be his guardian divinity. But one morning, when he came to look at his cocoon, he found it rent and empty; but near by there sat a beautiful butterfly—the angel of his prize. And, in blind rage and disappointment, he killed the lovely creature, because it had spoiled his cocoon. The history of progress, in every age, is just the story of the Indian peasant and his cocoon. The spirit of truth, with the hues of heaven on its wings, is always sacrificed to the very human form or thing, by the blind devotee who values the husk more than the kernel—the fading leaf above the enduring oak. To put it otherwise—it is as if the bridegroom were to prize the bridal dress, and the bridal gifts, and the orange blossoms, more than the charming and beautiful bride, whom he had vowed at the altar to love and cherish above all else.

The leaf-stripped trees to-day speak of a time when we also shall be like them, stript of all adornment, and be taking our places before the Great Judge of all. Shall we then be like the oak—a well-matured, and stately work of the great Master? Shall we have fulfilled the divine purpose, and stand before God with self-respect untarnished, knowing that we have faithfully fulfilled our part? We are each to-day helping to make an answer for these questions. For the answer will not be uttered by our lips when the Judge enquires, "Hast thou fulfilled the chief end of man?" The oak makes no reply to the woodman, when he appears to judge of its fitness to build a frigate, or adorn a shrine. The "result of life," is before the feller, and he satisfies himself by that. So it will be the " result of human life," appearing in the character, which will approve or condemn us at last. That result is not to be reached by any amount of outward service merely, nor by sacraments, nor priests, nor pious offices. It is not to be gained by fitful spurts of devotion, nor by much zeal for theological formulas. The oak grows slowly, and builds up surely into itself the materials necessary to give close grain and hard fibre to its wood. Little by little, day by day, this process proceeds secretly and silently; and, at the fit time, the tree is ready to help in the construction of the most permanent works. Lay up for yourselves, said Jesus, little by little, and day by day, treasure in heaven—that is, build up into the spiritual character such spiritual materials, so to speak, as will make you meet for earth and heaven. From youth to manhood, and into age, add constantly to your spiritual store—ever adding more, and adding better. Then when the time comes that your work is to be tested, and you are presented to the Judge, "just as you are," blessed are they to whom the welcome will come, Servant of God! Well done! That is surely a result worth striving for, above all other results of time. That is something surely, for which we ought to weigh carefully in the scales of truth, all that is permanent and all that is transient, all that can go with us out of this world, and all that cannot. For it is only by so weighing these things that we shall discern which is more precious, and which is less so ; and so be able to use without abusing each good gift of God.

III.—HIS COLD.

"Who can stand before his cold?"
—Psalm cxlvii., 17.

In former days, religious people were too much given to introducing the Deity directly into the workings of nature, and the movements of history. The consequence was, that our forefathers made the Creator responsible for details, rather than for great leading principles, and modes of action. As we understand the methods of the divine government, in this learned and scientific age, that old conception reduced the Deity very much to a human stature. Their God was really, in his attributes and modes of procedure, very much a hugely exaggerated man. In these last days, there has been a marked recoil, among thoughtful people, from the old ideal. In certain intellectual quarters some have even gone to the other extreme; and, as usually happens in extremes, these cultured people of to-day have dropped into as great errors as their less cultured predecessors. As they represent Deity oftentimes, it would seem as if they had divorced him from both nature and history; so that it is impossible to discover where his operation comes in, if it comes in at all. Such an ideal of God seems to exalt him so much, that he disappears from human ken in the depths of his vast immensity. I do not say that these are irreligious people—in point of fact, they are very sensitive lest they should be called irreligious. They conscientiously believe that they have hold of a personal God; but many earnest and thoughtful Christians fail to discover his personality. Surely, there is a standing place somewhere between the extremes. There must be a third alternative. Mankind cannot be shut up between the God of petty detail, often inconsistent and capricious, always tinkering at the faulty constitution of his universe, making improvements to-day, and to-morrow, finding them to be no improvements, but the reverse, and the God dwelling in awful repose, in "the vast alone," indifferent to the universe which owns his sway, and fettered by chains of his own forging from exercising governmental authority. If this latter be the God of the "Reign of Law," then I would rather have the God of the psalmist, who knew very little of law, but a great deal of the personality which he introduces so frequently into this psalm, and whose almighty power he symbolizes in the simple, pregnant words of my text—Who can stand before his cold? Surely, it is better a thousand times, to hold by a personal God, though superstitious notions may gather round his name, than by a God who is no better than the undefined, and unthinkable God of the agnostic. In the rich religious light of the nineteenth century, it ought to be possible surely to bow before a God walking in the dignity of infinitely wise laws, and working in the silent majesty of infinite power; but also thinking, feeling, loving, in the interest of creatures, on whom he has conferred a dignity first among living things. Surely, it is possible to believe in a God dwelling in the highest heaven, directing his universe by wise laws, and, at the same time, dwelling among men, who is to be accurately enough described, for all practical religious purposes, in such phrases as these,

"He giveth snow like wool ; he casteth forth his ice like morsels ; he scattereth his hoar frost like ashes ; who can stand before his cold ?" I believe it is possible, and therefore I have taken this text, as the best symbolism I know, of a present God almighty in power, infinite in wisdom, and boundless in his goodness.

1. *His cold as a symbol of power.* The climate of Palestine must have been very different in ancient times from what it is to-day, if the psalmist was justified in employing the phenomenon of cold to symbolize the divine power. However that may be, he was right in his figure, all the same, as we Canadians can abundantly testify. The power that can, in a few hours, bridge over the mightiest rivers with a pavement secure and stable, in strength and smoothness surpassing far the grandest of engineering feats ; the power that can split up the rocks of the mountains, like cordwood under the axe of the feller ; the power that can laugh at all known human powers, or forces arrayed against it ; that must surely be a fit emblem of him, who sitteth upon the circle of the earth, and before whom the inhabitants thereof are as grasshoppers—him who weigheth

the momntains in scales, and the hills in a balance. Cold destroys vegetation, that all the winds of heaven and all the heats of summer cannot kill; cold works more havoc in the human form divine, than any other agency whatever. Only one thing, living or dead, that I know of, can resist cold, and that is the eye. That delicate member, so sensitive that a grain of dust can blind it, is so insensitive to cold, that it alone can defy the Ice-King to do his very worst. It has been said that the eagle, so keen is his vision, can gaze on the meridian sun. I doubt the assertion; but it is well-known that the eye of the explorer, who has pushed his way far beyond the limits of animal life, has, uncovered and undaunted, braved both cold and snow, without incurring the least injury. When every precaution has to be taken to protect less sensitive parts of the body, from the often most serious, and always most distressing results of frost-bite, the delicate eye can face every danger with impunity.

Well may men stand awe-stricken, as they contemplate the almighty power of the cold, and mark it for the symbol of a great attribute of Deity. Well may we, as winter approaches,

see in the cold the visible presence of the
Almighty One—a yearly Emmanuel, teaching
us lessons of awe and marvel, and bringing to
us a message of infinite love and goodness.
May we have the true religious vision to see
him, and the ear to hear his voice. May we
contemplate the winter's severity, as not "cold,"
merely, but "His cold," so that even this
inhospitable season, with nature's sleep so like
death, may suggest some helpful truth, to promote our spiritual life, and specially to develop
our sentiments of reverence and adoration.
Pious men and women should find God everywhere, and they will find him presiding gravely
in the power and mystery of winter's cold, as
truly as he sits smiling in the spreading leaf
and blossoming of the spring.

2. *The wisdom of "His cold."* Demonstrations of power excite wonder not unmixed with
fear. They cannot evoke the spirit of reposeful
trust. Wisdom suggests, to rational men, a
higher vantage ground for, "Faith in God."
The *wisdom* displayed in "His cold," is as striking at least—probably some will think it more
striking—as the wonder of the *power* of the
cold. The general law of cold, in its action upon

matter, is contraction. You may have read in the newspapers, quite recently, that the fitting of the girders to the cantilevers of the Forth Bridge was dependent upon a low temperature, when the metal was at a high point of contraction. We were told that the junction was performed successfully, because the morning was appropriately cold. But the mighty power of cold, as winter presents it to Canadians, consists not in the contraction, but in the expansion. Water alone among bodies expands under cold. That anomaly explains, how a small quantity of water getting deep down into the crevices of a mountain, will, on freezing, split up its adamantine rocks, as easily as a child sunders the petals of a buttercup. It explains, why ice floats and does not sink ; why the clayey soils so retentive of moisture are pulverised in winter, and made ready for the harrow in spring ; why myriads of insects secreted in the soil, are killed off in the torpid state where their parents thought they had found a secure nest for hem, against the rigors of the cold ; and why cold is the best disinfectant if it be intense enough— destroying instantly the germs of disease as they appear in decaying vegetation, or foul garbage, or impure drainage. In eastern countries, the best scavengers are the vultures, who gather about the towns, and fatten on the foul refuse lying around. Cold is our best scavenger. What foul and hurtful thing can stand before " His cold ?" In these ways, we readily perceive how great a benefactor the Deity is to us, in making the symbol of his infinite power a symbol also of his infinite wisdom. Were it otherwise, the cold would preserve rather than destroy much of our most injurious decaying matter ; it would positively cherish rather than destroy the army of noxious insects which prey upon vegetable growth and pester human-life, making even as it is a frostless winter the precursor of a fruitless summer.

The greatest blessing of all, however, is to be seen in the freezing of the flowing river. Because water expands under cold its specific gravity diminishes in the process of freezing ; and so, frozen water floats upon the unfrozen and heavier water below. By that means the ice-pavement is formed, which, on the one hand, is of immense value both to animals and man, and, on the other, preserves for the finny tribes their natural habitat intact. Let us suppose, that, following the general law of expansion and contraction, water should contract under cold, and the most disastrous results would follow. The surface water freezing first, the ice would sink to the bottom, because in contraction it would become heavier. Our rivers would, therefore, be frozen from below upward, instead of from above downwards; and where there might be a great depth of water, such a mass of ice would accumulate, in the course of one Canadian winter, that all the heat of our hottest summer could never melt it. Moreover, the beds of our rivers would be universally raised, by the sinking ice, and their waters sent careering over the dry land, freezing and sinking as they spread, till, in a few hours, or days, it may be, the valleys of the great rivers would become huge ice seas, such as we see in the upper Swiss valleys, on which all the heats of summer seem to make little impression. Under such a catastrophe all life would disappear from the face of the earth. Tropical regions would become arid wastes through their rain-supply failing, and the seas would be vast ice-fields. Even where streams were shallow, and the summer's heat might thaw them out, no living thing could survive in their waters; for, as the rivers froze, the fish would be crushed to death by the descent of the sinking ice. What infinite wisdom then in this one exception to the law of contraction ! Almighty wisdom regulating almighty power, and making it the slave of the living creation. Who can stand before the power of the destroyer cold ?, I said, in the conclusion of my former head. Who can stand before the power of the saviour, cold ? I say now at the close of this. Of a great salvation, as well as of a mighty destruction, speaks the cold of winter, to the pious soul.

3. *The goodness of " His cold."* Power the most marvellous, wisdom the most beneficent, we have already found in " His cold." Shall we stop at these, and seek for no other attribute of the Great Creator ? We have hardly a basis for Christian trust in power and wisdom. Goodness will help us, however ; for it indicates character, and character must be the great attraction for beings whose true glory is in their character. Power we may wonder at or fear, wisdom we may praise and admire, but goodness calls out the homage of the God-like in us. In the wisdom displayed in the cold we have

found several good things. That standing exception of water alone expanding under cold, while other bodies contract, is not the least of many clear tokens of our all-mighty, all-wise Father's care and goodness, in the operation of his cold. Indeed, we might call it, the greatest material blessing we can enjoy in that connection; for it is essential to our very existence. Still, after all, it is in the spiritual blessings, which the material blessings suggest, that the best blessing lies for devout souls. What stimulus to our spiritual nature, in the contemplation of the Deity putting forth his mighty power, and exercising his mighty mind, to protect and provide for his creatures as well as to expand and elevate their thoughts, by the grandeur of his power, in the works of his providence. I defy any mind, capable of being impressed by the presence of a divine being, to follow the line of thought we have been pursuing, without being overwhelmed at the sublimity and condescension of the Great Creator. And if we combine with this conception the Fatherhood of God—an ideal pre-eminently Christian—we shall certainly find living truth, it may be for the first time, in the words of the Master :—" Consider the lilies of the field how they grow. If God so clothe the grass of the field shall he not much more clothe you ?" And that other word :—" Are not five sparrows sold for two farthings and yet not one of them is forgotten in the sight of God ?" A simple soul may be unable to reason its way, through many of the intricacies of the divine government. A philosopher may easily corner him with his puzzles. But the pious soul will always reply, " God is here and God is good. I see his footsteps, as he walks upon the waters in wintry majesty ; I see his hand in the frost-sealed earth, which protects living root while it destroys dead corruption ; and in the ice-vaulted stream which builds a house for the fishes and spreads out a pathway for man. I recognise his goodness, as well as his power, in " His cold," and I walk the earth with a firmer tread, that I know my Father is here besetting me behind and before, and laying his hands upon me."

4. *The method of "His cold."* This mighty power which operates to destroy, and to save, on the most gigantic scale, is the most silent of all nature's great silent forces. Thousands of tons of rock are dislodged from the mountain

side, as in the recent disastrous rock-slide at Quebec; but no ear heard the discharge of subterranean forces, no human being felt the shock of the rending earthquake. Silently in the stilly night, under the jewelled canopy of heaven, a giant's hand is laid upon rippling stream and solid land. Then, without the slightest sound of contending forces, or cry of pain, the vastest display of power under the mighty heaven is presented to thoughtful mortals, when the morning breaks, and eager life awaking to its daily toil, finds the throne of the ice-king set up once again. What need we, more impressive, to inform us of a present divinity, than such a feat of divine workmanship? What a sublime consistency in work proclaiming abroad the sublime worker! It is everywhere the same throughout the universe, if we could see things as they are. The dawn breaks in radiant splendour upon a slumbering world; but no salvo of artillery ushers in the smiling morn. With rosy fingers, she draws aside softly the dark curtains of the night, and, on the sleeping ear of refreshed labour, steals tenderly the balmy whisper of the opening day. The soft breath of coming spring passes through an ice-bound land, and, as if by magic, the fetters of the ice-king are broken. The trees hang out their banners, to welcome the passing queen, and every brake is vocal with her anthem. But no ear heard the stroke of the hammer which broke the chains, nor the sound of the busy life which burst forth spontaneously, to greet the coming of the spring. All silent might; resistless power revelling in silence. What a lesson here also of the divine majesty! No noisy demonstration in his grandest works; no straining after effect; no giant-like effort to secure success. In all his wide dominion self-confident, self-possessed, and modest, the Great God marches silently through all the seasons working wonders as he goes.

These are some of the suggestions which naturally spring up in the mind, as one reflects on, " His cold." Let us try to verify, and apply them in the winter now upon us; and we shall grow into higher conceptions of the majesty and humility of our God. Rightly appreciated, they will offer one reason more from the seasons, for magnifying the character of Him, who hath made all things so fearfully and wonderfully. But I must not forget to emphasize the warning word implied in the question :—" Who can stand before his cold ?" No season tries and searches out our weak points like winter. A single night's frost will silently strip the grove of its foliage, better than a whole week's gust and blast, in November. Accordingly, the death rate of a city rises with appalling rapidity, in a season of unusual severity. Who can stand before his cold ? many sufferers are made to groan in their agony, and many mourners to sob in their tears, after a cold, hard winter. The elderly and the delicate ought to use all care that they may stand before " His Cold." Life is too precious a gift to be recklessly exposed to danger. Fight with some other foes as you please ; but this foe is only to be met and successfully resisted, clad in the best panoply. Stand guard against this enemy incessantly. He watches your every movement, and the subtlety of the serpent is nothing to his craftiness. The young and strong may go out into the open to stand before "His cold," and gain fresh vigour and elasticity of mind and body by the exercise. But the aged ought to keep within their entrenchments, and fight through the embrasures.

The usages of modern society invite another warning word. Reasonable care and vigilance will do much to preserve health and vigour even in the coldest winters ; but it is not using care, nor vigilance either, when we subject our systems to the frequent strain of unseasonable hours, or expose ourselves to the cold in unseasonable dress. Fashion is a despot ; and when her sway means evidently disease and death, they are the wise who break her bands asunder and cast her cords from them. Burning the candle at both ends, soon makes an end of the candle.

PART V.

SERMONS ON SPECIAL OCCASIONS

I.—THANKSGIVING DAY.

"A man's life consisteth not in the abundance of the goods which he possesseth."—S. Luke xii., 15.

Our Lord is here warning his hearers against one of the most insidious and dangerous mistakes into which an individual can fall—the mistake that "having," is "possession." He includes within his admonition everything which man can possess; and he exposes most forcibly, yea, even tragically, the folly of the human being who lives in such a delusion; as also the inevitable disaster which is sure to follow. The rich fool was the victim of such an absurdity. He is presented standing, as we are to-day, among the abundance of a luxuriant harvest. His idea of the uses of abundance is to hoard it. So when he finds his barns inadequate to store the season's produce, he determines promptly to build larger. A very right and proper resolution, to preserve the abundant return until he can utilise it; but an absurd conclusion if hoarding only in his motive. He is faithfully proceeding, however, on what he conceives to be a sound business principle; and he is not ashamed to confess, that his ambition in the larger buildings is to provide the one thing needful for his happiness and peace, by increased facilities for greatly increased hoarding. He believes that the new barns will minister greatly to his happiness in the most effective manner. Accordingly, he is gratified, as he anticipates the day when his new buildings completed and full to overflowing, he shall sit down among the plenty and soliloquise, "Soul thou hast much goods laid up for many years, take thine ease." "Soul take thine ease,"—as if human life were an ignoble, aimless existence lower than that of the beast of the field, or of the worm that wriggles in the slime. There were two false principles at work in bringing him to this miserable conclusion; and it is specially becoming to point them out, and emphasize their falsity, at such a celebration as this.

1. He confounded the meaning of the terms, "having," and "possessing." He thought they meant the same thing. But he was in error.

This rich agriculturist had obtained a rich return for his labour; and by every principle of common sense, he should have set himself to employ it to the best advantage. But no. His idea of "having," is not "using," but "hoarding." "This is mine," he says practically, "and I propose to do with it just what I please. I owe responsibility, in connection with it, to neither, God nor man. I shall enlarge my storage accommodation, and shut up my fruits there safely under lock and key. These are mine and I mean to keep them for myself alone." That was how he conceived of property in God's harvest, produced by God's earth, and cherished, and watered by God's sun and rain.

His principle was false even from his own point of view. He claimed the harvest for himself, and he hoarded it for himself. A moment's reflection might have shown him, however, that hoarding is not possession, in the living, true, religious sense. God has endowed man with certain faculties and gifts, which are to be exercised and developed by certain things, which this world of His produces. Our bodies are to be sustained and developed, by lawful food; and for them Mother Earth caters, by her yearly supply of the good things of the harvest. Our minds are to be cultivated and matured by observation and study, and for these God's book of nature and the works of genius, the broad fields of history and human experience are the pasture grounds, in which the human soul is to feed. We have, moreover, a spiritual character to develop; and for that, Jesus is the very bread of our life. But neither body, soul, nor spirit of man or woman, possesses anything, which it does not take up into itself, and utilise by making part of its being. The demands of the body are satisfied when it has used certain elements of food; but all food besides, is for the time being, practically nothing to the body, because it can use no more. An invalid may have spread out before him the choicest and most toothsome viands which can be obtained, and yet what are these to him, but a mockery and a sham, since he cannot partake of them? These dainties are his, because his money purchased them; and yet they are not his, for he cannot taste them. No one ever realises, like the bed-ridden sufferer, that one really owns only what he can use, and that one can get out of his possessions only as much as his nature can absorb, and nothing more. So is it in the case of an illiterate man who has inherited a valuable library, or of the uncultured owner of a fine collection of paintings and other works of art, or of the millionnaire, who is unable to enjoy his vast treasure. The law will recognise the property of all three, confirm their title to it, protect them in the possession of it ; and yet it is not theirs, beyond the very limited use they can make of it. Likewise, in the matter of spiritual possession, it is the using that is the possessing. Religious observances, special opportunities for worship, the best books, and the privileges of superior Christian fellowship may all be at an individual's disposal ; but, unless he utilize them, so little are they his, that it were better far that he did not enjoy them ; for without them he would be relieved from an intolerable care, or spared a perilous snare. To own a bible is to possess a precious treasure ; but he, who fails to feed his spiritual nature on the truth of the bible, till it can be said that the bible possesses him, cannot be said to be a real owner. The dead book which one holds in his hand, must become a living book in his soul, before it can be really his property. The Christ of the Gospels can only be your Christ, and mine, in the fullest sense, when we have incorporated his spiritual personality with ours, and are "living, moving, and having our being," inspired by his divine spirit. Any ecclesiastical or theological identity with Christ is a mere figment; this personal, spiritual union is the only, because the religious, reality. Our Christ is ours, because we are his.

Here is the conclusion of the whole matter,— the human being can only get out of any thing, or any personality just what his nature can take in body, soul, or spirit and nothing more; and his nature can take only according to its particular ability. Just as the rose can take from the sunbeam its blush, the lily its virgin whiteness, and the violet its imperial purple, and nothing more; so the individual can only get out of his surroundings, his possessions so-called, and his opportunities, just what his nature can take, and only that; and all else besides is as nothing to him, because his nature cannot take it up into itself. An old Scotch proverb puts this thought in a nut-shell:—"A man has nae mair gudes than he gets gude o'." This rich fool piqued himself on the abundance of the goods which he possessed ; and yet, after all, he only possessed a very small portion of them. All that he could not use personally, or did not choose to dispense as a steward, was only nominally his ; and nominal possession like that is often the greatest misery of all. Look at the miser whose burning desire is to hoard up daily more and more ; and yet, with a dark and terrible inconsistency, he has constantly the more burning desire to use ever less and less. What more horrible verdict could there be, on the utter falseness of this principle, than his miserable fate! He is well called, *Miser*, for misery is his name, and wretchedness must ever be with him.

The Christian ideal of possession is stewardship. A steward acts for another ; and his duty is to utilise all his master's possessions entrusted to him, and to utilise them for the very best to his master. The Christian is, in the strictest sense of the term, a steward. Whatever he possesses, he is to use. Be it life, or talents, or riches, all is to be used in the spirit of the faithful steward. That much-abused word, *usury*, conveyed originally the precise idea of the Christian steward. It means the *using*, with discretion, all the gifts entrusted to us as human beings. He who cannot be a Christian usurer, ought to call in the help of others. Our Lord, you remember, chid the one talent man who hid his talent in the earth, because he did not take the counsel and help of others, to enable him to fulfil a trust, the duties of which, he could not himself perform. That unfortunate man was a hoarder simply, and our Lord convicted him of breach of trust. He *had* a talent and yet he *had it not*, for he did not *use* it. Far better for him that another should have had it who could have used it. Lying hid in the ground it was a heavy load on his heart. Used, it would have been his, and it would have brought into his life a gleam of true happiness; unused, it was not his and it shot through his soul the fiery dart of all unhappiness. His is the dark fate of all, who confuse the terms *having* and *possessing*. "To have," is, "to hold, to hoard, to grasp in one's hand," saying, "this is mine." To possess," is, "to be lord of," "to order about," "to put to good purpose." The true hoarder is lorded over by that which he hoards; he is the slave of slaves. The true possessor is lord over all that is his; he is the master, and whatsoever he possesses is his humble servant. Possession of strength, or position, or wealth, with him means diligent using, and not idle abusing—manly exercise, and not unmanly sloth—actual wearing-out, if need be, rather than rusting-out.

2. He looked for the reward and blessedness of life in the wrong direction. He expected to find his happiness in the goods he possessed. He said to himself, "There is my reward, for all the care and labour I have bestowed. In my swelling garners shall I find happiness. 'Soul thou hast much goods laid up for many years, take thine ease, eat, drink, and be merry.'"

Most certainly God means his creatures to eat, drink, and be merry. All animate nature is a standing testimony to the fact. But eating, drinking, and merrymaking, are all to be done with the one motive — the perfection of our life. Beast, bird, and fish eat, drink, and are merry to make themselves better beasts, birds, and fishes. Man ought to eat, drink, and be merry to make himself a better man. The rich fool meant to eat, drink, and be merry for quite another reason. His ambition was not to be a better man ; his practice certainly tended to make him a worse man. Happiness he was seeking in dead things; he had not learned that its seat and centre are in the living soul. Poor Burns knew better, though his conduct belied his knowledge, when he sang :—

> " If happiness hae not her sea
>   And centre in the breast,
> . . . . . .
>   Nae treasures, nor pleasures,
>   Could make us happy lang,
>   The heart ay's the part ay,
>   That makes us right or wrang."

All our happiness lies in the extent to which our spiritual nature is developed; and the right use of everything we have ought to be an element in the great process of spiritual development. Our Blessed Lord is our standard of character, and towards his sublime height should all our energies continually tend. Accordingly, the use of everything any one possesses, is only to be regarded as genuine, is so far as it is directed to promote true life; and whenever anything possessed tends to hinder the progress of our spiritual life, or to drag it down, making it corrupt where it should be pure, and selfish where it should be sympathetic, then that thing is not used, but abused, and there can be no real happiness springing out of abuse.

The rich fool, like every one, naturally desirous to be happy, took the worst way of attaining his object. If he had put his produce to use, it would have done something for him, even though it had not done the best it could do; but hoarded only, it really was nothing to him, except in the security it offered against future want, and there was very little in that for him after all. Ere his plans were executed, and he had time to sit down and congratulate himself on his success, the dread fiat went forth which neither rich nor poor can disobey,—" This night thy soul shall be required of thee." His happiness was nipped in the bud, as by a chilling frost; from his goods, which were his reward, he was cruelly torn, and launched into the world of spirits poorer than the meanest peasant who toiled upon his lands, and infinitely more miserable. So passeth the glory of the world.

There was a very vicious element in this rich man's resolution, which, even though he had been spared for many years to enjoy his treasures, must have gradually undermined his spiritual nature. At his own estimate, these enlarged barns were to be instrumental mainly in placing him in a position of independence both of God and man. Come blight, or famine, or drought in future years he was safe ; let men do what they pleased he had his barns full, and what cared he? In such a spirit, he could not be thankful. How can a man offer thanksgiving at the feet of God, for the bounties of the harvest, if his whole aim in life is to attain independence of God, so that come good seasons or bad he can never want? There can be no gratitude where no sense of present benefit exists. The Lord's prayer runs, " give us this day our daily bread," or as it may be rendered, "our bread for the coming day." No farther than that can the enlightened worshipper go, and no farther would he wish to go ; for he knews that daily thanksgiving is bound up with daily bread, and true dependence on the Power Divine with the daily offering of the tribute of thanks. In so far, therefore, as this rich man's goods created in his mind the spirit of independence of God, they were a terrible snare. Well for him that he was called away suddenly and unexpectedly! Had he lived out the full term of his days, it had been in all probability worse for his spiritual nature. Most certainly it would have been the worse for his happiness, till the very end.

It is as great a mistake to decry abundance in itself, as a snare, as it is to esteem it in itself, as a blessing. Abundance, whatever form it takes, is a great blessing from on high, if the possessor have the spirit to receive meekly, and to use wisely, the gift. This rich man was highly favored of God His swelling barns were a great good in their precious fruits of the earth. They had for him, also, the elements of choicest happiness, if he had had the heart to perceive it. But he knew not the value of the good gift put into his hand; and, in his ignorance and blindness, he converted God's blessing into a curse, and the possibility of choice spiritual gain, into the reality of deep spiritual loss. Let no one despise any great gift, as if it could possibly be, of itself, a danger, or a curse; but let every one cultivate the spirit which can recognise in every treasure, the gift of God, to be used for his glory, which must always be for our good. Then, whether it be ten talents, or twenty, or though it be only one which God has entrusted to us, we shall thankfully receive the gift, and conscientiously administer it. We shall not vaunt our treasure, nor shall we hide it in a napkin; we shall not weakly squander it, nor selfishly hoard it; but we shall, as God the giver is our judge, frugally and wisely discharge our trust according to our light. In this matter, we are to follow no leader's bell, and call no man master. We are the trustees; God is the truster; between our souls and him the whole matter lies.

Doubly erring was this unfortunate man as we have seen; and disappointed inevitably in both ways must he have been, had he lived long enough. Had he been spared, he must have found to his cost (as so many are finding every day of their lives, who have not the heart or the power to mend it) that real possession is only in real use, and that true enjoyment of anything depends upon its right use in the promotion of our true life. He would undoubtedly have been taught by rough experience, that a man's life is not in these things; whether or no he ever discovered, that these could be valuable helps to develop his higher life, and sweeten it as well.

Nationally as well as individually this

great truth holds. We are to-day rendering thanksgiving for a bountiful harvest, and it is most proper that we should do so with lusty joy. For, after all is said and done, the grand fact stands eternally true, that in God we live, and move, and have our being. On his bounty we hang, on the regular recurrence of his seed-time and harvest we depend, and, when smiling plenty crowns the plain, there can be no fitter acknowledgment of our individual and national stewardship, than when as a people we offer at our Father's feet the fit tribute of grateful praise. Our national thanksgiving is that, or it is nothing. But national life consists not in the wealth which a nation possesses. Poor Rome was living Rome, because of the stalwart virtues which alone can dignify a people. Rich Rome became dead Rome, because of the vices which plunge the most promising nation into degradation and shame. The nation which does not realise its great mission, as the vicegerent of God to promote righteousness and virtue, is a nation that never can be strong, and never can be truly thankful for any good gift. Its, will be the spirit of the Rich Fool, who hoarded that, like the prodigal, he might lavishly indulge his selfish tastes, or like the miser whose mind is engrossed and racked how to add to his pile the most, while taking from it the least. It is thus our better nature revenges herself for our sin, by making the vices which we cherish to scourge us with scorpion thongs.

The right use of things considered in relation to the present which is ours, means no extravagance in charity and no blindness to the future, no neglect of ourselves and no indifference to our wants. But it means sound sense and discrimination, wise dispensing and earnest consideration, how the better always to fulfil our trust. Mingled with our national thanksgiving, as with all thanksgiving, there should ever be prayer for a riper spirit of stewardship, without which we shall never be made to understand that "a man's life consisteth not in the abundance of the goods which he possesseth."

Dominion Thanksgiving Day,
Nov. 17*th,* 1887.

II.—THE HOLY SABBATH.

"The Sabbath was made for man, and not man for the Sabbath."　　　　St. Mark, ii, 27

The distinction here drawn by the Master is of the utmost consequence in the discussion of what is called the "Sabbath question." Indeed, rightly apprehended, to my thinking it settles the question for ever with any intelligent person. To begin with, my text arranges things in their proper order. A most important service is that, in any statement of truth or duty. It puts the individual before and above the institution; and, by that simple circumstance, suggests how the institution is to fulfil its function relatively to the individual. The institution, it rightly exhibits, as dependent upon the individual. Without the individual, there could be no need for the institution. Without man, there could be no Sabbath. Called into existence then for man, the Sabbath must ever be regarded as subservient to man's true interests. It is called the *holy* Sabbath and no term could better bring out the deep true meaning of the institution. For *holy* just means *helpful*, and it would be easy to show, that in this capacity, Theodore Parker spoke a wise word when he declared that "the Sabbath is the most precious legacy ever bequeathed to man." Physically it is helpful, morally, mentally, religiously, it is helpful: and that individual is guilty of a gross wrong against humanity who lends his influence to rob us of its blessed helpfulness. As a helper then the Sabbath is meant to fit-in to the widely diversified and chequered lot of mankind. For every rank, condition, and race of men it comes breathing the same holy and refreshing benediction.

But whenever men reverse the dictum, and make it run "man was made for the Sabbath," they turn things upside down. In a moment, the blessed helper becomes a usurping despot, the loyal servant a hard task-master. Instead of the Sabbath adapting itself to the highest interests of man in every necessity and exigency of his being, man is told to fit himself, into the Sabbath, as into a hard metallic mould, incapable of expansion or adaptation to his varying conditions and circumstances. Multitudes have professed to follow this false doctrine, and honestly tried to honour the Sabbath, with the inevitable result which follows all error—ignominious failure. " The Sabbath was made for man," to be a bright, blessed day of rest and refreshment for body, soul, and spirit, said the great Master who knew so well what was good for man's body, soul, and spirit. " Man was made for the Sabbath," said blind priests and scribes who knew so ill what was good for man's body, soul and spirit, that in their false Sabbatarianism they poisoned the sweetness of the holy day and converted its most devoted observers into knaves and hypocrites.

I might illustrate the distinction our Lord draws here by the theory of the divine right of kings, once so popular a doctrine in Great Britain, especially during the Stuart period. The theory of those days was, that the "people were made for the king, and not the king for the people"—that is, that the sovereign had a divine right to rule, and that his subjects were under a divine obligation to obey ; and that in consequence, no uprising by an oppressed people against monarchical authority could ever, in the nature of things, be justifiable. Accordingly, after the execution of King Charles the first, the Church of England inserted in her liturgy a special collect, to be read annually on the day of King Charles the Martyr, which order was regularly obeyed until quite recent times. But that old idea of the age of chivalry has been dead for generations; and now the civilised world will only follow the leader or king, who can justify his claim to the title, by a policy which reveals his belief, that he is made for the people, and not the people for him.

Until quite recent times, the Protestant church among English-speaking people tried to maintain the reverse dictum of my text saying, "Man was made for the Sabbath," and said it as consistently and persistently as if the Master had never said, "the Sabbath was made for man." In this effort, the theory was maintained that the Jewish Sabbath is of perpetual obligation all the world over. But that doctrine like the divine rights of kings, so dear to the

Stuarts, is now exploded, at least among those who choose to look at this question from a common-sense rather than from a traditional point of view. The absurdity of that contention may be readily perceived by taking a single leading feature of the Jewish Sabbatical laws, such as, the inhibitions against lighting a fire on the Sabbath, and the cooking of food. Such laws might do very well in an eastern land where people live simply, and heat is a standing trial; but where would we be in winter, with the thermometer at twenty below zero, in houses without fires and condemned to eat food at freezing point? Nothing else need be quoted to show how entirely local were the Jewish Sabbatical regulations. Even the fourth commandment betrays in its very phraseology, its adaptation and restriction to a primitive and agricultural people. Who will assert that in the days of a complex civilization like ours, it is possible to observe the command absolutely not to do any work on the Sabbath? Let the most intelligent and conscientious person in this church try to realize what is meant by these words, "Six days shalt thou labour, and do all thy work; but the seventh is the Sabbath of the Lord thy God; in it thou shalt not do any work, thou, nor thy son, nor thy daughter, thy manservant, nor thy maidservant, thy cattle, nor thy stranger that is within thy gates," and let him say whether it is possible to fulfil the fourth commandment in Canada to-day. This is a great and an important question. It cannot be pooh-poohed or put aside, but must be looked squarely in the face, and answered manfully. Is it possible to keep the fourth commandment, according to the letter of it, in this complex civilization of ours? Is it possible to cease entirely all work in our homes on Sabbath? Is it possible to cease entirely all labour in certain large public works such as gas-works, bakeries, etc., or in the great means of intercommunication such as railways and shipping? The ancient Jews were in a position, with regard to the Sabbath, as different as possible from ours. They could keep the fourth commandment literally; but we cannot, and there is no good in disguising the fact—deluding ourselves with the idea that we are keeping the commandment when we are not, and indeed cannot keep it, let us do our very best. What then? Are we to have no Sabbath? says the believer in a Jewish Sabbath still. Are we to take refuge in our complex civilization, and say that the Sabbath may be as other days? Where can you stop if you abolish the Jewish Sabbath? Well I answer, it is not now a question of abolishing the Jewish Sabbath? The Jewish Sabbath is abolished already. Nobody, I know of, keeps, or can keep, the command literally as the Jews kept it. Our servants do certain domestic duties on the Sabbath which cannot be dispensed with safely, or decently. Our cooks prepare our dinners, as on other days. Our milkmen bring to us their necessary of life, as on other days. Railway journeys are continued, or completed on the Sabbath; and labour, in some departments of industry, has to be continued from necessity on the Sabbath, else the week-day toiler would be deprived of his employment for part of the week. Ships cannot come to anchor in the Atlantic at midnight on Saturday, and remain so till midnight on Sunday. Telegraphic intercourse between great cities cannot be dispensed with, in the public interest. These works are, one and all, direct violations of the fourth commandment, read it as you please. The Jewish Sabbath, therefore, is gone; and nobody of intelligence, or breadth of mind, proposes to restore it, even if it were desirable. It is not desirable however. The late Dr. Norman McLeod once pointed out, in his own forcible and graphic way, that the fourth commandment was essentially a local institution for Jews in Palestine; and that it was never intended to be binding on other peoples in very different circumstances. About the original institution of the Sabbath I will not pause to speak. Suffice it to say that it has lived and been honoured all through the historic period; and there could be no better certificate of its intrinsic worth than that fact. This we can affirm emphatically, that the Sabbath was not instituted by the fourth commandment, and the Sabbath cannot be abolished by abrogation of the fourth commandment. The Sabbath was made for man, and its authority lies not in tables of stone, but deep down in the necessities of human nature. It is the birth-right of every human being to have one day in seven for rest, and no one is at liberty to deprive another of his birth-right wantonly, thoughtlessly, selfishly. So far as it can possibly be done (and those who have the authority over others are to give their earnest thought to the subject), every man, woman, and child should have a Sabbath rest safely conserved. It may not be possible to give that rest on the Lord's day. The clergy, for example, cannot have rest either bodily or mental on the Sabbath; but they who must labour on the first day of the week should have a corresponding period for rest on some other day. Special cases have to be met in that way, because they cannot be met in any other way. One day in seven is the demand of human nature, and while the Christian community as a whole prefers for good reasons the first day of the week, there is nothing absolutely or essentially sacred in the first, more than the fourth, day of the week. Indeed, the day was changed at the beginning of the Christian era, by whose authority we know not: and the day can be changed again to suit altered circumstances. The one grand point which must be insisted on, and maintained, in its integrity, is the essential necessity for one day's rest in seven for every human being. It is for the toiler's vital interest to have his Sabbath rest; and it has been to me a matter of profound wonder and regret, that while day-labourers are constantly speaking up for increased wages, they have, in many cases, allowed their Sabbath rest to go without protest, and been quite willing to forego it for the chance of getting seven day's wages in the week instead of six. The workers themselves have been greatly to blame for many senseless forms of Sabbath work, without any week-day equivalent of Sabbath rest. But masters have been also greatly to blame, and wherever they have ordered Sunday labour without an equivalent of week day rest they have prosecuted a very blind policy. Every wise master will desire to get the best work out of his servant, and he is justly entitled to it. But the best work comes only from the man who is physically, morally, and mentally at his best in all the circumstances. The master knows that the Sabbath rest is a blessed help to him, and that when deprived of it he does neither justice to himself, nor to his work. Consequently, from very selfishness, if from no higher motive, a master ought to be as careful of his servant's Sabbath rest as of his own: and if he cannot give the rest on Sunday, let him give it on Monday, or some other day of the week. To use a commercial phrase, it pays, to safeguard that interest. It will bring the master better work from his servant, and it will always deliver his conscience from a grave sense of responsibility.

Now, to clear our minds and help our consciences, we must keep firm hold of these three results :—

1. That the Jewish Sabbath was a local institution.

2. That there is nothing exceptionally sacred in one day more than in another under the Christian system.

3. That every one is entitled to claim and to receive his one day's rest in seven; that no one can justly deprive another of his Sabbath rest; and that no one is at liberty to surrender his Sabbath rest for any selfish interest.

If we keep firm hold of these three conclusions, the main points in the Sunday labour difficulty will be minimised greatly, if they be not entirely removed. If certain public officials must work in the public interest on Sunday, the public service ought to be so adjusted that these men will receive a full equivalent, not in *pay*, for no man can buy or sell his Sabbath rest, but in *time* on another day of the week. Moreover, there should be the most scrupulous alternation of men on duty, on the Sabbath, so that there may be the greatest amount possible of Sabbath rest for each on the legal Sabbath day. Associated with the Sabbath rest, there is the important element of the religious uses of the day, and on the principles of sound Christian fraternity that " no man liveth for himself," and that all are " to look not only on their own things but also on the things of others," as Christians it is. our bounden duty, to promote the Christian celebration of the Lord's day, by ourselves and by all over whom we have influence, to the utmost of our ability. It is a sin against our Christian name if we fail in that regard; and it may be our Christian duty even to sacrifice ourselves, for the good of others more or less dependent on us. For the faithful discharge of this, as of every stewardship, God will call us into judgment; and woe be unto us, if we have not done to others, and especially to those under our authority, as we should wish to be done by. In the Old Testament appeals on this subject, the prophets are constantly forecasting the doom that must come upon the nation that forgets the

Sabbath; and chiefly, it appears, because the toiling classes were systematically deprived of their rights by their superiors. Again and again, are their fiercest denunciations directed against princes, priests, rulers of the people, and masters, because they robbed their subordinates and servants of their inalienable Sabbath rights. And it is, I fear, a word to be spoken still, as pointedly as old Isaiah, or Jeremiah spoke it to the Jews, that they who heedlessly, or needlessly deprive themselves, or others, of a day of rest in the seven, are guilty of a flagrant sin against God and man, and that retribution must inevitably descend on the heads of those who do this wrong.

I have not spoken directly of the various forms of what is called Sabbath desecration; because I think great principles are sometimes lost sight of by dwelling strongly on details. I cannot, for example, see how one can condemn the street railway on Sundays unless he is prepared to condemn all carriage traffic as well. The poor man, who believes it to be for the good of his health to take a car ride on Sunday afternoon, is no more blameworthy than the gentleman who gives an invalid an airing, or takes out his own carriage to drive himself to church.

Indeed, a good deal more is to be said for the poor man, because while his rich neighbour can drive every day in the week, he can often only do it on Sunday; and there is no more hardship, on principle, in a man driving a car for part of the Sunday, than in a coachman driving a carriage. Besides, it ought to be carefully considered, whether, in abolishing street cars, Sunday labour may not be inevitably increased rather than decreased; for many, who use the cars at present, might employ cabs for church-going and other purposes: and thus, for every man at present employed in Sunday labour, there might be employed ten times as many. Of traffic on railways, or in shipping, and labour in certain great public works, only gross ignorance or stupid prejudice would say, that either can be dispensed with entirely. Probably it is true that more labour is performed on Sunday than is necessary. There is a tendency to thoughtlessness in matters of this kind. It ought, therefore, to be the duty of those at the head of large concerns, to do their very best, so that such labour should be kept at the minimum.

But in all matters of Christian duty, the only real court of appeal is the court of the

Christian conscience. If people are so ill-instructed, that they set small price by the Sabbath, then it is for the Christian Church to enlighten them : and the Sabbath will only be conserved, by the education of the community to appreciate the precious blessing and privilege of the institution. Society must realize the good before it will stand up for it. Most strongly do I feel that, when the community has in its wisdom legislated on any topic of public morals, the law ought to be rigidly enforced; and notably in this matter of the Sabbath. But repressive measures alone will never make a Sabbath-loving people. Neither will the authority of any law make a gladsome appreciation of this good thing. Here, as in all religion, the spring of all good service and duty lies within. The soul must feel the advantage and enjoy it, before the man will strike for his rights and liberties.

"The Sabbath was made for man," and never did man need its hallowed quiet and rest more than the sons of the nineteenth century; for never did men spend more brain, muscle and nerve power in the six days of business worry and excitement. Guard it, I beseech you, as a sacred trust. Enjoy its privacy for the choicest family and social delights. Do not allow it to become a reduced copy of a gay and sensational week. Turn the current of your thoughts on the Sabbath into other grooves, and thereby gain refreshment for your minds by the very change. Give tone and elevation to the day by the devotions of the sanctuary. No doubt a man can be religious out of church as well as in it of a Sunday; but I never yet knew a man whose religious life grew apace, or whose religious character was elevated, under neglect of public worship. Of this I am sure, moreover, that the man who is likely to make a right use of the later hours of the holy day, is the man who in its earlier hours has struck the key-note of heavenly aspiration, among his fellow men in the place of prayer, and praise, and holy meditation.

But as I have already said, while the national observance of the Sabbath is a matter for the national conscience, the individual observance is a matter for the individual conscience. As St. Paul said to the Colossians, "Let no man judge you in meat, or in drink, or in respect of a feast day or a new moon or a Sabbath day."

Every man must be a law to himself: for where the spirit of the Lord is there is liberty. The one rule of the Sabbath is that of the Master, " The Sabbath was made for man." It is God's good gift to us; and is for every person to judge how the Sabbath is to be made to do the best for him. From that responsibility, nothing can absolve any one of us. Who shall dare to treat lightly so solemn a trust, or thoughtlessly profane so great a privilege?

III.—THE ANGELUS.

"Simplicity and godly sincerity."—2 Corinthians, i, 12.

"Simplicity—
Thou better name than all the family of fame."

Simplicity taken literally means unfoldedness. It is the opposite of duplicity or foldedness. Though society may not care much for simplicity, it seldom fails to do justice to the simple one; and it never fails to distrust the double man or woman. Simplicity in things is openness, plainness, or if I may be allowed the word spread-out-ness. In character, it means frankness, naturalness, transparency. The simple character is to be recognized at a glance, its openness disarms suspicion, its candour invites trust. The simple man, in the proper sense of the epithet, is the true man. In his presence you feel that you have before you a genuine living manhood.

Sincerity has a similar signification. It is a word taken from the rural life of the old Romans. The Roman peasant was always an apiarist. His finest quality of honey—the purest and the best strained— was called, "sincere," because it contained no wax. The sincere Christian, is the Christian pure in thought, and feeling, he whose character is like the finest quality of honey, when purified from all waxy ingredients, unmixed, unadulterate. Godly sincerity is Godlike purity of character.

It is very suggestive, to note the constant use which the New Testament writers make of such terms as these, to indicate the genuine, Christian spirit. They never speak in commendatory terms of wise Christians, nor of learned Christians, nor of aristocratic Christians. Their favorite characteristics of the model Christian are pure, simple, sincere. They knew no Christianity which was not spiritual; they found no seat for religion but in the character. Their ideals of perfection are men and women of simple and true spirit, whose conduct matches their character.

There are no other features of human character more truly esteemed, and that even by some whose own characters are neither simple nor sincere. It is the spontaneous tribute, which humanity pays to that which is best and most human in itself. There are no other graces so attractive, and so efficient in commending our holy religion. Indeed, simplicity and sincerity are so inalienably associated with Christianity, that an unsimple or insincere Christian is a contradiction in terms. The model Christian ought to be, above everything, a model of simplicity and sincerity, in character and conduct

The most effective lesson in these virtues, which I have been taught for many a day, is being taught to our citizens by "The Angelus,' now on exhibition at the Art Gallery. In an age like ours, when the tendency is so strong to weigh everything in the golden scales of mammon, the chief interest of this transcendent work of genius consists, to very many, in the sensational story of its last purchase, and the large price paid for it. Some few see in its fortunes on American soil, a striking illustration of the strange methods which an enlightened Government, in this nineteenth century, can adopt, to promote civilization and culture. But just as neither money nor a protective tariff ever created a work of art, so they cannot immortalize a work of art. The mere fact that the sum of one hundred and ten thousand dollars was the last purchase price of the Angelus, can no more enhance its real value as a gift of God to man, than the original price of three hundred and fifty dollars could diminish it.

1. The first impression made upon the spectator is that of solemn awe, at the sublime simplicity and sincerity of the picture. The scene is most common-place. A potato field, with a peasant and his wife in the foreground, and, in the distance, bathed in the soft radiance of the setting sun, a church spire. Any scene less romantic, indeed more matter of fact, than that simple picture of rustic life one could hardly imaginē. This is the picture which has created so much excitement among an unsimple, artificial, and superficial generation. Had it been a scene of courtly splendour, or high historic interest; or had the artist been a master of the so-called tricks of drawing or colouring ; or had he worked in the meretricious spirit of the hireling, making "pay," his first concern, and "work," a secondary consideration so long as it paid,

one could have understood the chorus of applause with which the advent of this picture has been greeted on American soil. Nothing but its solid simplicity, however, is the charm of the Angelus. Two human beings, lowly and simple as God made them, stand there ready to step out of the canvas, so truly has the artist put a portion of his own being into theirs. The "Angelus," or evening call to worship, has just sounded from the distant spire, and these busy toilers have caught the sound. Promptly they turn from toil for home and children, to communion with God their Father. The husband uncovers, and, with a look of uncouth, but deep reverence, breathes the well-known words of devotion. The wife, with bowed head and clasped hands, stands a very picture of prayer. Never did Saint or Madonna of the old masters, at holy shrine or on chapel wall, breathe a more exalted spirit of religious fervour, than this peasant wife of Barbizon amid the symbols of her rustic life. Every line of her figure is alive. One almost expects to catch the whisper of her lips. It is a sublime religious spectacle. I defy any truly fervent soul to study these worshipping peasants without having his faith purified and his better nature elevated. Their spontaneous and unconstrained devotion, the simplicity with which they hail the holy light of religion as it comes into the close of a hard day's toil, the pathos with which they uplift their souls to God, are a grand, silent, but speaking testimony to the reality of our common faith, and to its blessed ministries in this work-a-day life of ours. I can imagine few scenes so likely to recall the reverent doubter to devotion, and to plant a rock beneath his feet, that, standing thereon, he may learn to doubt no more. Nothing in art could better put to the blush that flippant religious indifference, which defaces so many characters, and drive its victims to their knees in abashed humiliation and penitence, than this picture. I can imagine the deep religious thrill, which, as it comes, transfigures that plain potato-field, for a moment, into the house of God and the very gate of heaven. I can see toil consecrated and brightened. I can see common life take on a heavenly glow, and wedded love grow into a truer mutual blessing. as I contemplate that worshipping peasant pair. I can realize that to them life is not all a rigorous struggle for potatoes and bread, and the close of life's brief day not what Mirabeau called "the beginning of an eternal sleep." As the pealing of the Angelus comes across the peaceful fields, its voice like the spire from which it comes, lifts the minds of these worshipping rustics to heaven, "our home," and helps them to find in their humble home, "a heaven." Millet himself is there in these devout peasants. He knew what religion had been to him, in the miseries of a hard and bitter lot; and he vivifies his canvas, to express the deep-rooted faith of his nature, in the abiding power and blessing of man's one stay and consolation. He becomes, therefore, the preacher of great gospel truth, as well as the exemplar of deep personal piety.

For this age there is really no more needed lesson than that. That solid worth is personal and spiritual; that a man's life consisteth not in the abundance of the goods which he possesseth, or in the want of them; that the day laborer's lot may be lit up by a heavenly radiance as truly as the millionaire's; and that the world ought to be something more to all of us than a kitchen, or a store, a paraded splendour, or a theatre of varieties and amusements—are hints that should be dropped by the way in all our streets, and offices, and homes, and fashionable places of concourse. Our men and women need to be constantly reminded that "Man doth not live by bread alone," and that his true life is only to be sustained and matured by the word of God. They need also to be reminded in the frantic struggle for riches, that to be simple and sincere, godly and true, it is not in the least essential to be rich and prosperous; just as it is to be constantly reiterated, in spite of the monkish gospel of poverty, that to be poor is not to possess the sure passport to the kingdom of God and his righteousness. The Angelus conveys these reminders in a marvellously effective and pathetic manner. The soul of a living man preaches from the canvas in all the simplicity and sincerity of his being. He has a message for old and young, high and low, rich and poor, and these are its brief pointed terms:—"Be true and simple. Don't labour with all your might to be somebody else, but stand upon your own feet. Don't be ashamed to be natural; esteem it your true dignity to be unaffected and sincere. Despise not religion, but cherish it as your first good. Never dream that it is manly far less womanly, to boast glibly of your ability to go through life's toils and trials without heavenly help and solace. Prize life as a sacred trust, to be enjoyed and spent most sacredly. In the highest place, as in the humblest, let the Angelus, as it tinkles, awaken within you a true echo, which rising high above the hubbub of the world's voices will reply—"I am for Christ."

It is this message for true men and women which is to lend immortality to this great work of art, and not any adventitious circumstance. The Angelus will live, not because it is of great marketable value, which after all is a very variable quantity; but because it cannot die. Heart of man and woman will never fail to respond to its mute appeal; and in the soul of humanity it is in the best and safest keeping. True to human life, it must ever have attraction for human nature. High-born lords and ladies will be content to sit at the feet of this peasant preacher of Barbizon, and not be ashamed to own that this prophet of low degree is worthy of all exaltation. A true man, though dead shall live to speak, through the centuries, to lighten burdens on weary shoulders, and enlighten hearts that are wearier still. The spirit of a simple piety will march onwards through the years to discredit the shams and the trickery, the delusions and the snares which so desecrate both life and religion. Moreover, it will be ever seeking, to present man to his brother, and to his God, as our Lord presented him when taking Nathanael by the hand he declared :— " Behold an Israelite indeed in whom there is no guile." The man, whose consecrated genius renders such a service to his age and people, is one of humanity's great masters and benefactors. It is surely very good for the world that such an one is born into it; and it is surely good for him that there is such a world to be born into, where crowns are to be won which cannot fade away. Such an one will abide the tests of the great stewardship, and will be greeted at length by the Great Steward himself, Servant of God, well done!

It has taken thirty years to bring the Angelus into the full view of society ; but, though it had taken thirty more, it was sure to come to the light some day. Very imperfectly have men yet realized the ideals of our Blessed Lord ; and yet nineteen centuries have run their course since a blind world nailed him to the cross·

Nevertheless, nothing, that can live by reason of its truth, shall ever be lost to the great God, to the great world in which his Son was crucified. However lowly its origin, the real work will live and fulfil its mission. Though it may seem insignificant to man, no true thing is insignificant in the eye of God. It is the small, true thing, which time and again has conquered the great, false thing. David with his true, young heart, and his patriot's sling was more than a match for the bully of Gath, with his mailed armour. Depend upon it, no true thing, which you do in simplicity and godly sincerity, can ever die. If you breathe into it the spell of a living soul, it shall live in spite of every foe, and awaken new life in pining brothers and sisters. And though the fathers in their unwisdom should refuse to see your good work, yea, though they may let you die in misery beside it, their children will honour your name and build you a monument.

2. Another strong feature of this wondrous sermon in oil is the absolute repose it breathes. The motto of Millet in all his work was— "Truth of expression will do it;" and the truth of the Angelus is most impressive. The artist

has in his mind one of those summer evenings we can remember so well, when earth and sky combine to breathe calm upon the weary and worn toilers of humanity. Such an evening, we can imagine the night of the Transfiguration to have been, when, as the sinking sunlight melted into the glow of heaven, the weary Master stood forth to his astonished disciples in the robes of shining peacefulness. The present bishop of Peterborough once said at an art meeting:— "When I was a young clergyman I spent a ten pound note, which I could ill spare at the time, on a little landscape which struck my fancy. Since then I have obtained untold soothing out of that little picture. When I am troubled or perplexed, vexed or irritated, the sight of that scene of deep repose works like a charm in my being. I have been thankful, a thousand times, that I had the good fortune to make that purchase when I did." How many weary men and women have the same tale to tell! In the heart of nature's peaceful beauty the human soul finds its only medicinal balm. No voice is half so inspiring as the deep and awful silence of the mountains. There the mind drinks in its richest refreshment, and its noblest thoughts well up till ordinary prose is all too tame to find expression for them. It is in the depths of nature's loneliness, where the hum of the bee or the chirp of the cricket falls on the startled ear, that a man feels his faith, and learns to know better, both himself, and the God who made him. There it is that he does not believe simply; he sees. Millet produces just such a scene of repose in the Angelus. The tinkling of the bell breaks upon the startled air like an intruder's foot on our morning prayer. It is like the breaking of a spell—so deep and true is the sense of nature's repose.

Never did society need more the repose of this picture. In the breathless rush of the busy life which surges all around us, and bears us along, willing or unwilling almost, on its strong stream, it is an unconscious tribute to the innate craving of humanity for repose, that the least reposeful of civilized peoples should have hailed so enthusiastically, the advent of a picture' which, in its every lesson, teaches just the very opposite of the life they are living day by day. It teaches simplicity and sincerity; their life is very largely unreal and artificial. It teaches fidelity and truth in human nature. Infidelity and error taint the springs of both their social and religious life. It suggests the reposeful, calm, meditative spirit in ordinary life and in devotion. "Hurry up," is their motto in everything—even in their holidays. "The Angelus" is therefore a real satire upon modern society. American hurry and Barbizon repose can never agree. Let us hope that the story of this picture will bring to many a toilworn, strained mind and body just the balm it needs. Sad tokens are abroad, that the strongest and the loudest warnings on this subject come not a moment too soon. As life speeds along on this continent at the gallop, commercially, socially, religiously, the opportunity for seclusion and meditation, which are so essential for the mental and spiritual development of the true man or woman, seems rarely to come, and still more rarely to be desired, by those who need it most. Even the sacred calm of the holy Sabbath is far too little safe-guarded by social and political leaders. How very few meditate, like Isaac at even-tide, to find, like him, the rich reward of a new light coming into their life, as the tinkling of the camel's bells heralded the home-coming of his fair young bride!

Most Christian art is this of Millet's; most Christian truth speaks this master-piece of his. Like our Blessed Master, the artist was perfected through suffering. Terribly tragic was the fate of this man of many sorrows. Disappointment, privation, hunger, were almost to the last his close companions. The wife of his youth succumbed to trial inexpressible, and his own premature death, doubtless, owed its origin to the same cause. This weary man and full of woes was painting almost against hope. Still he painted, by a commission from Heaven; and his work lit up with glory those gloomy days of suffering and sorrow. He had a work to do for humanity; and he did it with all his heart, though the load he carried often threatened to crush him.* But the pressure of hard poverty, and cruel neglect, and an inappreciative society, which many a time have driven the son of genius to the swine's trough and its shame, only proved the Gethsemane of Millet to bring out all his virtue. His trials made him a man and a master, though they killed him in the making.

It is a misfortune of our time that so many have greater difficulty in touching the secret of simplicity, than they have in realising the purport of things elaborate and artificial. Tens of thousands have seen the Angelus, on whom its simple story made no more impression than the daisy on the ox that crops it. Had the subject been some great classical myth, they might have spent hours before it, and days praising it; but a scene of lowly life and devotion demands a much greater effort of study, to enter into its life and spirit, than most so-called educated people are willing to give. More particularly is that apparent in this case, where the subject is in antithesis with the sentiment of modern society. The Pharisees could not know the simplicity of our Lord; they knew too much to condescend to study the thought of one so sublimely unpretending. Tens of thousands of Christians to-day, like those old Pharisees, scout a simple gospel, and set themselves deliberately to elaborate a Christianity, as complex and as hard to be understood, as they can make it. Fatal error surely, this attempt to be unsimple in thought, and life, and religion. Human life in its design, its wants, its aims and its hopes is simple enough. "We brought nothing into this world and it is certain we can carry nothing out," is a simple enough beginning and ending for most of us. Humanity in development towards the divinity of Our Lord as the standing model to help it to develop, is a simple enough truth of practical religion. A character to win, a Christ to follow, a God who is our father—these make up the sum of saving knowledge for all plain practical purposes. Is our duty not simplicity and sincerity themselves? What more simple can any one desire, or have? A Christly character, a Christly life, a Christly father in heaven. The Angelus speaks of all these in terms that can never be forgotten. Blessed are they who enter into the artist's spirit! Blessed are they who in an unsimple age can dare to be simple; and among artificial men and women are able to bear the cross of simplicity!

Parents! Ye can write no better motto over your threshold than, "Simplicity and Godly Sincerity." Ye can have no better scroll, to place before your children's eyes, the last thing at night, and the first to greet them in the morning. Ye can set them no better example than simple and natural manliness and womanliness. That is your special responsibility; no other can do what you can in that respect.

God bring to you in the faithful discharge of this trust a crown of everlasting glory.

Young men and women ! Simplicity and sincerity are the richest charms of fresh, young life. Make my text your guiding star, I implore you, as ye step forth into the world's "broad field of battle." Take to your heart of hearts the advice of Polonius to his son :

> "This above all,—to thine own self be true ;
> And it must follow, as the night the day,
> Thou canst not then be false to any man."

Keep a heart true as steel for the love of God and man ; a mind true to duty as the dial to the sun ; a conscience true to right as the needle o the pole ; a foot true to the kindred points of Heaven and Home ; and a hand true and strong to labour for the good of human kind. Then shall your path in life grow brighter ever and better. In your experience the words of the psalmist will be fulfilled:—"Mercy and truth have met together, righteousness and peace have kissed each other."

May 25th, 1890.

www.ingramcontent.com/pod-product-compliance
Lightning Source LLC
Chambersburg PA
CBHW032142010526
44111CB00035B/902